A Nation's Paper

The Globe and Mail
in the Life of Canada

Edited by John Ibbitson

SIGNAL

McCLELLAND
& STEWART

Contents

An introduction *to the* History Project

At its heart, *The Globe and Mail* is a contract between readers and journalists built on trust. That relationship has helped us thrive.

You hold in your hands one of *The Globe and Mail*'s most ambitious undertakings: thirty essays involving dozens of writers, editors, researchers and designers that explore the role this newspaper has played in the progress of our nation since George Brown founded *The Globe* 180 years ago.

Our goal was not to write a history of Canada or a history of *The Globe and Mail*. Instead, we searched for issues and events in which the paper intersected with the life of the country, influencing its course.

The essays that have been published by *The Globe* throughout 2024 and that are contained in this book seek to illustrate that principle.

But which issues? Which events? Our readers helped with that, sending in many dozens of suggestions when we first announced this project in the spring of 2022. Deputy editor Sinclair Stewart, a team of departmental editors and I came up with the thirty topics and matched them with writers. In some cases, we asked journalists who were deeply familiar with the subject to provide us with an essay. So Gary Mason, who has written extensively on environmental issues, wrote on how *The Globe* has covered the environment through the decades, while Konrad Yakabuski, who is based in Montreal, wrote about our coverage of Quebec during years of constitutional negotiations and referendums.

In other instances, we sought fresh eyes and perspectives. Ann Hui gave us a thoughtful essay on the Catholic-Protestant tensions that dominated political and social life through much of the country's history. Evan Annett offered insight into how Sir Wilfrid Laurier and Sir John Willison, *The Globe*'s editor at the turn of the last century, worked out a solution, however imperfect, to the crisis over the use of French in Manitoba schools. Jana G. Pruden told us about Kit Coleman of *The Mail*, Sara Jeannette Duncan of *The Globe* and Faith Fenton of *The Empire*, three pioneering women journalists of the Gilded Age in the late 1800s who broke out of the so-called women's pages to cover, among other things, the Klondike Stampede and the Spanish-American War. Vanmala Subramaniam told the story of the great General Motors strike of 1937, in which *The Globe*'s editorials backed the losing side.

Though we limited ourselves to thirty essays, we could easily have written thirty more. An essay on how *The Globe* covered the social upheavals of the 1960s would have been welcome. David Parkinson wrote a splendid piece on how publisher George McCullagh fought and lost a battle with the censors during the Second World War. But there was room for another essay on the paper's role in the conscription crises. And one of the most delightful moments in *The Globe*'s history, when dance critic John Fraser helped renowned Russian ballet star Mikhail Baryshnikov defect after a performance at Toronto's O'Keefe Centre in June 1974, didn't manage to make it into an essay.

The Globe and Mail has been deeply involved in both the good days and the bad days of this country's progress. George Brown and his paper envisioned a future for British North America that would stretch from sea to sea to sea and helped realize that vision. His paper was also at times anti-French, anti-Irish and anti-Catholic. But Brown and The Globe matured together, eventually embracing a more accommodating vision for the new Dominion.

In times of war and peace, the paper has fought for a free and independent press, open borders, a market economy and a compassionate society. We are at our best, as a paper and as a country, when we champion such principles.

But Willow Fiddler's essay showed that, even though The Globe ran stories as far back as the early 1900s detailing unsafe and unhealthy conditions endured by Indigenous children at residential schools, the paper only started giving those schools and other Indigenous issues proper investigative coverage in the 1980s. Dakshana Bascaramurty told us about the paper's blinkered approach to Africville in Nova Scotia. Patrick White explained why it took so long for The Globe to understand the people and lands of the North. Kelly Cryderman examined the sometimes-strained relationship between The Globe and Western Canada. Elizabeth Renzetti wrote that the paper often championed the cause of women everywhere but in its own newsroom.

The paper grew along with the country it covered. Temur Durrani explored how The Globe took advantage of technological advances, from the telegraph to satellites to the internet, to become an ever-more-national paper. Marsha Lederman wrote that The Globe has a solid, though not unblemished, tradition of supporting immigration and racial diversity, while Rachel Giese revealed that Pierre Trudeau was stealing from a Globe editorial when he said that the state has no place in the bedrooms of the nation.

Of course, there is far more to the newspaper than news. Cathal Kelly explained why sportswriters love to make predictions and don't worry if they're wrong. Barry Hertz delivered a moving tribute to film critic Jay Scott. Tony Keller and Cliff Lee each wrote about the inner workings of the paper: Tony told readers about Junius, the guiding spirit of the editorial board, while Cliff gave us a delightful exploration of letters to the editor.

Finally, Ian Brown meditated on which is more unlikely: that such an improbable country as Canada somehow succeeded, or that *The Globe* somehow succeeded in covering it.

We offered each writer, all of whom are present or former *Globe* staff, two weeks to research their topic, conduct interviews and complete a polished essay of about 2,500 words. What fools we were. Some writers started their essays when the winter snow was still on the ground and completed them as the autumn leaves began to fall. Yet somehow, over the course of a year, everyone came through, often working away on their essays even as they completed other assignments on their beats. Also, we were saved by news researcher Stephanie Chambers.

The first stop for most essayists was the editorial library, where Stephanie unfailingly provided indispensable research materials. She and her colleague, Rick Cash, mined the paper's archives and located reams of other material. We quickly came to realize that without the editorial library's contribution, this project would have failed.

I first proposed a series of essays based on *The Globe*'s history to David Walmsley, the paper's editor-in-chief, in a phone call in August 2021. I had barely gotten into my pitch before David started riffing on possible essay topics. He took my subsequent memorandum to then-publisher Phillip Crawley, who green-lit the project on the spot. Phillip and David backed our writers and editors through thick and thin. After Phillip retired in August 2023, David and Andrew Saunders, who succeeded Phillip as CEO, shepherded the project to completion.

Nancy Janovicek, professor of history at the University of Calgary, agreed to come on board as consulting historian, and she proved to be invaluable, offering insight and enlightenment to essayists who consulted her. We are also indebted to the University of Toronto, which made its libraries available to our writers. To Information Services manager Craig Butosi and deputy chief librarian Julie Hannaford, our sincere thanks.

Tamar Satov edited the essays, demonstrating her abilities as one of Canada's finest editors time and again. Sandra E. Martin took over from Sylvia Stead as supervising editor when Sylvia retired in June 2023. Photo editors Liz Sullivan and Solana Cain guided the search for images to complement the essays. Many *Globe* editors worked countless hours to help polish the manuscript. Finally, *The Globe* is grateful to Douglas Pepper and to everyone on the team at Signal/McClelland & Stewart who turned the essays into this book. Royalties will be donated to Journalists for Human Rights, a Canadian non-profit organization that assists journalists in covering human-rights issues around the world.

Early in the development of the project, an editor asked what would become a foundational question: What is *The Globe and Mail*? In 1844, it was four pages, cranked out once a week on a hand press. By 1980, it was being transmitted by satellite to printing plants across the country. Today, most people read it on their smartphones.

Over the course of the project, we came to realize that, however it is delivered, *The Globe* at its heart is a contract between readers and journalists built on trust. We investigate, report on and interpret our communities, our country, our world. Our readers trust that what we are telling them is accurate, fair and important. At a time in which many newspapers have been forced to close, and others have become wraiths of their former selves, *The Globe* continues to thrive, through the trust and support of our readers.

You make what we do possible. You made this book possible. Thank you.

John Ibbitson
General Editor
The Globe History Project

A Nation's Paper

ABOVE, LEFT TO RIGHT: George
Brown; Sir John A. Macdonald.
(Hunter & Co./Library and Archives
Canada; Notman Studio/Library
and Archives Canada)

One: **Making *a* country**

George Brown, *The Globe* and Confederation | **John Ibbitson**

T he whippings drove some prisoners insane. Seven floggings over fourteen days for one inmate. A fourteen-year-old girl whipped five times within three months. One prisoner received 720 lashes during his imprisonment. A boy of eight was confined to the dreaded "box" for staring. A ten-year-old boy was whipped for laughing. And the food was so vile that inmates stole from the pigs' trough.

All these abuses and many others at the Kingston Penitentiary – "this den of brutality" – George Brown chronicled in his newspaper, *The Globe*.

"Who can calculate the amount of pain and agony that must be imposed in the pandemonium?" he wrote in 1846. "Who can tell the amount of evil passions, of revenge and of malice that must be engendered by such treatment?"

Three years later, Brown headed a commission that led the government of the United Province of Canada – the recently created amalgamation of Lower Canada (today's Quebec) and Upper Canada (today's Ontario) – to fire the warden, ban excessive corporal punishment and hire professional inspectors.

But the report offended the member for Kingston, thirty-four-year-old Sir John A. Macdonald, who was a friend of the warden. From then on, Brown and Macdonald were at each other's throats. Their rivalry almost destroyed the Canadian experiment. Their reconciliation saved it. And *The Globe*, by far the most influential and successful newspaper in British North America, drove the story.

Brown was only twenty-four when he and his father, Peter – a reform-minded Presbyterian fleeing religious orthodoxy and his own financial embarrassment – arrived in Toronto in 1843 from Scotland via New York to establish the *Banner*, which championed religious freedom.

But George was more interested in politics than religion and the next year launched *The Globe*. The weekly paper was a critical and commercial success from the very beginning, owing to its closely reasoned editorials, its honest reporting and its owner's willingness to invest in improved presses and an expanding roster of reporters.

There was plenty to report on. Upper Canada was a raw and rollicking land of immigrants and huge ambitions. The earliest settlers had fled the disloyal United States; then came English and Scots and Irish who were hungry for a new start and to get ahead.

Everything was newborn. Settlers carved frontier farms out of forests in the southwestern peninsula. Bone-shaking roads connected those farms to Toronto, an emerging city of church steeples; muddy, stinking streets; fine brick buildings; sheds and shacks and slums. Everyone argued loudly and at length, fighting over schools and religion and the shape that this newfound land should take.

The Globe supported the Reform, or Liberal, Party and championed secular education, representation by population and annexing the Hudson's Bay Company's northwestern territories (now the Prairie provinces) to the united colony.

The Conservatives, or Tories, favoured established religion, equal representation of French and English in the legislature and government by oligarchy, they being the oligarchs. But the Tories were already in the minority in Upper Canada, pushed aside by the flood of newcomers.

The Roman Catholic Church dominated Lower Canada, already two centuries old. Conservative Bleus ruled here, with the reformist Rouges very much a minority.

French versus English, established versus new, sectarian versus secular. The British had mashed these two cultures into a single colonial province, a shared political space. How were they supposed to get along? It turned out they couldn't.

Brown, who by the late 1850s led the Reform Party (it was standard fare in those days to own a newspaper while engaging in partisan politics), was solid, mutton-chopped, determined, stiff-necked, hot-tempered, principled. Macdonald, who led the Conservatives, was the very opposite: subtle, smooth-shaven, calculating, ambitious, a politician to the core. The two men clashed year after year. Macdonald always won.

Brown "remained a journalist in politics," his biographer, J.M.S. Careless, wrote a century later, "the forceful wielder of words and mass opinions, not the skilled master of men and tactics."

At his best, Brown and *The Globe* championed free speech, representative democracy and a Canada that might one day rise as a great nation.

"We have passed into a position in which we must think and act for ourselves," the paper declared in April 1848. "We require men at the helm who feel a nation is being formed, and that as we now choose, so shall our national character be.

"The people of Canada must be *nationalized*."

At his worst, he was anti-Catholic – "in its very nature, the Popery is utterly opposed to civil liberty" – and anti-French – "the French . . . rule over, insult and plunder the loyal English."

Over the years, however, Brown and his paper mellowed. "We want neither English nor French ascendency, neither Protestant nor Catholic domination," *The Globe* declared in 1860. "We contend for equal rights for all, equal protection to all."

From the first, Brown was determined that his newspaper would reach beyond Toronto to readers throughout Upper Canada and even into Lower Canada. He poured money into the latest technology: fast presses; swift delivery by coach and, increasingly, the new railroads; telegraph dispatches that damned the expense.

Within two years of its founding, the weekly had become a semi-weekly. In 1853, it became a daily. By 1861, *The Globe*'s circulation had surpassed thirty thousand, three times that of any other newspaper in the two Canadas, with a fully staffed newsroom and pressroom, an Ottawa bureau and a writer sending dispatches from London.

Canada and *The Globe* were both prospering, but political paralysis threatened the colony's future. Election after election produced a hung legislature: Bleus and Conservatives, Rouges and Reform, in equal balance.

In 1864, matters reached the breaking point. There had been four governments and two elections in less than three years, and the latest Conservative coalition was set to fall. Although Upper Canada now had a considerably larger population than Lower Canada, both sections were guaranteed equal representation in the legislative assembly to protect the rights of the French minority, increasing tension and instability.

Some advocated a return to two separate colonies; others, annexation by the United States, where a great new power was emerging from civil war and looking hungrily to the north. If Upper and Lower Canada could not resolve their differences, neither might long survive.

Brown had changed. Two years before, at the age of forty-three, he had met Anne Nelson, the thirty-three-year-old daughter of a prosperous book publisher, during a visit to Scotland. They were soon married. Brown's friends noticed how his opinions and temper began to moderate. Anne spoke French, had lived in Paris and surely understood the fears of French Canadians, marooned on a continent of English speakers. She brought a sense of empathy to the partnership, a quality that Brown sometimes lacked.

"Perhaps the real father of Confederation was Mrs. Brown," the historian Frank Underhill jested in 1927. Biographer Careless, in all seriousness, agreed. Brown's "public conduct was so much affected by his private concerns, centred in his wife and family, that the former cannot be properly described without reference to the latter," he wrote in 1960.

For Carmen Nielson, a historian at Mount Royal University who has studied the Fathers of Confederation, "looking at these men as fully formed humans" means looking at how their family and social networks helped shape their politics. In Brown's case, that meant transitioning from obstinate bachelor to husband and father, concerned about his wife's approval, "which gives us a clue to how important family relationships and the broader social-slash-family-slash-political network was," Nielson believes. She speaks not of the Fathers of Confederation but of the matrix of relationships that brought about Confederation.

With the legislature paralyzed, Brown proposed an all-party committee that would examine alternatives to the existing, broken model. Most committee members supported a proposal that Brown had been advocating for years: dissolving the united province and replacing it with separate governments for Upper and Lower Canada, with "some joint authority," as Reformers called it, responsible for matters of common interest. A federal, rather than a unitary, state.

Brown let it be known that he was willing to co-operate with Macdonald in supporting a government that sought constitutional reform. The two men agreed to meet, even though being in the same room together was painful for both of them.

Macdonald, who for years had resisted dissolving the united province, now set forth a proposal of vast ambition: incorporating not just

Lower and Upper Canada but the Atlantic colonies, the northwestern territories and eventually British Columbia into a continent-spanning federation, with separate governments for each province and a central government for issues of national concern. To achieve this, he proposed a Great Coalition of all the parties in the assembly that would bring Brown and other Reformers into the cabinet.

George-Étienne Cartier, leader of the Bleus, decided that the French in Lower Canada would have a better chance of preserving their language and culture within a federal state than they would yoked to Upper Canada. But what of Brown?

Macdonald was proposing something more daring than anything he had in mind. Was it a trick, a scheme to stave off federating the two Canadas by proposing something so grandiose it could never be realized? And could George Brown possibly sit at the same cabinet table with John A. Macdonald?

Brown faced the most difficult political decision of his life. If he supported Macdonald's plan, he would be betraying many of his most loyal supporters. But he knew better than anyone that things could not go on as they were. Canada must either move forward or fail.

On June 22, 1864, Macdonald put before the legislative assembly his proposal for a new government dedicated to constitutional reform. Then Brown rose.

"For ten years I have stood opposed to the honourable gentlemen opposite in the most hostile manner," he told the assembly.

But "a great crisis has arisen in the Province; that election has followed election; that one ministerial crisis has followed another, without bringing any solution for the difficulties in carrying on the government of the country."

Brown would cross the floor, he declared, and join the coalition dedicated to establishing a new federal union. With that decision, Canada became possible. Men from both sides of the House cheered and crowded around Brown, shaking his hand and clapping him on the back.

"A great good has been achieved," *The Globe* pronounced in its editorial endorsing the coalition. "The gloom of a week since has given place to a bright prospect of a speedy and harmonious settlement of our difficulties."

The rest is our history. The boozy, party-filled meetings between Canadian and Maritime leaders at Charlottetown that year. The tough negotiations in rainy Quebec City to hammer out the details of the new federal state.

The Maritime provinces soon regretted their earlier enthusiasm, rightly seeing Confederation as a solution to a central Canadian problem that would leave them on the margins. But Ottawa and London were determined to make the union happen and arm-twisted Nova Scotia and New Brunswick back in.

In December 1866, delegates representing the two Canadas, Nova Scotia and New Brunswick began final negotiations with the British in London for a new federal, self-governing Dominion, as it would be called. It took until February for colonial and imperial legislators to work out the details of the British North America Act.

On February 25, in the greatest scoop in the paper's history, then or later, *The Globe* published the entire text of the act, four days before the government in Ottawa received its copy. Newspapers and politicians howled. Who had leaked the BNA Act to *The Globe*? An editorial impishly pointed out that its proprietor knew the highest authorities. "For instance, could it not have occurred to our contemporaries that a most gracious lady – but we forbear!" To the best of our knowledge, *The Globe*'s source was not Queen Victoria.

Brown, Macdonald and the other Fathers of Confederation offered the world a unique alternative to empire or rebellion: a new federal Dominion that recognized from the moment of its creation the linguistic and cultural rights of a minority at a time when most national and imperial powers sought only to deny and suppress minority rights. This "was something quite remarkable," says Marcel Martel, a Canadian historian at York University. "The rest of the world paid attention to Confederation."

But not all minorities were respected, not all voices heard. The Fathers of Confederation gave little thought to the rights of Indigenous Peoples, simply assuming they would be assimilated into the larger European, Christian society. Even the stoutest rep-by-pop Reformers saw no reason to grant the vote to women or to men who didn't own property.

"People estimate that only about 15 per cent of the population were able to vote," says Patrice Dutil, a political scientist at Toronto Metropolitan University. "It was a Confederation for some, but not for others."

Though as both Dutil and Paul Litt, a historian at Carleton University, remind us, while we can't avoid filtering the past through present values, we should at least try to view it through the lens of those who lived within it.

"Democracy was only in its infancy in Canada" at Confederation, observes Litt. "Canadian elites feared that if given the vote, the rabble would be manipulated by populist demagogues."

For Brown and his peers, the tumultuous politics of the republic to the south had to be avoided at any cost.

On July 1, 1867, as bands played, bells pealed and fireworks flashed across darkened skies, *The Globe* published a nine-thousand-word editorial to mark the birth of the new Dominion. "Old things have passed away," Brown wrote, ". . . and this day a new volume is opened, New Brunswick and Nova Scotia uniting with Ontario and Quebec to make the history of a greater Canada already extending from the ocean to the headwaters of the great lakes, and destined ere long to embrace the larger half of this North American continent from the Atlantic to the Pacific."

Macdonald's Conservatives beat Brown's Liberals in that summer's first national election, ending Brown's political career. He remained influential in the debates of the nation through *The Globe* until his voice was cut short in 1880 when a former employee, objecting to the terms of his dismissal, shot Brown in the leg during a struggle. The wound became infected, and after weeks of agony and delirium, Brown died on May 9, at the age of sixty-one.

There were a number of fathers – and mothers and sons and daughters – of Confederation. But it was George Brown who realized that the United Province of Canada must dissolve if a greater Canada were to arise. It was George Brown who overcame decades of hostility to cross the floor and sit beside John A. Macdonald.

It was George Brown who founded the newspaper that has told the story of Canada to Canadians, from his day to ours.

John Ibbitson is writer at large at *The Globe and Mail* and general editor of The Globe History Project.

ABOVE: Orangemen celebrate in Toronto on "The Glorious Twelfth," July 12, 1958. (*The Globe and Mail*)

Two: **Orange v. Green**

The battles between English Protestants and Irish Catholics ultimately gave rise to multiculturalism | **Ann Hui**

I n February 1856, a group of about one hundred Irishmen met at a hotel in downtown Buffalo, New York, to discuss the hundreds of thousands of Irish famine refugees who had landed in North America in recent years. Many were living without means – poor, in Canadian and American cities, in dire need of aid.

At the meeting, the men – about half of them Canadian – proposed a number of solutions. One was to settle the refugees in then–Upper Canada, along the Ottawa Valley. *The Globe*, reporting on the meeting later, was aghast.

This would "flood the province with a population likely to be as great a curse to it as were the locusts to the land of Egypt," declared a *Globe* editorial. "Settle the Roman Catholic Irish in masses and we should have a second Connaught, a second District of Quebec, a second Naples."

Such sentiments were common for Upper Canada at the time. Many among the primarily Protestant, largely British population felt a strong distrust toward Catholics. And many were particularly disdainful toward the Irish Catholics, whom they blamed for a wide variety of social ills, from poverty and crime to disease. Other newspapers of the day, particularly *The Toronto Telegram*, were also vocal about their contempt.

But *The Globe* was a particularly important voice among the anti-Irish-Catholic chorus. Publisher George Brown was a staunch believer in the notion of a secular state – of the separation between church and state. He was vehemently against the idea of the Catholic Church wielding any influence over Canadian affairs. And he wasn't shy about using *The Globe* as a platform for his message: the newcomers were a hindrance to national unity.

It was the first time the young country, then just a group of colonies, had faced such a large influx of outsiders. As such, it serves as an important lesson. Canada's response, as reflected in *The Globe*, would reverberate throughout the country's history. Newcomers would repeatedly be seen as a threat – not just to their neighbours in Toronto, or Montreal, or cities and towns in which they were settling but to the very idea of Canada.

"People like to think Canada was always welcoming and tolerant," says Allan Levine, historian and author of *Toronto: Biography of a City*. "When sometimes the exact opposite was true."

In the mid-nineteenth century – around the time the Irish refugees first began appearing in Upper Canada – it was common to see buildings with orange roofs dotting the country's landscapes. The buildings, which were across Ontario and concentrated especially in cities like Toronto, were meeting places, clubhouses of sorts for a fraternity called the Orange Order.

The Orangemen (named after William of Orange, the Dutch Protestant king who defeated the Catholic king, James II, in the Glorious Revolution) had first appeared in Northern Ireland in the eighteenth century. In the face of religious tensions, the Orange Order served there as a kind of Protestant defence organization, viewing themselves as guardians of Protestant rights and liberties. Earlier waves of Irish-Protestant settlers brought the group to Canada, where local Orange Orders became a symbol of an allegiance to the Crown, Britain and Protestant conservatism.

Toronto, with its large British-Protestant population, emerged as a particularly Orange city. The organization had a stronghold on the city's power centres – from City Hall to the police department to the fire stations. For decades, only Orangemen – or those allied with them – filled senior positions in these institutions. Until the 1950s, almost every mayor of Toronto was a member of the powerful Protestant organization.

So in the summer of 1847, the arrival of about 38,000 Irish refugees in Toronto in the span of just a few months sent shockwaves through the city. Until that point, Toronto's population had been just 20,000. And while many of the refugees quickly moved along to other parts of the country, the thousands who stayed – many of them Catholic – quickly transformed the face of the city.

Around the same time, the Catholic Church had begun making moves in Europe. The Vatican was rebuilding, appointing bishops across the continent, including in Britain. *The Globe* reported on these "papal aggressions" breathlessly. "Protestants in Upper Canada felt that not only was their homeland being taken over – with the Catholics on the march in Europe – but that they were on the march here too," says Mark McGowan, a professor of Celtic studies at the University of Toronto.

The largely British and Scottish population had a specific contempt toward the Irish – one that seemed to extend beyond religion.

"Irish Need Not Apply" signs, for example, were common in Toronto storefronts at the time. A series of cholera epidemics in the early 1850s, blamed on the arrival of Irish immigrants, further fuelled these attitudes. "There was a sense that they were poor, ignorant, feckless people who were a drain on British society," says McGowan.

Newspapers, including *The Globe*, fed into this perception. In 1856, the paper published this: "Irish beggars are to be met everywhere. And they are as ignorant and vicious as they are poor. They are lazy, improvident, unthankful; and fill our poorhouses and prisons." The words came from a letter first published in the *News of the Churches* – which *The Globe* later chose to reprint. They've been mistaken, often, for Brown's own words.

A decade later, in 1866, a *Globe* reporter's tour of Stanley Street referred to the almost entirely Irish enclave as "a plague-spot of filth and misery, that cesspool of disease."

Within a few years, Irish-Catholic communities began to organize in response. They created their own groups, like the Young Men's St. Patrick's Association, to defend themselves and provide aid to those who needed it. They organized Catholic parades and marches to celebrate and protect their culture.

The Panic of 1857 – an economic depression that rippled across the border from the U.S., leaving many suddenly jobless – had only aggravated matters. "You had lots of people out on the streets without work and looking for some sort of release," says William Jenkins, a professor of history at York University.

The long-simmering hostilities eventually boiled over, from street brawls to full-on riots. From the late 1850s until about 1880, violence between Orangemen and Irish-Catholic groups was commonplace.

The 12th of July parades ("Orangemen's Day," when Protestants would march the streets of Toronto to commemorate the victory of King William of Orange over King James II) became an annual site of violent conflict. At an 1858 St. Patrick's Day Parade in Toronto, an Orangeman drove a horse and cart into the procession, and an Irish-Catholic man died in the violence that ensued. In 1878, shots were fired at a celebration for the Papal Jubilee in Toronto.

These "Orange v. Green" clashes took place in Toronto and across the country, too – particularly at centres for Irish labourers in the Niagara Peninsula, Kingston and around Montreal. Across the country, battle lines were drawn, often along city and town boundaries. A town was either Orange or Green.

The town of Cavan, for instance, was deeply Orange. Irish Protestants had first settled in the town – about halfway between Toronto and Kingston – in 1816. It was generally understood that Catholics weren't welcome. And in case there was any confusion, the Cavan Blazers, a vigilante group of local Orangemen, was there to enforce the understanding.

The Canadian Statesman would later describe the Cavan Blazers as "social regulators" who considered their duty "correcting persons acting in a manner injurious to the community." In the 1850s, for example, the Blazers took it upon themselves to crack down on a local Cavan farmer who had begun holding monthly Catholic masses at his home. They set fire to the farmer's house one Sunday during a mass. Decades later, the story would become inspiration for the writer Robert Winslow in his play *The Cavan Blazers*. The play is still staged almost annually in nearby Millbrook, Ontario.

In a paper titled "United in Oppression: Religious Strife and Group Identity," University of Alberta professor Albert Braz explores the question of whether the tensions between the Orange and Green might have been avoided. Braz describes a scene from Winslow's play, in which the head of the Blazers says to a Catholic leader, "We should have talked."

He wonders whether simple conversation might have ended the conflict. But in the end, Braz decides, the answer is no. "Not because the two groups have conflicting collective memories," he says. "But because they both see themselves as victims, of each other."

———

Orange versus Green represented a fight over religion, loyalty and race. But above all, the fight was over identity – and over the idea of a Canadian identity.

The Loyalists, whose vision for Canada was a British North America – a British colony that followed a British way of life – treated the arrival of the Greens as a threat.

Part of it was insecurity. "It wasn't yet a foregone conclusion that 'Canada' would survive," says Jenkins. Canada was still a young country – not even a country but a group of colonies, unsure of what might become of them. It was warding off threats of annexation from the U.S. And for Upper Canada in particular, it wasn't yet clear whether the English-speaking Protestant colony would successfully counterbalance the French-Catholic population of Quebec.

Another factor was loyalty. *The Globe* and other newspapers at the time would endlessly debate whether the Catholic newcomers were loyal to the Queen or to the Pope. The debate around separate Catholic schools, for instance – an idea that Brown ardently opposed – only fed into this sense of distrust.

And then there was the kind of Canada they wanted to build. The British colony the settlers had envisioned was one of high moral order, where the problems of the "old country" – vices such as crime and prostitution – could be weeded out. Toronto, in particular, was preoccupied with the notion of a perfectly moral, ordered city.

"It was this idea of: Do these people fit the mould of what a 'good Canadian' is?" says Levine. "People in Toronto had a particular vision for their community, and the attitude about outsiders was: How are they going to ruin this?"

This fear of outsiders would repeat itself throughout Canada's history. Lawmakers, with the support of newspapers like *The Globe*, wrote the fear into legislation, deciding whom to include (recruiting Ukrainian settlers to Canada's West, for example) and exclude, based on the idea of assimilation.

"It very much had to do with the question of who they thought was capable of assimilating," says Laura Madokoro, a professor who teaches the history of migration at Carleton University. Some cultures, they felt, were unassimilable. And those decisions were made, she says, based largely on religion, class and race (and, in particular, *whiteness*).

Indigenous communities in Canada, of course, felt this first and most indelibly. Theirs was a population the British settlers felt they needed to be protected from, one that needed to be "civilized."

Later, with the arrival of Chinese labourers in the late nineteenth century, *The Globe* warned of "inferior people" corrupting local populations, reminding readers of Canada's goal of "building up a nation, founded on a superior standard of manhood." And in 1914, when a steamship carrying hundreds of mostly Indian men arrived at a harbour in Vancouver, the newspaper described them as "infuriated Hindus" who had to be "beaten back with showers of coal and other missiles."

"Each time, the reaction was 'They're not like us,'" says McGowan. "And the question was 'And can they ever be?'"

On the question of Irish Catholics, *The Globe* would eventually evolve. By 1870, the paper was debunking questions of "disloyalty" aimed at Irish Catholics. And by 1878, *The Globe* declared itself "the true friends of the Irish-Catholics" and called for greater representation of Irish Catholics in Parliament.

By then, word had already spread around Ireland that Canada – and Toronto, in particular – was deeply Orange. The numbers of Irish immigrants had dropped off. Orange and Green tensions had begun to ease.

By the 1880s, the violence, for the most part, had dissipated. Towns or neighbourhoods were often still divided across Orange and Green lines, but the borders could be decided upon mutually. (Even today, there are still nine active Orange Lodges in Canada, according to the group's website. Most are in Ontario, though their presence appears to be mostly symbolic.) The existing Irish-Catholic communities became settled and better established in their new homes. They "assimilated" – to an extent. They became "Canadians" but also maintained – through their own perseverance – a religion and culture of their own.

Other waves of migrants – Ukrainian, Jewish, Italian and Greek – would eventually arrive in large numbers. The differences became less noticeable.

Brown would even come around to view the Irish Catholics as a valuable constituency in his political career. By the 1870s, Brown and the Liberal Party had positioned themselves as allies to Irish Catholics, promising to improve the community's standing – in exchange, of course, for their votes.

Much later, under publisher George McCullagh, *The Globe* would in fact become so strongly associated with the community that when the paper merged with *The Mail and Empire* in 1936, Protestant Conservatives responded with alarm. In *Big Men Fear Me*, author Mark Bourrie describes the reaction of competing newspapers at the time: *The Kincardine News* called the merger "a menace to Protestantism."

It wasn't until the latter part of the twentieth century that Canada would officially replace the idea of "assimilation" with a new one: "multiculturalism." Newcomers were still expected to embrace Canadian cultures and traditions, but they could expect to do so while maintaining their own cultures and traditions.

To Madokoro, multiculturalism is not only an idea but also a continuing process "of negotiating difference and accommodating difference."

So in that process, we trudge along. Toward the lofty but elusive ideal of a Canada that's inspired by difference, not threatened by it. It's an ideal that millions of immigrants have spent many decades fighting toward. And first among them were the Irish Catholics, there to pave the way.

Ann Hui is demographics reporter at *The Globe and Mail*.

Three: **Queens *of* *the* Gilded Age**

Kit Coleman, Sara Duncan and Faith Fenton pioneered women's journalism in Canada | **Jana G. Pruden**

The legion of newspapermen covering the Spanish-American War in June 1898 received some shocking news. A reporter was arriving by train to join the 150 or so other correspondents gathered in Tampa, and *she* had official papers from the U.S. War Department.

"A lady war correspondent!" wrote Charles E. Hands, one of the newsmen reporting on Cuba that summer. "The idea was too comic. We could not believe it. . . . After all, we said, there were limits of the sphere of women's usefulness."

His story about the new reporter's arrival ran under the headline: "Mrs. Blake Watkins, Lady War Correspondent."

Kathleen Blake Watkins – who would in a few months become Kathleen Blake Coleman, after she married for the third time – was better known to newspaper readers in Canada as "Kit of the *Mail*," a beloved columnist at one of the publications that would become today's *Globe and Mail*. Coleman was part of a rising tide of women boldly breaking into pages that, until then, had been seen as a man's domain.

Disgruntled newsmen aside, journalism was changing. Newspapers of the day were loosening their connection to political parties and becoming more independent business operations funded with advertising dollars. At the same time, the place of women in society was evolving, and editors had indeed begun to see the "usefulness" – or at least the potential revenue – to be had from women reporters writing for women readers.

"This was a period in which there was more and more emphasis on trying to make the newspaper appealing to women, because advertisers realized that women were spending a good portion of the domestic dollar," says Misao Dean, a specialist in nineteenth-century Canadian women writers. "They were creating features and columns specifically for women readers, and this was going to get them more advertising dollars."

Women's pages also came about at a time when there was increasing awareness of what women writers could contribute to society more broadly. On pages and in columns such as "Woman's World" at *The Globe* and "Women's Empire" at *The Empire*, female writers were tasked with producing "articles of interest to women" – or at least about the things male editors thought women wanted to read.

"There was grudging appreciation of their intelligence and their world view as being somewhat different from a male view," says Barbara Freeman, an adjunct research professor in the School of Journalism and Communication at Carleton University. "And maybe something worth considering from time to time."

———

In Canada, Kit Coleman of *The Mail*, Sara Jeannette Duncan of *The Globe* and Faith Fenton of *The Empire* (each paper a predecessor of *The Globe and Mail*) pioneered the place of women on the page, waging their own battles for respect, ink and the opportunity to write about more than the latest styles of hats – as glorious as the hats of the day may have been.

"Kit hated covering fashion, but twice a year, at least, she had to go down to the department stores and write up all the fashions," says Freeman, author of *Kit's Kingdom: The Journalism of Kathleen Blake Coleman*. "She always said that women should be able to write about politics and business."

It seems Hands would come to agree. Despite his early misgivings about Coleman's arrival in Tampa, he would, by the end of his story about her, admire her chops as a journalist and commend her ability to be "one of the boys."

Jill Downie, author of *A Passionate Pen: The Life and Times of Faith Fenton*, says it can be easy to forget the controls that existed on women's lives at the time and, in that environment, how truly revolutionary women in the reporting ranks would have been. She notes that women faced restrictions on what they wore, where they went and how they lived – with marriage still considered to be the ultimate goal. "Thinking outside that tiny little box was a very dangerous thing to do," she says.

Downie says the women's pages, sometimes known as the "lace-collar ghetto," was a section of the paper where women became trapped writing about domestic subjects, and they had limited opportunities to do serious work.

But there were great possibilities to be found in the women's pages too. Serious and even subversive matters were being addressed alongside – or even within – columns about cooking, gardening, social happenings and fashion, right under the noses of the men running the paper, or husbands leaning in for a look.

One *Globe* women's page from 1885 includes a story about dressing little dogs in fancy attire; instructions on how to make coffee syrup; tips on cleaning rooms where someone has been sick; a story about suffrage in the United States and why women should vote; an analysis of the wardrobe of a famous actress; much news about hats; an encouragement to women to try outdoor activities, including cycling; and an anecdote about a tall and "majestic-looking" female rancher travelling with her female companion to a cattle show, in which the rancher is quoted saying: "Men are all frauds. I wouldn't marry the best one of them that ever lived."

Dean says *The Globe*'s Duncan had an editor who allowed her to write what she wanted in her column, and "she went for it," even writing on suffrage about forty years before most women got the vote. "I think in these articles about appearance or about fashion, she was trying to suggest to women that many of the standards of beauty were themselves oppressive and were reinforcing more serious limitations on women's lives," says Dean, who has written extensively about Duncan's journalism and works of fiction.

When her male editor passed along a letter from a female reader asking for a household beauty remedy for freckles, Duncan made it clear in her response she had no such advice to give and instead questioned why the woman would want to get rid of them at all. "Don't you know that Cleopatra was freckled? . . . I like to think of you there against the sunset, with your bare arms akimbo on the gate, freckles and all," she wrote.

Her perspectives were daring, even revolutionary, and there was no small degree of pushback. As Fenton wrote in *The Empire* in 1891, after a reader raised the idea of a women's column that could be written without any restrictions: "I pictured the face of the managing editor were I to go to him with a request for such a column. Visions of woman suffrage, communism, libel suits and general anarchy would flit before him in swift succession."

Fenton understood that women themselves were still coming to terms with such bold ideas. She wrote in 1895 that it was hard for the average Canadian woman "to loosen the old conventionalities, the old-time proprieties and properness in which men have so carefully swaddled her."

It may be for this reason that Fenton's most subversive columns begin softly, using what Downie calls "her comfort words," asking whether women should be able to vote, to belong to certain clubs, to go out without male escorts. "She's trying to coax women that these are not dangerous thoughts," Downie says. "She's saying, 'It's safe to think like this. It's interesting to think like this.'"

But while she wrote of women's liberation, Fenton herself lived a double life for nineteen years. By day, she was a spinster teacher known by her real name Alice Freeman, and by night, Fenton, the popular newspaper writer. Downie says having two jobs was financially necessary because her salaries as a journalist and a teacher were less than half what her male colleagues made. The secrecy was similarly required because Fenton would have been fired from her teaching job had it been revealed that she was also writing for the newspaper.

This split between a woman's work and personal life wasn't unusual for the time. Coleman's identity was so mysterious that debate raged in the papers over who she was, and in 1890, *The Globe* ran a series of drawings asking, "Which is Kit?" – imagining who the real Kit of *The Mail* might be. Four of the eight images were men.

Freeman, the Carleton University professor, says Coleman had "a bit of the Irish blarney in her" and enjoyed the speculation about her age, appearance and gender. The differences between the woman and her byline were so stark that Freeman writes about her as two different characters: Kathleen in real life, Kit on the page.

Other female reporters in Canada, such as Vic Steinberg of the *Toronto News*, used male bylines and regularly went undercover as men to experience and report on things they couldn't have access to otherwise.

Duncan began her career writing under the name Garth, and later, Garth Grafton. Though it was apparent in her articles that she was female – she writes, for instance, about being a woman attempting to buy insurance for herself – the masculine pen name suited the convention of the time, even if readers knew the author was female. Dean says Duncan could be "quite snippy" about what she thought of as excessively feminine or frivolous pen names for women. "She took herself very seriously as a journalist," says Dean.

Although being a woman was a serious impediment in some ways, it also provided perspective and access that male reporters didn't have, such as when Fenton visited women's prisons, so "readers of the Empire might know something of the daily lives of those restless, broken-winged birds, the imprisoned women of Ontario."

When Coleman was being dispatched to cover the war in Cuba, a story in *The Catholic Register* noted that as a woman among the nurses, "she will be in a position to gain information of intense interest about the hospital service such as no male war correspondent has ever yet been able to gather on the field at first hand."

Still, Coleman wrote that she was "very keenly made to feel her inferiority" by some men of the press, who harassed her and tried to prevent her from doing her work, and that military generals brushed her away "as though I were an impertinent fly."

As one of two women covering Parliament while writing for *The Washington Post*, Duncan described an environment of choking cigar smoke, blue language and hostility that drove the women out of the press pool and into the library instead. She left Canada in 1888 to tour the world with another female journalist, and she married a man in India, moving away from journalism to become an accomplished fiction writer.

At the same time Coleman was breaking out of the women's pages to cover the war in Cuba, Fenton – then forty years old, unmarried and laid off during the merger of *The Mail* and *The Empire* in 1895 – journeyed to Yukon with a group from the Victorian Order of Nurses and became *The Globe*'s correspondent in the Klondike. It was a period that would come to define her journalistic career, in which she witnessed and covered serious, front-page news. That came to an end when she met a doctor and became "Mrs. John N. E. Brown," leaving her career as a journalist to, as she described it, be "the wife of her husband."

Coleman continued to write for newspapers and magazines until her death in 1915. Her final column, which ran a month before she died, talked about the babies fathered by soldiers overseas, describing the children as "The cruel outcome of our nonsensical wars, our absurd and shocking 'civilization,' our conventional mock modesty."

The women's reporting – informed by their past experiences and also by the time in which they lived – was not without its flaws. There are, in places, inaccuracies, insensitivities and patronizing attitudes. But while Dean says it's easy to either dismiss or excuse these writers, the reality is more complicated. "They were all individuals, and some of them were more progressive than we might expect," she says. "It's only by studying them in their historical context that we can come to understand how they represent the roots of our own ideas and prejudices."

Downie describes the early women reporters as "imperfect people who needed to make a living and managed to carve out an increasing role for women in the newspaper industry, despite continuing limitations because of their gender." She says examining the women's views and writing in the context of their time also gives a clear picture of how the present world has advanced and changed. "One cannot rectify or justify," she says. "One can only try to understand and explain the world she lived in."

In that restrictive world, the pioneering newspaperwomen of *The Globe*, *The Mail* and *The Empire* led serious and groundbreaking public discussions about issues such as spousal abuse, pay equity, poverty and women's independence, which would ignite the women's movement in the century to come.

The long-term impact of this early journalism by women is impossible to measure, but Downie recalls a story shared by a young woman after Fenton's death in 1936 that may give us a glimpse. The woman described her mother showing her a photo of Fenton journeying to the Klondike, part of "a human chain of persons going up an icy slope to a terrifying path between mountains, people looking like tiny black dots in the formidable scene."

"She remembered her mother saying, 'One of those tiny black specks is Faith,'" Downie says. "So there's a little girl being shown that picture of Faith Fenton the journalist doing this, and her mind will never be the same again. She will never think along the same lines. I would like to think that was the influence she had on a generation of women."

Their work didn't change everything – women journalists would continue to face serious hostility and prejudice on the job – but Dean says it helped create a market for women's voices and a place for women who said what they thought and who were direct about it. Because of that, she says, "It became less and less possible for newspapers to keep them out."

Coleman was the founding president of the Canadian Women's Press Club, formed in 1904 so female journalists barred from male press organizations could meet and support each other. There, the young women reporters gathered around Coleman, who encouraged them in their work and urged them to keep going in their careers, even when it was difficult.

"They really looked up to her, and they, in turn, did their best," Dean says. "And that whole generation inspired the next generation, which inspired the next generation."

Navigating male-dominated newsrooms herself in the 1970s, Freeman says the example set by persevering female journalists such as Coleman continued to help set the course for the women who followed.

"If we have so many women in journalism today, it goes back over one hundred years, one hundred and twenty years, to when these women started out," she says. "It was really due to them, because they kept trying."

Jana G. Pruden is a feature writer at *The Globe and Mail*, based in Edmonton.

ABOVE: A school near Brandon,
Manitoba, ca. 1900–1910. (Canada
Dept. of Mines and Resources/
Library and Archives Canada)

Four: *The dynamic duo of "sunny ways"*

John Willison, Wilfrid Laurier and the Manitoba Schools Question | **Evan Annett**

C anadians of the twenty-first century might think that "sunny ways" originated with Justin Trudeau. It did not. The phrase entered Canada's lexicon more than a century earlier, at one of the nation's gloomiest times. The 1890s brought new strife between anglophone Protestants and francophone Catholics angered by Métis leader Louis Riel's execution after the rebellions he led in the West. Canadians had to decide whether their bicultural bargain could last.

Into this came the Manitoba government's illegal decision to abolish French-language, Catholic-run schools, the crux of what became known as the Manitoba Schools Question. Could a province do this, inflaming half the country, or should Ottawa invoke its constitutional right to disallow the legislation, incensing the other half?

The governing Conservatives, in disarray after Sir John A. Macdonald's death, leaned toward the second answer. Opposition leader Sir Wilfrid Laurier, however, sought a deal with Manitoba that he likened to Aesop's fable *The North Wind and the Sun*: whereas the wind (disallowance) would make a man grip his coat tighter, the sunny way (friendly negotiations) would coax him to remove it.

But imagine if Aesop's contest had been rigged. Imagine that a mountain blocked the wind while advising his friend, the sun, on how to shine to maximum effect. That mountain was Sir John Willison, *The Globe*'s editor and one of Laurier's most important Ontario apparatchiks. From 1890 to 1896, the Protestant newspaperman and the Catholic politician haggled over a policy that could break Canada if they got it wrong.

For *The Globe*, *The Mail* and *The Empire* – all ancestors of the modern *Globe and Mail* – the 1890s radically shifted the balance of media power, testing newspapers' relationships with the parties that paid their bills. "Sunny ways" would not change Canada as much as Laurier hoped. But for Canadian journalism, it was a moment that moved mountains.

When Willison and Laurier met in the 1880s, one was *The Globe*'s correspondent in Ottawa, the other a promising MP who, in 1887, became Liberal leader. Willison "was quite fascinated by Laurier's abilities" from the start, says Carleton University historian Richard Clippingdale, author of the Willison biography *The Power of the Pen*.

In his 1919 memoirs, Willison remembered an early visit to Laurier's home in Arthabaskaville, Quebec, that impressed upon him Laurier's "knowledge of men and of books, his clarity and vigour of mind." Laurier, doubt-stricken about whether English Canada would accept a francophone Catholic leader, valued the insight of someone like Willison, who could explain the Ontarian perspective.

The friendship deepened Willison's ties to a party he had supported since his youth. When he was a teenager in Southwestern Ontario's rural

Huron County, a visit to an uncle's house introduced Willison to *The Globe*, the antithesis of the Tory-allied *Leader* and *Daily Telegraph* that his parents read at home. When the Tories established a more formidable Toronto organ, *The Mail*, in 1872, Willison read that paper too. But his dream was to one day become a journalist at *The Globe*, the Dominion's most influential English-language paper and an ally of, but never totally beholden to, the Liberal Party.

Now that he was *The Globe*'s man in the Parliamentary Press Gallery, Willison not only reported on what the Liberals were doing but advised Laurier on what the public was thinking. And the Liberal leader took that advice. "Even if somebody in Ottawa, in the caucus, told [Laurier] differently, he tended to think that Willison probably knew what the opinion in Ontario was better than they did," Clippingdale says.

Willison needed to know plenty about Ontario's politics just to survive in Toronto's cutthroat newspaper business. In the Gilded Age, at least five and briefly seven newspapers fought for attention in a city with fewer people than modern-day Regina. Ontario's capital and largest city had been dubbed "the Belfast of Canada" because of unending feuds between its Orange Protestant ruling class and Catholics, immigrants and the poor. A paper could flourish or fail depending on whose side it chose.

In 1887, Macdonald and his Conservatives created a new paper, *The Empire*, when *The Mail* broke away to pursue a more anti-Catholic, anti-French course than the Old Chieftain would allow. *The Mail* wanted French abolished as an official language in anglophone provinces and even advocated the creation of a third federal party that might break up Confederation to keep the "British column" supreme.

On June 6, 1891, shortly after winning his sixth general election, Macdonald died of a stroke. Over five years, the Tories cycled through four replacements. First was Sir John Abbott, a septuagenarian senator who resigned after a diagnosis of terminal cancer; next, Sir John S. Thompson, a fortysomething MP who died of a heart attack in 1894. Then came senator Sir Mackenzie Bowell, a veteran newspaperman and owner of *The Belleville Intelligencer*. Bowell saw no need to keep both *The Mail* and *The Empire* going in Toronto. On February 6, 1895, *The Empire* announced that it was finished, and the next day, *The Daily Mail and Empire* took its place. All *Empire* journalists lost their jobs.

Weeks earlier, after a fire had destroyed the *Globe* building at Yonge and Melinda Streets along with much of the surrounding block, the Conservative *Empire* had offered space in its newsroom to its Liberal rival. Citing the two staffs' "exceedingly pleasant relations" when they were working together in the same office, Willison's paper declared *The Empire*'s end "a matter of unusual regret to *The Globe*."

The instigator of the Manitoba schools crisis, premier Thomas Greenway, had been an acquaintance of Willison for more than a decade, once offering him a job in the Manitoba town Greenway had founded. Willison refused. Now, thirteen years later, the premier was poking at one of Confederation's sore spots, and Willison, *The Globe*'s editor, sought to understand what was happening in Manitoba and to help Laurier respond.

When Manitoba was made a province in 1870, its francophone population, mostly Métis, was roughly equal in number to anglophones. Riel and his allies had secured for each a separate school system: one Catholic and French, one Protestant and English. But new English-speaking settlers, mostly from Ontario, quickly became the majority, especially when Métis, denied land that Canada had promised, moved west.

In 1890, after a rally in Portage la Prairie energized anglophones against all things French, Greenway defunded Catholic schools and stripped French of official-language status. Parliament could have disallowed this immediately. Instead Macdonald, and later Thompson, punted the issue to the courts, hoping they would sort it out.

Initially, *Globe* editorials were quiet on the subject. Laurier, writing to Willison in June 1890, had warned him to avoid "irritating questions" of language and religion. The final judicial answer came from Britain five years later, in January 1895: Franco-Manitobans had a real grievance, and it was up to Parliament to decide whether to remedy or ignore it. Macdonald, Abbott and Thompson were all dead now, and Bowell was in a bind. He was a former Orange grand master, so doing nothing would look like Protestant prejudice, but national disunity would ruin his party's legacy. In the end, Bowell tried, and failed at, everything at once. His efforts to reach a deal with Greenway went nowhere; he waffled about whether and when to use the remedial law his cabinet was preparing to disallow the Manitoba law; Quebec MPs who wanted swifter action threatened to resign or revolt.

Through early 1895, Laurier and Willison argued through the mail about the Liberals' next moves. Laurier asked that *The Globe* leave room open for remedial laws in case a Liberal government needed them. Willison pushed back, careful to stress that this was for political and not sectarian reasons. "I do not object at all to Separate Schools for Manitoba," he wrote on April 1. ". . . But Manitoba has taken a course, and so long as she chooses to adhere to that course interference from Ottawa, in my humble judgement, will be futile and mischievous, possibly disastrous." The best outcome, Willison believed, would be "some sort of an agreement between Manitoba and the Dominion Government."

Laurier lost his patience over a July 17 *Globe* editorial that dared Bowell to dissolve Parliament and accused politicians in Ottawa of stoking Quebeckers' sectarian grudges over Manitoba. That, Laurier wrote Willison in an angry letter, seemed to be "as much an attack on the Liberal Party as on the Conservative Party." Willison apologized. "I would just about attack my own father," he wrote back.

In the fall of 1895, Willison went on a tour of the Prairies, where Greenway squired him around Manitoba's wheat fields. In a report from Banff in the September 20 *Globe*, Willison concluded separate schools were a non-starter: "Here, English must be the commercial tongue, and English sentiment dominate, and English institutions grow and flourish." To oppose this would be "a vain battle with the gods and provoke retaliation when the west reaches the full measure of its strength."

Laurier did not need more convincing. He had resolved privately to oppose remedial legislation; now, it was a matter of bringing that message to voters. Laurier tested his Aesop metaphor at a speech in Morrisburg, Ontario, on October 8: "The government are very windy," he said. "They have blown and raged and threatened, but the more they have threatened and raged and blown, the more that man Greenway has stuck to his coat. If it were in my power, I would try the sunny way."

In the next day's *Globe*, those words ran a few columns over from a big Eaton's department store ad for winter coats and blankets. The metaphor-muddling coincidence was also a reminder: cold days were coming. There was still time for Tory disallowance legislation to make compromise impossible. Unless Laurier acted first.

In Toronto, *The Mail and Empire* struggled to make sense of its new circumstances. Journalists who once amplified Orange Protestant francophobia were now aligned with a party seeking to rescue Franco-Manitobans. Ontarians noticed: the paper's circulation stagnated in the first six months of 1896, while *The Globe*'s grew.

Soon it was Bowell who needed rescuing. A faction of ministers, fed up with his equivocation on Manitoba, forced him to cede power to elder statesman and diplomat Sir Charles Tupper. Tupper pressed ahead with the remedial bill, now dubbed C-58, but Laurier's Liberals were able to filibuster the legislation until Tupper's time was up and an election was scheduled for June 23, 1896.

The Globe got busy touting the Liberals as the party of provincial rights. As Willison predicted, it was a winning issue, even in Quebec. In 1896, provincial rights trumped French-language rights in the eyes of French Canadians. The Liberals got a majority, and Tupper became the shortest-serving prime minister in Canadian history. The next day's *Globe* called Laurier's victory "a bond of union between the two great divisions of the people."

Laurier and Greenway worked out a compromise that kept a single non-denominational school board but added some French-language

Catholic instruction in regions where demand warranted. Laurier's solution may have averted a national crisis, but it was not the deliverance francophones hoped for. Manitoba made its schools English-only again in 1916, when Laurier was in opposition, and it would take decades of Franco-Manitoban activism to undo that. As for Indigenous people in Manitoba – whose children were forced to unlearn their mother tongues in residential schools that mostly taught in English – neither Laurier nor *The Globe* spared much thought for their minority language rights.

Still, the Manitoba solution was critical to Laurier's reputation as a great conciliator, a legend that Willison helped to build in a 1903 biography of his friend. In later interviews, Willison boasted that "sunny ways" couldn't have happened without *The Globe*, that without its opposition, Laurier would have supported remedial action from the start.

The events of 1895–96 put *The Globe* on a new path to success. Its competition was in disarray, its incinerated headquarters was rebuilt, and patronage and printing contracts – which governing parties of the era would often use to reward their own newspapers – flowed from now-Liberal Ottawa. But one thing Laurier's election couldn't change was Willison's propensity to argue with him. They clashed over trade, the Anglo-Boer War and *The Globe*'s even-handed coverage of the Conservatives in the 1902 Ontario election. That was the year Willison decided he had had enough: he left to run the rival *News*, whose owners promised him more independence.

In leaving, Willison wrote in his memoirs, "I had no thought of a political separation from Sir Wilfrid Laurier." But they had a new argument brewing over Laurier's wish to guarantee separate French schools in Alberta and Saskatchewan. "I doubted if he would ever give effect to his intention," Willison recalled, but in 1905 Laurier did just that in the acts that created those provinces. To Willison, this was the kind of federal meddling that he and Laurier had worked so hard to avoid in Manitoba, and *The News* came out hard against it. "I regard with no respect at all the contention that we are constitutionally obliged to create an educational system for the Western Territories," Willison told Laurier in a terse exchange of letters that would be their last for three years.

But in 1908, Willison, nostalgic in his advancing age, wrote to the prime minister that "my personal affection for yourself has not been overcome," and he considered their feud settled. "I cannot find fault with a friend if he differs from me, but loss of friendship is painful; in your case it was particularly painful," Laurier replied. "But no more of this: let it rest in oblivion until such time as meeting again as of old at the fireside, talking of this, that and the other thing, that one may also turn up."

Even when their political opinions clashed, Willison and Laurier never lost respect for each other. For all the frosty rhetoric between their cultures and creeds, sunny ways prevailed.

Evan Annett is an editor on the visuals team at *The Globe and Mail*.

ABOVE: Uprooting of Japanese Canadians, 1942. Japanese Canadians say their goodbyes at a Vancouver train station. (Library and Archives Canada)

Five: **Warm welcomes, cold shoulders**

The Globe often offered a humanitarian view of immigration but in its worst moments urged Canada to close its doors to certain people | **Marsha Lederman**

T he front-page headline demanded action: "Time to close the gates." It was March 26, 1908. Centred on the page, a list of three recently murdered men and their four "supposed slayers" – their non-Anglo-Saxon, ethnic names unmissable in all-caps. "The Goth is at our own gates," *The Globe* editorial warned.

"One has only to glance at this list to see that the Slav and the Italian are swelling the statistics of crime in this country."

The only effective cure for the "invasion" would be "the closing of the gates on the offscourings of the Slav and Latin races."

Canada was in the midst of an immigration boom and a nation-forming discussion about the country's racial makeup, with much hand-wringing about keeping it British. "Slavs" was a term the paper – and others – used to describe a large swath of Eastern Europeans.

One hundred years is a long time in this young country's history. But a century has its constants. On March 26, 2008, exactly one hundred years later, *The Globe and Mail* was still weighing in on immigration. It supported Conservative reforms that would give the immigration minister broad powers over the prioritizing and processing of applications in an effort to deal with a huge backlog.

"This will not sit well with some ethnic communities, for whom the Liberals have made sacred the right to bring in aging parents and grandparents. But it stands to benefit our economy," the paper stated in another editorial that month. "Immigration policy, not to be confused with refugee policy, should first and foremost fit Canada's needs."

While the backgrounds and originating locales of Canada's newcomers have changed over time, immigration has always played a role in this nation – and played out in the pages of its national newspaper.

Frequently using language excruciating to read today, *Globe* reports, editorials and opinion columns – sometimes written by newsmakers themselves – have covered and even led the immigration debate. *The Globe* often, although certainly not always, offered a progressive, humanitarian view, long before the tide of opinion seemed to turn.

But if it was at times more favourable toward immigrants than were many Canadians – including government officials – the paper also at times amplified fear and panic. In its worst moments, it urged Canada to close its doors to certain people.

The narrative many Canadians have been raised on, the fairy tale we like to tell ourselves, is that this is a nation built by newcomers on vast, empty land – a myth that stings for Indigenous people. A country that is accepting and open to immigrants – all too often, another myth.

"Immigrants were not always welcomed with an outpouring of compassion for the world's downtrodden, oppressed and displaced," wrote

Globe reporter Victor Malarek in his 1987 book *Haven's Gate: Canada's Immigration Fiasco.* "They were brought here to work and Canada was not about to coddle them. . . . They were sometimes shunned, patronized and exploited."

As *The Globe* marks its 180th anniversary, questions around immigration continue to populate its pages. Who gets in, who doesn't. On what criteria. Deafening in its absence for many years: discussion of who was displaced by settlers as Canada formed and evolved.

From the Chinese head tax to Roxham Road, a trip through the pages of *The Globe* offers the real story in black and white. Canada – if it opened its gates at all – has often been inhospitable, even hostile, to newcomers.

For Canada, underpopulation would be "a constant and lasting problem," *Globe and Mail* journalist Doug Saunders noted in his 2017 book *Maximum Canada: Why 35 Million Canadians Are Not Enough.*

At Confederation in 1867, Canada's population was 3.5 million. The vast majority were white: French, Irish, English and Scottish. But Chinese men began coming to British Columbia in large numbers in the 1880s, primarily to work on the railway.

Newspaper coverage at the time displays striking antipathy toward those men, often referred to as "John Chinaman." Even pieces supporting Chinese immigration employed dodgy language and stereotypes. In 1878, when the B.C. government wanted to restrict and regulate Chinese immigration – a proposal that predated a national Chinese head tax – *The Globe* wrote: "If every one who is comparatively ignorant with rather demoralized religious ideas and a spirit that is content with little, is to be excluded from Canada for instance, where shall we begin, and where shall we end? Levy a prohibitory tax upon the Chinese, is the same thing to be done with the negro or the East Indian, with the Italian or the Irishman?"

The paper contained contradictions within its own pages and was not always enlightened. "It is not easy to see how we shall escape being overrun by them," read an 1884 piece by a *Globe* correspondent.

"Nothing but restrictive legislation against Chinese immigration will suffice for our protection."

The Chinese Immigration Act of 1885 – the first piece of legislation to exclude immigrants based on ethnic origins – imposed a stiff $50 head tax. It increased in 1900 to $100 and in 1903 to a staggering $500 (about $15,000 today). Later, the 1923 Chinese Immigration Act severely restricted entry to Canada. It was repealed in 1947.

There was also much written about the "Japanese crisis" at the turn of the last century, as Japanese people (Canadians frequently used a different term, as did some *Globe* headlines) began to settle in B.C. When rioting targeted Vancouver's Chinese and Japanese neighbourhoods in September 1907 and some victims fought back, one *Globe* story announced, "Very bad news from Vancouver: Japanese were buying firearms yesterday." An editorial called for prevention of further disturbance, punishment for the guilty and compensation for Japanese people who were hurt or had property damaged. But it added: "We must show that we have institutions, conditions, and standards of conduct worthy of being preserved from the deteriorating influences of foreign admixtures."

That same editorial called on Ottawa to oversee the contentious issue of Japanese migration. "This would remove a great source of irritation," the paper stated.

In 1908, Canada negotiated a deal that saw Japan voluntarily restrict immigration to Canada to four hundred people annually. It was called a "Gentlemen's Agreement."

A huge influx of other immigrants came to Canada during the early twentieth century. From 1896 to 1914, nearly three million arrived, almost half between 1910 and 1913. While most came from Britain and the U.S., many continental Europeans arrived too. Coverage of the time is rife with references to hordes of "Slavs" and "Galicians" and comments about Ukrainian immigrants in sheepskin coats. (The people were sometimes simply called "Sheepskins.")

That these newcomers were largely white was no accident. While Canada launched an aggressive campaign to lure farmers, it wanted white farmers. Black people, officials said, were not suited to Canadian conditions. "But colour, of course, was the real obstacle," wrote Valerie Knowles in *Strangers at Our Gates: Canadian Immigration and Immigration Policy, 1540–2015*. Indeed, Canadian policy was overtly discriminatory.

The Continuous Journey Regulation of 1908 required prospective immigrants to enter Canada directly from their country of origin, effectively blocking immigration from India – no ships sailed directly from there. The Immigration Act of 1910 prohibited immigrants deemed "unsuited to the climate or requirements of Canada." (An order-in-council the following year, which was adopted but never implemented, sought to ban Black immigration outright.) In 1919, the government amended the act to exclude immigrants from enemy alien countries and gave officials the discretion to prohibit immigrants based on nationality, race, class or "peculiar" customs.

The effects of these laws led to some of the darkest stories in Canada's immigration history. Sometimes, *The Globe* spoke out against these injustices, other times not.

In May 1914, the *Komagata Maru*, carrying 376 Indians, arrived in Vancouver. As British subjects, they believed they could immigrate to Canada. But they were stuck on board for two months while the courts heard arguments and the public fumed – fuelled by often hysterical and racist reportage.

While a 2017 examination of the 1914 media coverage found local newspapers to be far worse, *Globe* headlines included "The Hindu peril and the relief" and "Obstinate Hindus make fresh demand." (The demand? Better food.)

Yet *The Globe* urged readers to "Treat the Hindus generously." (Those on board were, in fact, overwhelmingly Sikh, not Hindu.) And it ran a scathing editorial questioning why Canada claimed the right to enter their country "and not let them enter ours."

The ship was ultimately sent back.

During the years of Nazi tyranny, Canada admitted fewer than five thousand Jews, reported Irving Abella and Harold Troper in *None Is Too Many: Canada and the Jews of Europe 1933–1948*. The book is named for a bureaucrat's response when asked how many Jews Canada should let in.

Following Kristallnacht in 1938, *The Globe* called for relaxed regulations to admit some German and Austrian refugees who could farm: "Silence is not possible when people are being treated like animals."

After Canada refused to help more than nine hundred German-Jewish refugees aboard the doomed MS *St. Louis* in June 1939, a *Globe* headline read "Canada condemns Jews to suicide."

During and after the Second World War, *The Globe* repeatedly called for increased British immigration – and help for European refugees. Many Canadians, including Prime Minister Mackenzie King, were against this, despite the Holocaust's horrors. Eventually, doors opened.

The Globe's narrative regarding Japanese Canadians was starkly different. Once at war with Japan, Canada forced about 21,000 Japanese Canadians into internment camps.

In a November 1943 editorial, *The Globe* – stating British Columbians would be unhappy to see their former Japanese neighbours returned to their former properties, vocations or community status – wrote "wholesale deportation may become the only feasible option."

When readers accused *The Globe* of being "cold-blooded," the newspaper doubled down: "We agree that the deportation . . . would be a departure from accepted traditions, but the Japanese present a very special problem."

It's an ugly contradiction. *The Globe* championed European refugees entering Canada but couldn't imagine reintegrating Japanese Canadians who already lived here – without any evidence of disloyalty. The editorial was titled "Disposing of the Japanese."

"You dispose of garbage," says Canadian author Mark Sakamoto, who wrote about his family's internment in *Forgiveness: A Gift from My Grandparents*. "So here's the paper of record saying that a whole group of people are garbage that should be disposed of."

Sakamoto notes that authorities seek public support by degrading the humanity of those targeted – calling them rats or garbage. "It's so sad that Canada was doing that at the same time it was fighting on the side of angels against people who were doing the same thing."

Such contradictions in Canadian immigration policy continued after the war.

In 1956, when Soviet tanks crushed an anti-Communist rebellion in Hungary, sending thousands fleeing to Austria, *The Globe* campaigned to bring them to Canada.

"For shame!" a Saturday front-page editorial cried, noting that Canada – a "half-empty country" – was promising only "top priority" to Hungarians who met immigration requirements, and interest-free loans for travel costs. The government, *The Globe* charged, "has displayed the warmth and generosity of a codfish."

It urged an airlift and for Ontario to house and feed them. "Let it fling the door wide, wide open."

By Monday, *The Globe* got "Action!" its headline stated. A provincial official was heading to Austria. By midweek, Ottawa announced it would pay the airfare for all those from Hungary who wanted to make Canada home.

Canada accepted more than 37,000 Hungarians.

This warm Canadian welcome (and that for thousands of Czecho-slovakians later fleeing the Soviet invasion) was no doubt informed by the Red Scare and skin colour – these immigrants were white.

Under the Immigration Act of 1952, the government could still limit or prohibit immigrants for reasons that included nationality and ethnicity.

But *The Globe*'s attitude was changing, and the paper started calling for change. A March 1956 editorial asked "Who's prejudiced?" Not Canadian people, *The Globe* said, naively asserting that individual acts of discrimination were "so rare in most parts of Canada as to make headlines and arouse public wrath." It concluded: "There is, in fact, only one place where racial prejudice is powerfully entrenched and racial discrimination sweepingly practiced; and that is in official Ottawa."

The paper applauded new policies introduced in 1962 eliminating overt racial discrimination but found the resulting increase in immigration from what was then the British and other West Indies in 1962 and 1963 "disappointingly" small.

In 1967, Canada implemented a new immigration points system, which evaluated applicants in categories including education and employment prospects. When that brought more arrivals from the Caribbean and Asia the following year, *The Globe* wrote: "The diversification they bring to Canada is an exciting and a maturing influence."

In 1979, a new crisis: "boat people" fleeing Vietnam, often in makeshift vessels. *The Globe* called on Canada to help, citing its shameful record on Second World War refugees. "Will the [Joe] Clark Government of 1979 look as gutless to the Canadians of 2009 as the Mackenzie King Government of 1942 does to us today?" wrote foreign affairs columnist Stanley McDowell in July 1979.

"People are drowning, starving, being raped and beaten and set adrift to be dehydrated by the sun or eaten by sharks."

Immigration minister Ron Atkey distributed copies of *None Is Too Many* to his cabinet colleagues, urging them to save the day.

They did. In 1979 and 1980, Canada welcomed sixty thousand Southeast Asian refugees. In 1986, the United Nations gave its Nansen Refugee Award to the people of Canada – the only time it has been awarded to an entire country.

But, as *The Globe* reported, the immigration system was marred by bureaucracy, queue-jumping and bogus claims. Changes tightening immigration rules in 1987 enraged refugee advocates – and the opposition. Liberal MP David Berger said the Conservative measures would bar even "Jesus of Nazareth."

In a *Globe* column, Berger wrote: "Which country will maintain a generous attitude toward refugees if Canada doesn't?"

On September 3, 2015, an image appeared on *The Globe*'s front page – and in newspapers around the world. It was a Syrian boy, Alan Kurdi, dead on a beach in Turkey. The two-year-old had drowned seeking refuge in the West with his family. (This hit home for Canadians even harder when they learned that the boy's aunt, who lived in B.C., had attempted to sponsor other family members but was rejected.)

While some *Globe* readers were furious about the A1 photograph, then–public editor Sylvia Stead responded, "a newspaper has a responsibility at times to show the horrors of war and death." There have been times throughout history, she wrote, when publishing a photo has changed public understanding or opinion of a world event.

Indeed. Between November 4, 2015, and December 31, 2016, close to forty thousand Syrian refugees were admitted to Canada – in many cases sponsored by individuals or groups of Canadians. Many more followed.

In 2022, Canada welcomed more than 130,000 Ukrainians fleeing Russia's invasion.

That same year also saw more than 39,000 asylum-seekers from more than one hundred countries cross at an irregular border – the vast majority at the gateless New York-Quebec border at Roxham Road.

Writing in *The Globe*, Quebec premier François Legault stated, "We have reason to be proud of our tradition of welcoming refugees." But, he added, Roxham Road had become "a real problem," and he called for the crossing to be closed. Not long afterward, Canada and the U.S. announced an agreement to do just that.

Border barriers are not merely physical. Canada erects walls with policy, politics, attitude.

On one Roxham Road story, before the policy change, a reader typed an online comment, asking where the sympathy was for Canadian taxpayers. One wonders – assuming this reader is not Indigenous – how their ancestors came to Canada. Were they refugees, labourers, early settlers? Were they met with support? Hostility?

And what sort of lives and opportunities do their descendants enjoy because someone made the journey, fraught as it was and is, to Canada?

Marsha Lederman is a columnist at *The Globe and Mail*, based in Vancouver.

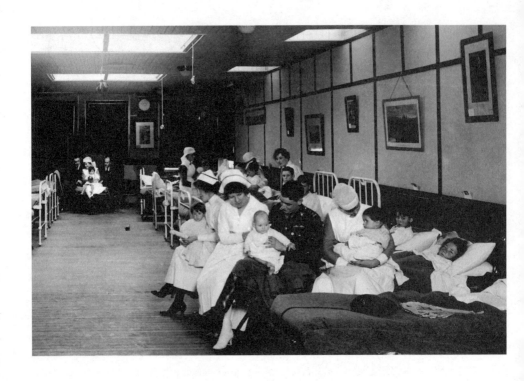

ABOVE: Women and children
receive treatment at Kingston
Emergency Hospital in the fall of
1918 during that pandemic.
(Kingston Emergency Hospital/
Archives of Ontario)

Six: *The* tale *of* two pandemics, *a* century apart

The Globe's underplaying of the Spanish influenza pandemic, far deadlier than COVID-19, seems puzzling today
| **Kelly Grant**

O n the morning of October 25, 1918, *The Globe* ran a letter on its front page from the widow of an army chaplain who died of Spanish influenza.

"Canada can well be ashamed," the headline read, quoting what the widow said were some of the last words of her husband, Captain Roy Kain. He perished at a military base hospital in Toronto, crammed in a room with five other dying men and, according to his wife, ignored by doctors struggling to care for more than eight hundred soldiers in a building fit for three hundred, at most.

"I shall never forget the horror of that room," Lillian Kain wrote. "Can any front-line trench be worse than to be placed in a room with the most advanced cases, to hear the cries of the dying, to realize your own time is coming as surely as the sun will rise, to feel that you are suffering and dying from the neglect and carelessness of others?"

The letter is one of the few front-page items that *The Globe* – the newspaper that would later absorb a competitor and become *The Globe and Mail* – ran about the catastrophic wave of influenza that swept across Canada and the world in the autumn of 1918.

There should have been far more of them. Despite killing an estimated fifty thousand Canadians over two years at a time when the country's population was just over eight million, the Spanish influenza pandemic was often relegated to *The Globe*'s inside pages.

To be fair, it's not as though *The Globe* ignored the flu's toll on civilians. It carried 356 articles mentioning influenza in October 1918, the height of the pandemic. Many of those stories would be hauntingly familiar to anyone who lived through the COVID-19 pandemic. Schools, theatres, dance halls and other public gathering places were closed. Hospitals were overrun. Gauze masks came into vogue. Toronto's medical officer of health, Charles Hastings, encouraged people to shop by phone and pleaded with bosses to let their symptomatic employees stay home, lest they spread the flu to more workers.

However, such stories rarely received front-page treatment.

Moreover, *The Globe*'s editorial pages in 1918 lacked the kinds of crusading columns, editorials and investigative reporting that would mark its coverage of COVID a century later. Veteran health columnist André Picard set the tone on March 11, 2020, when he called on Canada's leaders to "Shut it down," a few days before officials began closing schools, businesses and major public events in the face of the frightening new virus.

In contrast, the paper's editorials at the peak of the Spanish influenza crisis were uncharacteristically tepid, sometimes amounting to little more than the reprinting of public-health advice and the commending of volunteers for tending to the sick. "Effective methods of combatting the Spanish influenza must be mainly personal," wrote Junius, as *The Globe* calls the authors of its unsigned editorials, on October 9, 1918. Closing schools, churches and other public gathering places hadn't saved Boston from the ravages of the flu, so a "minimum of community disturbance" should be the order of the day in Toronto, Junius wrote – though when the city's medical officer of health began enacting closings a week later, *The Globe* didn't push back.

Looking back at the coverage from the vantage point of a journalist who reported on COVID-19 nearly every day for eighteen months, *The Globe*'s underplaying of the far deadlier Spanish influenza pandemic seems puzzling. But unlike reporters in the COVID era, *Globe* journalists and editors in 1918 were consumed with covering a world war that was weeks from ending as Spanish influenza peaked in Toronto. They were also working in a different media world, one shaped by the space limitations of a physical newspaper instead of the infinite space of the internet.

Today, medical historians believe the Spanish influenza first came to Canada in a spring 1918 herald wave mistaken for a bad season of "la grippe," the French word for influenza. *The Globe*'s first mention of an unusually dangerous type of flu was contained in a May 29, 1918, news brief out of Spain that described Madrid's business sector as paralyzed by a "grip" that had infected a third of the population, including King Alfonso.

The true origins of the 1918 pandemic are still contested, but what is known is that it didn't begin in Spain. However, that country's neutral status made it the first place from which correspondents could report on the disease's toll without their stories being quashed by wartime censors. Throughout nearly two years of coverage, *The Globe* referred to pandemic influenza as being of the "Spanish" type.

In early twentieth-century Canada, protecting public health fell to municipalities and provinces. Ottawa's only relevant job was enforcing quarantine regulations for ships of immigrants presumed to be carrying contagious scourges such as cholera and smallpox.

There existed no national health department at the time. Some reformers, led by recently enfranchised women, pushed for the creation of one during the war years, partly to stem the spread of venereal disease in anticipation of infected soldiers returning from Europe. *The Globe* supported the establishment of a Dominion health department and the prosecution of a national war on the "social diseases," as the paper often referred to syphilis and gonorrhea.

"This evil," Junius wrote of venereal diseases on August 30, 1917, "ramifying through every class, stalking unseen where least expected, and lying in ambush to spring upon the innocent and helpless, who are cursed for the sins of the guilty, has reached such dimensions that it must be brought under control to save society from devastation."

In January 1918, C.K. Clarke, dean of the University of Toronto's Faculty of Medicine and director of the Toronto General Hospital, described the toll of venereal diseases in a four-part series in *The Globe*. He heaped blame on prostitutes, 60 per cent of whom he labelled as "mentally defective" girls who ought to be isolated on industrial farms.

The Globe's drumbeat of editorials, written against the backdrop of an Ontario judge's inquiry into legal means of controlling VD, used similar language. They bemoaned the "feeble-minded" and "fallen" women who spread disease to men who couldn't control themselves – men who went on to infect their innocent wives and unborn children.

There was no such moralizing in the pages of *The Globe* when a terrifying new incarnation of the flu reached Canada. "The big difference? Sex," says Heather MacDougall, professor emerita of history at the University of Waterloo. "Influenza was indiscriminate in who it attacked and who it killed and didn't have anything to do with sex."

Nor did the arrival of Spanish influenza have anything to do with immigrants from overseas, frequent scapegoats in past infectious-disease outbreaks, or with soldiers returning from the battlefields of Europe, a common misconception about the pandemic's origins in Canada.

In truth, as historian Mark Humphries explains in a 2013 book optimistically titled *The Last Plague*, influenza spread north to Canada from the United States. The virus arrived in Canada in mid-September 1918, in four different places around the same time: the Quebec town of Victoriaville, where a Eucharistic Congress seeded a civilian outbreak *The Globe* didn't cover; Sydney, Nova Scotia, where a U.S. ship bound for Europe dropped hundreds of infected soldiers on a small-town hospital; a military hospital in St. Jean, Quebec, where recruits from Boston likely brought the virus north; and Niagara-on-the-Lake, where a training camp for Polish-American recruits for the French army was the site of the first major outbreak in Ontario.

Captain Kain was ministering with the Polish camp, as *The Globe* called it, when he caught the flu. His wife took him to the base hospital, located inside a previously shuttered Toronto General Hospital building, hoping he would receive better care, only to see him die there.

Lillian Kain's letter in *The Globe* came via Toronto mayor Tommy Church, a colourful conservative who used the press to harangue military leaders over conditions at the base hospital and military camps, including one for Canadians at Niagara. He received the widow's letter in his capacity as head of the police commission and apparently shared it with the press.

Giving prominent play to coverage of the base hospital scandal was, for *The Globe* and other papers, a back door to criticizing Robert Borden's Union government without running afoul of press censors or condemning a war *The Globe* supported. Putting Kain's letter on the front page, "would have been a very political act," says Humphries, a professor of history at Wilfrid Laurier University.

At the time of Captain Kain's death, a coroner's inquest was already under way at Toronto's morgue, ostensibly into the death of one member of the Royal Air Force, twenty-six-year-old Cadet Freeman A. Davidson, a law student and conscript who died at the base hospital on October 13, 1918. The inquest morphed into an investigation of whether the facility was properly equipped to care for the crush of infected men who streamed through its doors when influenza struck.

The Globe covered every turn of the proceedings, from Church's testimony blaming Ottawa for "bungling everything," to the fire chief declaring the base hospital a "fire trap," to surgeon-general J.T. Fotheringham, the acting director-general of medical services for Canada, "flaying" the press for what he deemed their unfair coverage of the scandal.

"It is the duty of the Government not only to investigate and discipline the men responsible for this state of affairs," *The Globe* editorial board wrote on October 30, 1918, "but to see that they are replaced by men who are competent and ready to undertake, without a moment of unnecessary delay, the institution of a new and a better system under which Canadian citizens may be assured that their suffering soldier sons are being cared for as they deserve. The government must act at once."

Kain herself testified at the inquest on November 5, 1918. *The Globe* described the widow as a frank but "somewhat nervous" witness who "bore up well" under questioning, considering officials at the base hospital called a key aspect of her letter false. They testified that doctors examined Captain Kain's chest daily and that he received the best of care. She wrote that her husband went five days without a chest exam.

Realistically, there wasn't much doctors anywhere could do for the infected. Antibiotics for the bacterial pneumonias that preyed on influenza-weakened patients were more than a decade away. The pathogen that caused the flu pandemic wasn't even identified as a virus until the 1930s. The only recourse was preventing infection in the first place; cramming soldiers cheek by jowl into an old hospital building did the opposite.

When the coroner's jury in the base hospital scandal delivered its verdict, it exonerated local doctors and nurses and instead pinned the blame squarely on Ottawa "for not providing better hospital accommodation for soldiers after four years' duration of the war."

Spanish influenza, unlike COVID-19, struck young adults with a particular ferocity, further hollowing out the same demographic group felled on the battlefield. Medical historians can't say for certain why Spanish influenza was deadliest to people in their twenties and thirties, but a leading theory is that less-lethal versions of influenza A didn't circulate much during their childhoods, leaving their immune systems ill-prepared for the fight in 1918.

Whatever the cause, influenza's penchant for killing people in the prime of their lives meant *The Globe* regularly printed stories of children orphaned and parents devastated multiple times over by the war and the flu.

The paper also printed partial lists of the dead, often with street addresses – a violation of medical privacy unthinkable today. If the circumstances were tragic enough, the deaths merited their own stories, as happened in the case of the Hare brothers.

Young John William Hare of 147 De Grassi Street succumbed to pneumonia in mid-October 1918. "Scarcely was the funeral over," *The Globe* wrote, "when the news came from across the sea to an already heartbroken mother telling her that her other son, Gunner Arthur Hare, died in England on the same day as his brother, stricken by the same disease."

The final weeks of the war, which coincided with the height of the influenza pandemic, cast an inescapable shadow over *The Globe*'s coverage of the flu. Of twelve front-page stories in October and November of 1918 that mention influenza, three were about the base hospital scandal and four were about Victory Bond fundraising with the flu mentioned only in passing.

By contrast, *The Globe and Mail* ran 116 front-page stories about COVID-19 in March and April of 2020.

In 1919, as soldiers streamed home and Canada suffered sporadic outbreaks of flu and venereal disease, the federal government established a national department of health, a precursor to today's Health Canada.

Funding and political support for the department waxed and waned over the decades as public-health challenges of different magnitudes hit the country: tuberculosis, polio, the less-lethal influenza pandemics of 1957 and 1968, AIDS, the original SARS outbreak in 2003 and another minor flu pandemic caused by H1N1 in 2009.

The SARS crisis led to the creation of the Public Health Agency of Canada, the entity that would pilot the federal response to SARS-CoV-2, the virus that killed tens of thousands of Canadians and upended the lives of everyone in this country.

COVID emerged into a media landscape that would have been unrecognizable to anyone who read the old black-and-white *Globe* broadsheet as the Spanish influenza raged. Not only was there no headline-dominating corollary to the First World War to distract reporters and editors from COVID, but there had also been a sea change in how people consumed the news.

By 2020, the news was omnipresent, cacophonous and relentless. It spilled from earbuds, blared from TVs and buzzed from smartphones at all hours of the day. Yes, *The Globe and Mail* still published a daily paper. But it also had a website with infinite space, and in the first year of the pandemic, *The Globe* seemed determined to fill almost all of it with COVID content.

The pandemic dominated *The Globe and Mail* for nearly two years in a fashion that pushed all other stories aside. That didn't make sense in 1918, when Canada, and the world, were at war. The main exceptions to *The Globe*'s passive take on Spanish influenza were stories where the flu and the war collided, such as the paper's campaign on behalf of the soldiers dying inside the Toronto base hospital where Captain Kain spent his final days.

The Globe's coverage of influenza is a reminder of how a story can be shaped by the stories happening around it.

Kelly Grant is a health reporter at *The Globe and Mail*.

ABOVE: Louis Riel and his councillors, 1869–1870. (William James Topley/Library and Archives Canada)

Seven: How *the* West was – *and* wasn't – won

The Globe's early championing of the region gave way to coverage that sometimes took the tone of reporting on a foreign country | **Kelly Cryderman**

In *The Globe*'s earliest imaginings, the West was a land of rivers, plentiful game and fertile soil, a "magnificent empire" that lay between the Great Lakes and Rocky Mountains just waiting to be conquered.

"The wealth of 400,000 square miles of territory will flow through our waters, and be gathered by our merchants, manufacturers and agriculturalists," stated a particularly grandiose 1863 *Globe* opinion. "Our sons will occupy the chief places of this vast territory, we will form its institutions, supply its rulers, teach its schools, fill its stores, run its mills, and navigate its streams."

Hard pragmatism lay behind that rhetoric. In the years before Confederation, the Province of Canada, which encompassed portions of what is today southern Quebec and Ontario, found itself trapped between the western-reaching American colossus to the south – its Civil War ending and its ambitions endless – and the vast lands under the control of the Hudson's Bay Company to the north and west. If Canada could not expand, it might soon perish.

Globe founder George Brown's powerful, if blinkered, advocacy influenced Canada's successful fight to purchase and annex HBC-owned Rupert's Land, a western territory five times the size of France, creating the fantastically large, peaceful and prosperous country of today. But it came at a price.

The rush to profit from what *The Globe* viewed as a wilderness uninhabited and unvisited, "except by the wandering savage or hunter," ignored the long settlement and rights of Indigenous Peoples. The paper's claim in 1876 that Canada, in contrast to the United States, had "treated our Indians like human beings, and have scrupulously kept the faith in all our dealings with them," was patently false – a wrong we are still reckoning with today.

As the West developed, *The Globe*'s early championing of the Canadianization of the region gave way to coverage that alternated between in-depth stories and editorials, and articles that sometimes took the tone of reporting on a foreign country.

One particularly embarrassing contemporary example: a 2011 front-page story about Alison Redford being elected Progressive Conservative party leader, and therefore premier, that featured the infamous headline: "Alberta steps into the present."

The headline was speaking about the province that is the historical home of the Famous Five, Canada's most noteworthy suffragette reformers, in the Prairie region where women first got the vote and at a time when Ontario – and most other provinces – had yet to elect a woman premier. In reaction, *Calgary Herald* columnist Licia Corbella wrote Ontario "is in the midst of a provincial election in which the current Premier, Dalton McGuinty, is that province's 24th all-male, all-white Premier. His challenger is Progressive Conservative leader Tim Hudak, another middle-aged white fella."

If *The Globe* has had its bad days in Western coverage, it has had many good ones as well, stretching back to the years before Confederation. Brown, as both *Globe* proprietor and leader of the Reform, or Liberal, Party, pushed hard for incorporating the West into Canada, unlike others – including his archrival Sir John A. Macdonald – who were more inclined to let it drift away as a separate colony. According to biographer J.M.S. Careless, Brown feared that letting the West pursue a separate destiny would see it occupied by "American miners and settlers, and its trade carried off by the Red River to St. Paul and the Mississippi."

Preston Manning, the founder of the modern-day Reform Party, created as an offshoot of the country's conservative movement, says Brown's editorial and political positions had huge ramifications for the West we know today. "He advocated more strongly than Macdonald that the Rupert's Land at that time – all of the West under the control of the Hudson's Bay Company – should be made part of Canada."

Brown got his wish. In 1870, three years after Confederation, Canada purchased Rupert's Land from HBC – ending the company's two-hundred-year monopoly over the lands whose rivers flow into Hudson's Bay – along with the far less formally administered North-Western Territory, the massive region even further north and west of Rupert's Land.

Brown was aligned with other Western interests from the earliest days of Canada being a country. He opposed the Macdonald-authored National Policy that levied high tariffs on foreign imported goods to shield Canadian manufacturers – at the expense of agricultural exporters, first in Southwestern Ontario and then on the Prairies. "Brown was never successful in getting free trade," Manning says. "But the fact that he advocated it was something that the Western guys always wanted."

The Globe's assertiveness in its ideas about the West also led the paper to write enthusiastically about a new industrial school in Battleford, Saskatchewan, in 1884. "The system will gradually and quietly transform tribes of otherwise uneducated and intractable savages," it said in an editorial about the inauguration of a decades-long system of forced assimilation and familial separation for Indigenous people in poorly funded church-run schools, where preventable diseases ran rampant and many children were sexually or physically abused.

A century later, *The Globe* would write about the demands from Indigenous leaders for investigations into conditions at the same residential schools.

The newspaper was also tested by the resistance of the Métis, in what would become southern Manitoba, who weren't enamoured with becoming a part of Canada. According to historian Gerald Friesen, the new English settlers arriving in the province were "determined to claim the new land as a child of Ontario," and they displayed an intolerance to racial mingling that we now consider blatantly racist. Racial and anti-Catholic intolerance took hold despite the long history of intermarriage between French traders and Indigenous women in the area, Friesen wrote in his book *River Road*.

Early on, *The Globe* treated the growing restiveness that eventually led to rebellion with Pollyannaish optimism. "There is nothing which cannot be removed by the exhibition of a friendly and liberal spirit," the paper declared as major troubles flared.

By the time Métis leader Louis Riel was set to be hanged after the North-West uprising, the paper had adopted a much grimmer tone. An October 1885 *Globe* editorial – likely motivated in large part by a dislike of the Macdonald Conservatives – lambasted the prime minister for misgoverning while ignoring the reasonable land claims of the Métis.

In the decades that followed, *The Globe*'s coverage of the "Western situation" could be nuanced. In the 1920s, for instance, the paper argued the provinces of Manitoba, Saskatchewan and Alberta deserved control over their own natural resources, which Ottawa had denied them when they obtained provincehood and which they finally achieved in 1930. *The Globe* also supported tariff reductions and lower railway rates for struggling farmers, noting the rise of a secession movement, "perhaps not formidable, but important as a symptom of discontent."

But that did not prevent the paper from indulging in patronizing writing, such as framing Manitoba's decision in 1928 to increase the salary of the premier to at least $10,000 a year as "another sign that the West is growing up."

And in 1933, when Western farmers facing the Depression and drought complained about discriminatory banking policies crafted in Montreal and Toronto, *The Globe* found it baffling that they felt "head office location has something to do with influencing policy."

The paper astutely sent author and humorist Stephen Leacock to the West in 1937. "Sunny Alberta is a land of contrasts. In point of altitude it begins at the summit of the Rocky Mountains and ends at the bottom of Saskatchewan," he wrote, a particularly adept description of the province, which at the time was leaning over a financial abyss after years of dust bowls and crops devoured by grasshoppers.

"In temperature it will freeze you at a few hours' notice with forty below zero and then wipe it all out with a Chinook wind and beg your pardon for it," Leacock wrote.

"In point of latent resources, in and under the soil – coal, gas, metals – there's literally no end of it."

The thousands of kilometres between those latent resources and political leaders in central Canada has long been a point of tension. In 1971, celebrated *Globe* journalist Stanley McDowell wrote from Regina on growing Western alienation. He noted Parliament was squabbling over a bill that enabled a payment Western farmers saw as their due, while quickly passing other legislation for a similar sum that helped central Canadian manufacturers.

"Quebec separatists began calling their province a 'colony' in the early 1960s. But Westerners can cite a solid body of historical evidence that their region was developed as a colony from the start," McDowell wrote.

In the fractious days of the National Energy Program in the early 1980s – as the government of Pierre Trudeau pushed to Canadianize the country's energy industry in response to two energy crises – many *Globe* editorials were on the side of Alberta, then-premier Peter Lougheed and the oil industry.

"The National Energy Program that emerged . . . led to the dismantling of a good many energy projects, and to bad relations with our closest industrial partner, the United States, over changing the rules in mid-game," one *Globe* editorial declared. "More than anything, it extended alienation of the West, which had already wiped out the Liberal Party beyond the city of Winnipeg."

The Globe opened an Edmonton bureau in 1979, just before those fractious days, citing the need to cover "this fast-growing and increasingly important centre of Canadian commerce and industry." It opened a Winnipeg bureau two years later. Today there's a small but vibrant crew in Calgary and Edmonton, but *The Globe* has been more fragmented in its coverage of Manitoba and Saskatchewan.

In some ways, the Toronto-centred Canadian media still struggle to understand the West. For example, it tends to view populism on the Prairies as uniformly negative and through the lens of modern American populism – a Canadian analogue to Donald Trump whipping up intolerance and anger with false claims. Western Canadian populism has unique historical attributes, which gave rise to political movements on both the right and the left.

It was Saskatchewan's governing Co-operative Commonwealth Federation that famously introduced the publicly funded medicare system, Manning notes.

New Democratic Parties on the Prairies argue with justification they are different – more pragmatic – than some of their national brethren. Writing in *The Globe* about the 2023 election of Wab Kinew as Canada's first First Nations premier, NDP adviser Mike McKinnon said "his leadership is sure to follow a proud Prairie tradition passed down from Roy

Romanow to Gary Doer, Rachel Notley and now Mr. Kinew. Manitobans can expect their premier-designate to join a long line of pragmatic and (mostly) popular NDP governments on the Prairies." Kinew makes the distinction himself, referring to his party by the full name, "Manitoba NDP," with the province's name in the lead.

With the rise of sovereignty and autonomy movements in Alberta and Saskatchewan, the relationship between East and West has become more strained. In November 2019, for example, Alberta premier Jason Kenney spoke dismissively of the "Toronto *Globe and Mail*" criticizing Western politicians and their "preaching" on job losses and economic hardship.

In a speech that he spent all night writing, Kenney referenced historical complaints – including those of Frederick Haultain, the first premier of the North-West Territories – that Alberta and Saskatchewan became provinces in 1905 without the same powers afforded others and alluded to the "Laurentian elite" author of a *Globe* editorial who failed to understand how economic powerhouse Alberta had bolstered the Canadian economy in the past, even as other regions struggled.

After Kenney was pushed from office in 2022, Danielle Smith took over as United Conservative Party leader and premier. She won the provincial election in May 2023. Smith has become the most strident proponent of provincial autonomy measures – or Alberta First policies, as she has called them – to occupy the office of premier. She introduced "sovereignty" legislation to enable Alberta MLAs to vote on motions against federal rules they believe intrude into the provincial sphere. And she has had little qualm in launching advertising campaigns cheerleading for Alberta to consider leaving the Canada Pension Plan and create its own fund.

Historian and former Saskatchewan cabinet minister Janice MacKinnon says coverage of the Saskatchewan First Act and Alberta's Sovereignty Act in 2022 revealed a lot about how the West gets treated by Canadian media. "Would anybody from Alberta presume to fly into Ontario to write about a piece of legislation that they haven't read, but they just know it's going to be bad?" she says.

"There's the centre of Canada, and they feel free to tell us that we don't meet whatever their standard is. But they sometimes don't understand the place where we live."

Even before Smith became premier, *Globe* readers have been fascinated by the churn and combativeness of Alberta politics and its leaders. In that vein, stories that reinforce stereotypes about the West are often popular. But columnists from outside the province at times gloss over the scale and complexity of energy and climate questions – and the effect of federal policies on provincial economies.

The Prairie provinces are different from the rest of the country because of the vagaries of the global commodity markets on which they depend. That makes the region subject to sudden ups and downs; the economy can be cratering at one moment and flying high the next. It makes for fascinating and complex stories.

On that Prairie resource wealth, there is no monolith of political views, even in Alberta. Former Alberta Liberal leader Kevin Taft and others have argued the gusher of oil and natural gas money has resulted in democratic institutions being captured by private interests. Economists say the reliance on resource revenues leads to financial swings that play havoc with public budgets and make planning difficult. And environmental liabilities to clean up the oil patch loom large, an issue that has been covered in depth by *Globe* reporters and columnists in recent years.

The Globe, as a national newspaper, has to recognize not only regional economic differences but the interests and conflicts of environmental protection, resource development and Indigenous rights. The world's climate is changing in terrifying ways, and the looming global disaster is difficult to square with Canada's role in producing still-in-demand fossil fuels, in an era where there's a renewed aversion to relying on Russia or the Middle East for energy security.

Most of the country's city dwellers see the economy as focused on the auto sector, real estate or technology. But in the Prairie provinces, the connection to the seemingly old-fashioned yet still absolutely necessary work of resource extraction and farming remains stronger, and it plays a greater role in politics. What the world needs from Canada is plentiful in the West – natural gas, wheat, lentils, potash – but also the space and sun for solar power, the underground for carbon capture and the potential for an array of critical-mineral mines.

The old resource-based economy Brown wrote about is still the West's foundation and, in many regards, the country's. To neglect it, or to write it off as yesterday's news, is to ignore the present reality.

Kelly Cryderman is a columnist at *The Globe and Mail*, based in Calgary.

ABOVE: Former justice minister and attorney-general Jody Wilson-Raybould prepares to testify before the House of Commons justice committee regarding the SNC-Lavalin affair, February 27, 2019. (Blair Gable/ *The Globe and Mail*)

Eight: **Notes *on* four scandals**

Globe scoops made a difference in controversies over large infrastructure projects
| **Doug Saunders**

I t was the first and, to date, the only time the front page of *The
Globe* has brought down a federal government. Readers who spent
three cents for a copy on Friday, July 18, 1873, were greeted with
seventeen small headlines running down the right-hand column of the front page, topped with the phrase: "THE PACIFIC SCANDAL!"

Inside was the sort of journalistic dynamite that six-year-old Canada,
and the almost thirty-year-old *Globe*, had never seen. The paper had
obtained a trove of correspondence between Conservative prime minister Sir John A. Macdonald and his cabinet and the secret U.S. backers

of a Montreal company that had recently won a $30-million contract to build the Canadian Pacific Railway. Macdonald had assured voters the railroad was a purely Canadian venture.

The correspondence proved, after months of reporting and parliamentary accusations, that the CPR, nominally headed by Montreal transportation tycoon Hugh Allan, was a front for the U.S.-based Northern Pacific Railway Company. In exchange for the mammoth railway-building contract, the Americans provided a staggering $350,000 in secret campaign funds to Macdonald and his senior ministers to help them buy votes and win the 1872 election.

Among the documents *The Globe* reprinted were the prime minister's telegram to Allan reassuring him that he and his cohorts will get the railway but "the whole matter [was] to be kept quiet until after the elections" and Macdonald's urgent wire to Allan's lawyer as election eve approached: "I must have another ten thousand. Will be the last time of calling. Do not fail me."

The Globe's 1873 revelations weren't exactly what we'd today call investigative journalism. Those telegrams had been stolen from the lawyer for Allan by the lawyer's personal assistant, who then sold them to the opposition Liberal Party, which was then tightly linked to *The Globe*.

The Pacific Scandal had begun in earnest on April 2, when Liberal MP Lucius Seth Huntington rose in Parliament and declared, in *The Globe*'s summary, "that the Prime Minister of Canada had granted the Pacific Railway in return for a bribe." He demanded an inquiry.

Only after *The Globe*'s revelation broke did Parliament strike a full-fledged royal commission. That fall, Macdonald gamely cross-examined all its witnesses, frequently concluding by declaring, "These hands are clean!" By early November, many of his own party's MPs had turned against him, and on November 5 he reluctantly gave up his government.

If that sequence of events sounds familiar, it's because this sort of scandal – involving prime ministers, big public infrastructure projects and behind-the-scenes payments from the private companies that want to build them – has exploded onto the front page of *The Globe* on four notable occasions.

There have been other big federal scandals, including the customs scandal of 1926 and the sponsorship scandal of 1999 to 2005. But these four are united in several ways: each prime minister initially denied any wrongdoing, and only after a front-page *Globe* story appeared did the public become fully aware of the scandal's scope. And these controversies temporarily bruised the reputation and electoral standing of the governing party, although none has permanently ousted a party or its leader.

After Macdonald's resignation, the Liberals won the 1874 election and governed for four years amid a global economic depression, but the Conservatives returned in 1878 with a majority and would govern until 1896. The railway's last spike was driven in 1885, during the fourth of Macdonald's six terms.

The Pacific Scandal was in many ways the template of prime ministerial scandal: it established a pattern of executive misconduct involving infrastructure money that would recur throughout the generations.

Half a century later, another long-serving prime minister faced another enormous infrastructure project, and another expensive election.

In 1928, when Prime Minister William Lyon Mackenzie King was presented with a plan to build a hydroelectric dam across the St. Lawrence River at Beauharnois, west of Montreal, many Canadians, especially in Ontario, felt its cost and scale far exceeded Canada's fiscal capacity and energy needs. "The preferable plan would be to build the entire seaway in conjunction with the United States, as necessary, and reserve Canada's share of the power for public ownership and distribution," *The Globe* editorialized that year.

Instead, King's government became interested in a private firm run by Montreal businessman R.O. Sweezey: the Beauharnois Light, Heat and Power Corporation. As historians S.J. Donovan and R.B. Winmill put it in the 1976 book *Political Corruption in Canada*, Sweezey "set out to appropriate all the political influence he could summon," making an astonishing $700,000 in donations to King's Liberals.

The company also made a deal with Liberal senator Wilfrid Laurier McDougald, a close friend of King, and senior civil servant Robert Henry. The two men set up a dummy company that was theoretically in competition for the contract; that company was then bought out by Beauharnois, making McDougald and Henry its chairman and vice-president. King then appointed Henry the minister of railways and canals, which made him responsible for giving Beauharnois its charter – which it got in 1929.

Globe reporters had been hearing rumours, and in April 1928, Ottawa correspondent William Marchington wrote that McDougald "is reputed to be connected with the Beauharnois Power Company." The next day, the senator rose angrily in Parliament to deliver what he called "an immediate, unequivocal and absolute denial to the implication of the *Globe* dispatch," claiming "I have no interest in or association with that company in any way, shape or form."

In May 1930, as a summer election loomed, MPs from the left-leaning Labour and Progressive parties obtained documents that proved McDougald was on the board of Beauharnois. MPs rose to denounce the Beauharnois deal as "fraud," "financial brigandage," a "gigantic steal" and a "menace to Canada," *The Globe* reported. The paper's editorials argued the project would largely benefit American customers at the expense of Canadians, noting that Beauharnois was going to charge Ontario Hydro twice the cost of producing electricity.

Despite the huge donation from Beauharnois, King's Liberals lost the 1930 election, during the Depression, to R.B. Bennett's Conservatives. Bennett didn't hesitate to launch an inquiry into the Beauharnois affair. Despite being a famously detail-oriented micromanager, King claimed he was unaware of the source of most of the party's campaign funds.

That claim was blown apart by *The Globe*'s front page of July 22, 1931. "Mr. King's holiday bills paid by Beauharnois; Ex-premier didn't know, declares McDougald," said Marchington's story, which drew on documents released by a parliamentary committee. That included a receipt proving King had enjoyed a lavish vacation in Bermuda and New York, shortly before the election was called in April 1930, paid for by Beauharnois, in the company of McDougald and another Liberal senator, Andrew Haydon.

The Globe's editorial described the findings as "an indictment of political wrongdoing, a condemnation of prostitution of public office for private gain, the like of which probably never has been heard in the legislative halls of Canada."

To the end, King claimed he had known nothing. "The Liberal Party has not been disgraced but it is in the valley of humiliation," he told Parliament during a three-hour speech in 1931. "But we are going to come out of that valley."

His escape from it happened with surprising speed. The Liberals were re-elected in 1935 with a majority. King would remain prime minister until 1948, and the Liberals would stay in office until 1957. In the 1950s, the Beauharnois would become one of the major sections of the St. Lawrence Seaway. The scandal's only lasting legacy may have been the 1944 decision to establish the publicly owned Hydro-Québec.

The next big prime ministerial scandal took place a couple generations later and unfolded over two decades of reporting. In the early 1990s, after he'd left office, Brian Mulroney accepted envelopes containing cash totalling about $275,000, during three private meetings in hotel rooms in the U.S. and Canada with Karlheinz Schreiber, a businessman of German and Canadian citizenship.

Schreiber had a contract with the European consortium Airbus Industries to persuade the Canadian federal government to renew the fleet of Air Canada, then a Crown corporation, with Airbus rather than Boeing jets. Airbus paid Schreiber an estimated $20-million, deposited in his Swiss account, to sell politicians and bureaucrats on this huge transportation-infrastructure deal.

In 1988, Airbus won a $1.8-billion contract from Air Canada for thirty-four A320 jets. Schreiber provided a similar service for the German corporation Thyssen AG, also involving millions in fees, to persuade Ottawa to build an armoured-vehicle factory in Nova Scotia. (It was never built.)

After the deal was announced, Schreiber's cozy relationships with prominent Tories, such as former Newfoundland premier Frank Moores – who briefly served on the board of Air Canada – were chronicled by *Globe* columnist Stevie Cameron. Then, in 1995, the revelation of Airbus payments to Schreiber for political influence was aired by the CBC's *The Fifth Estate*. Later that year, news broke that the RCMP was investigating whether Mulroney received some of that Airbus money. The former prime minister then sued Ottawa for defamation, winning a settlement in 1996 that included an apology and $2.1-million in costs. He told the court he "had never had any dealings" with Schreiber while he was prime minister.

In 2003, *Globe* editor-in-chief Edward Greenspon commissioned lawyer William Kaplan, who had published a book defending Mulroney and criticizing Cameron's work, to write a series of articles on the two. In the third article, with the shocking front-page headline "Schreiber hired Mulroney," Kaplan revealed that, years after his exculpatory book about Mulroney was released, he learned that Schreiber did in fact make cash payments to the former prime minister – news that undermined what Mulroney had previously told him about their relationship. Kaplan later said he felt "duped."

At first, spokespeople for Mulroney insisted the payments had been in support of a putative pasta business. Later, Schreiber and Mulroney would say the payments were for help with the Thyssen armoured-vehicle contract – which, if true, would suggest they were not payoffs for deals made while Mulroney was prime minister, but advance fees for future work.

Greenspon later wrote that Mulroney had phoned him and urged him not to publish the story, adding that Mulroney "said he could give us a better story if we suppressed the one about the $300,000 dealing." Greenspon did not play ball.

In 2007, articles by *Globe* reporter Greg McArthur blew a hole in many of Mulroney's claims. They showed that there was a previously undisclosed fourth meeting between Schreiber and Mulroney, at a luxury hotel in Switzerland in 1998, in which, according to Schreiber, the former prime minister wanted to know if there "was any evidence that he received any money." They showed that Mulroney had not claimed the cash payments as taxable income until 2000, around the time the CBC was preparing to air a report on Schreiber's bank records from Switzerland. Other reporting showed that Mulroney had not only known and met with Schreiber multiple times while prime minister, but that Schreiber had funded Mulroney's 1976 and 1983 Progressive Conservative leadership campaigns.

These stories led Prime Minister Stephen Harper's government to launch an inquiry into the Mulroney-Schreiber dealings, chaired by Manitoba judge Jeffrey Oliphant, beginning in 2008. Mulroney made multiple appearances and insisted on his innocence, on more than one occasion breaking into tears.

In the end, Oliphant concluded that the payments to Mulroney were "not appropriate." However, the inquiry could not prove that Mulroney was aware of the source of the money, and Oliphant's terms of reference prevented him from examining the other millions Schreiber paid out. Notably, Oliphant also concluded, based on a forensic audit, that "the source of the funds paid by Mr. Schreiber to Mr. Mulroney was Airbus," not Thyssen.

Schreiber was deported to Germany, where he was sentenced to eight years in prison for having evaded about $10-million in taxes on many tens of millions he'd disbursed in "black money" – bribes and kickbacks – including those mysterious Canadian millions. He is the only Canadian figure to have faced legal repercussions.

Once again, a prime minister managed to dodge responsibility for a scandal until it appeared on *The Globe*'s front page – this time long after the fact.

Just after that scandal died down, at the height of the Libyan uprising against dictator Moammar Gadhafi in 2011, *Globe* reporter Graeme Smith found thousands of documents scattered in the bombed and looted remains of a Tripoli building belonging to the Montreal-based engineering corporation SNC-Lavalin Group Inc. They showed that the company had spent years developing a close relationship with Gadhafi and his family. It soon emerged that SNC-Lavalin had paid tens of millions in bribes and other payments to win contracts for major infrastructure projects, including a huge prison.

Weeks later, the RCMP raided SNC-Lavalin's Montreal offices. Canadian prosecutors would eventually charge the company and its executives with bribery and fraud – and SNC-Lavalin, if convicted, faced a ban from bidding on federal contracts for up to ten years. To prevent that outcome, SNC-Lavalin began aggressively lobbying Ottawa to introduce a deferred prosecution agreement law, which would allow mediation and fines rather than criminal trials for such corporate offences.

The lobbying also drew attention to SNC-Lavalin's outsized political contributions. In 2018, one of its executives pleaded guilty to having channelled $110,000 in illegal campaign donations to the federal Liberals (and $8,000 to the Conservatives) from 2004 to 2011.

Also in 2018, the Trudeau government passed legislation allowing deferred prosecution agreements; SNC-Lavalin was the first applicant for relief under the act. But federal prosecutors concluded the company was ineligible, because of the gravity of the allegations and when they took place, before the law existed.

On February 7, 2019, *Globe* readers were greeted with another explosive front page: a story by Robert Fife, Steven Chase and Sean Fine reported that Prime Minister Justin Trudeau and his staff had put pressure on the justice minister and attorney-general at the time, Jody Wilson-Raybould, to order prosecutors to grant SNC-Lavalin a deferred prosecution.

That morning, Trudeau appeared at a snow-swept podium outside a Vaughan, Ontario, event and declared, "The allegations in *The Globe* story this morning are false." Neither he nor his staff ever "directed" the attorney-general to drop the prosecution of SNC-Lavalin, he maintained.

But on February 25, Wilson-Raybould told the Commons justice committee that Trudeau, his top aides and eleven senior civil servants and party officials had aggressively put pressure on her to drop the prosecution. Trudeau himself, in a tense meeting with the minister, had told her of the political importance of SNC-Lavalin to the Liberal Party's fortunes. At one point, she said, "The prime minister jumped in stressing that there is an election in Quebec and that 'I am an MP in Quebec – the MP for Papineau' [a riding near SNC-Lavalin's head office] . . . I was quite taken aback."

Trudeau then demoted Wilson-Raybould in a cabinet shuffle. She quit the cabinet on February 12, later joined by fellow minister Jane Philpott. In late March, Wilson-Raybould released a recorded phone call in which Trudeau's Privy Council clerk Michael Wernick had warned her that the prime minister "is gonna find a way to get it done one way or another . . . he is in that kind of mood." On April 2, Trudeau expelled her and Philpott from the Liberal caucus.

SNC-Lavalin pleaded guilty to one charge of fraud in December 2019, in a plea deal that imposed a $280-million fine but meant the company could continue to bid on federal contracts. Four months earlier, the federal ethics commissioner had concluded that "the authority of the Prime Minister and his office was used to circumvent, undermine and ultimately attempt to discredit the decision of the Director of Public Prosecutions as well as the authority of Ms. Wilson-Raybould."

Trudeau would face no formal penalties and his Liberals would go on to win the election that October and another in 2021. But those would be minority governments – a shift, some believe, precipitated by a public sense of impropriety and not-so-sunny ways.

It resembled the shift in voter sentiments that had pummelled Macdonald's Conservatives in 1874, King's Liberals in 1930 and the Tories in 1993 after Mulroney stepped down. And it followed a uniquely Canadian pattern, one that combined big infrastructure, private and foreign money and the ever-shifting relationship between prime ministers and an inquisitive newspaper.

Doug Saunders is international affairs columnist at *The Globe and Mail*.

ABOVE: Striking General Motors employees walk the picket line in Oshawa, April 13, 1937. (John H. Boyd/*The Globe and Mail*)

Nine: *The* birth *of* Big Labour

The Globe's publisher was in the thick of the GM strike in 1937, but on the losing side | **Vanmala Subramaniam**

I n April 1937, at the General Motors plant in Oshawa, Ontario, workers frantically scrambled to move hundreds of cars off the factory floor, working all night at the command of their managers. The cars were lined up and then driven along a highway leading to Toronto – seventy-five cars per hour, travelling through the night. These same workers, up to three thousand of them, were poised to go on strike the next day, forming picket lines around the soon-to-be empty plant.

The remnants of the Depression lingered: a lagging economy and fast-declining social conditions. Almost a third of the labour force had been out of work, and a fifth had depended on government support merely to survive. Workers were frustrated, and unions capitalized on that anger, leading the charge in demanding higher wages and shorter work hours.

The GM strike of 1937 helped give birth to the modern labour movement in Canada, cementing the power of unions and paving the way for improved working conditions. *The Globe and Mail* was in the thick of this momentous chapter in labour history, taking a strong anti-union stand in editorials, many of which ran on the front page.

William Wright, a mining magnate who backed the paper financially, feared the GM strike would encourage workers in his Northern Ontario mines to mobilize. *The Globe*'s editorials became his instrument for fighting the arrival of Big Labour.

During the strike, *Globe* publisher George McCullagh frequently visited his friend Ontario premier Mitch Hepburn, the two of them scheming over how to break the strike, wrote Mark Bourrie in his book *Big Men Fear Me*, an account of McCullagh's life.

But there were two *Globes* during the strike: the publisher who editorialized against it, and the reporters who covered the struggle of the men on the line. McCullagh fought in vain to break the strike, but he didn't interfere with news coverage of what turned out to be a massive win for the labour movement in Canada.

To understand the editorial positioning of *The Globe* in the 1930s – the interwar years when communism and labour movements started to gain traction in North America – you need to know McCullagh. He was the son of a union activist whose agitation kept costing him his job. McCullagh wanted no part of that misery. Instead, he hustled.

As a teenager from the wrong side of the tracks in London, Ontario, McCullagh sold an astonishing number of *Globe* subscriptions by somehow convincing small-town folk and farmers on the ruler-straight concession roads of Southwestern Ontario to buy a big-city newspaper. The paper noticed, hiring him as a reporter. Before long, McCullagh was forging strategic connections with wealthy Bay Street financiers, some of whom were making a fortune in the 1920s by speculating in mining stocks during the Northern Ontario gold rush.

By the time *The Globe*'s publisher, William Gladstone Jaffray, fired McCullagh for smoking on the job, he was already established as a smart twenty-four-year-old operator within Toronto's financial circles. He especially impressed Wright, an eccentric mining tycoon, and Hepburn, a rising populist and anti-union Liberal politician.

In 1936, a year before the GM strike, McCullagh used Wright's money to buy both *The Globe* and *The Mail and Empire*, merging them into *The Globe and Mail*. The new publisher promised the newspaper would "not sell itself to politicians, nor would its editorial pages be offered up on the altar of advertising." But all newspapers have their biases, and under McCullagh, *The Globe*'s editorials favoured the interests of the business class.

Unions were already making a dent in the American labour landscape in the Depression-defined 1930s, in part because U.S. president Franklin D. Roosevelt made worker rights a core tenet of his New Deal. In 1936, the United Auto Workers (UAW), then a rather small arm of the Congress of Industrial Organizations (CIO), staged three bitter months of sit-down strikes at a GM factory in Flint, Michigan, in the wake of hundreds of deaths caused by a combination of summer heat and dangerous working conditions.

Workers typically put in shifts of ten hours or more, crammed into cramped spaces with little ventilation, which could lead to heat exhaustion and death. And without the protective equipment that we take for granted today, such as hard hats and workboots, accidents could be and often were crippling or fatal. The union's demands for safer conditions struck a deep chord with workers: UAW membership ballooned fivefold in 1937. Its next target was Oshawa, one of GM's largest North American factories.

The Depression had a huge impact on the ability of unions to organize. "It was a time where the legitimacy of capitalism was being challenged – ordinary people had suffered during the Depression, and the rich had largely emerged comfortable," says Sam Gindin, former research director of the Canadian Auto Workers union. "So there was a progressive reaction to that."

American unions – particularly the CIO, headed by activist John L. Lewis, and its UAW offshoot – led the charge in Canada, rallying workers in the mines and auto plants. Employees at GM's Oshawa plant demanded that the UAW be allowed to represent them. Management refused.

On April 8, 1937, the workers went on strike, demanding an eight-hour day, compensation by seniority and recognition of the UAW as their union. Almost immediately, the Toronto District Trades and Labour Council – a key labour body that sought to unify unions across the province – endorsed the strike. At a mass demonstration at Queen's Park on April 11, C.H. Millard, president of the local auto union, warned that the full weight of Toronto workers would be thrown against the vehemently anti-union Hepburn, who was now premier, and "his attempt to dictate to us."

Fear that a "communist" uprising in Oshawa could spread to northern minefields bled through *The Globe*'s front-page editorials, with the newspaper referring to Lewis as a "dictator" hell-bent on ruining the Canadian economy.

"The CIO invasion has struck at the mines, the present mainstay of Canada's prosperity, an industry which cannot be said to be connected with any in the United States," one editorial warned. "If the north mines close down, the result would be calamitous."

Though there was no direct evidence that Wright dictated editorial policy to McCullagh, the publisher knew his backer's mind and certainly knew his own. He believed organized unions spread socialism and threatened the rights of owners.

Unfortunately for McCullagh, the public disagreed.

The GM strike garnered widespread attention and support, at least according to various polls conducted by the *Toronto Star* and *The Globe and Mail* over the course of its three weeks. In the Oshawa area, according to the *Star*, more than 60 per cent of residents were in favour of auto workers forming a union. In the eastern Ontario towns of Belleville and Pickering, a *Star* reporter noted, stores displayed pro-labour signs supporting the UAW and the CIO.

Undeterred, Hepburn begged Prime Minister Mackenzie King to bring in the RCMP to break the strike. When King refused, Hepburn resorted to a rather novel tactic of hiring students from the University of Toronto to act as strike-breakers. Dubbed "Sons of Mitches" or "Hepburn's Hussars," the youths roamed the streets of Oshawa trying to look menacing, though without accomplishing much.

Everyone knew Hepburn and McCullagh were close. The premier had convinced the publisher to take up a seat on the University of Toronto board of governors. During the strike, McCullagh helped Hepburn behind the scenes, frequently visiting the premier's office to strategize on how to break it.

On April 23, the *Toronto Star* ran an editorial describing Hepburn as a "pawn in a larger game," insinuating that the premier was in fact taking instructions from McCullagh. In an interview that same week with *The Windsor Daily Star*, Hepburn denied that he was "being used by the *Globe and Mail* or whatever interests are behind that newspaper."

For his part, King was convinced that McCullagh was the power behind Hepburn's throne. "The truth of the matter is he is in the hands of McCullagh of *The Globe*, and *The Globe* and McCullagh in the hands of financial mining interests that want to crush the CIO and their organization in Canada," he wrote in his diary on April 13, 1937.

In contrast to its virulent anti-union editorials, *The Globe*'s reporters covered the strike in detail, writing hundreds of articles documenting the demands of workers, daily responses from GM's management and Hepburn's various policy responses.

One story detailed how Oshawa mayor Alex Hall received a "barrage of booing" from workers on the picket line when he warned them that their actions would damage the local economy, noting that the raucous response left him "flushed, grim, and perspiring before the strikers."

Another report presented allegations by GM's management that the UAW used "coercion of the most persistent nature" to enlist new members, which the union denied.

Lorne McIntyre, the lead *Globe* reporter covering the strike, met with striking workers in Oshawa as they waited for the CIO to present an offer that would lead to a ratification vote. "Gathering there, many of them expressed themselves forcefully that if the agreement did not include recognition of the international union, UAW, and thus recognition of the CIO they would vote it down," McIntyre wrote. "But if the advantages of the agreement and the importance of a Canadian labour organization are explained, it will hold."

It held. Workers voted 2,205 to 36 in ratifying the settlement reached between GM and the UAW. The deal increased hourly wages, limited shifts to eight hours a day and authorized overtime pay. And despite Hepburn's frantic efforts to prevent it, in mid-May, GM agreed to recognize the UAW as an official bargaining agent. The workers had won.

"In a few minutes after the ratification vote," wrote McIntyre, "the stewards were wiping out the visible signs of the strike. The tents that had sheltered men who took the cold watches of the night on the picket lines were struck. Stoves and equipment where pickets had made lunches, were dismantled. The strike was over."

In one of its final editorials on the strike, *The Globe* described Hepburn in glowing terms, as a premier who "must be given credit for fighting on behalf of Canadian labour as well as Canadian people." But the truth is McCullagh had placed *The Globe* firmly against the side of labour and on the losing side of his backers. Hepburn's loss was McCullagh's loss as well.

Over the course of the next five decades, *The Globe*'s attitude toward labour issues shifted. While it still tended to side in editorials with owners over workers, it devoted increasing coverage to labour issues. In fact, the paper hired one of the most prolific labour reporters in the country, Wilfred List, who was on the labour beat for roughly four decades until he retired in 1984.

In his coverage, List frequently wrote about the perks of unionization and praised large employers, such as the auto giants, who created superior work conditions for employees. He also highlighted how unions played a crucial role in forcing the hand of government and employers to introduce supports such as maternity leave, unemployment insurance and other benefits for workers.

"Paid maternity leave is becoming more important in union negotiations," wrote List in a 1981 report, detailing how the Canadian Union of Postal Workers won seventeen weeks of paid maternity leave in negotiations with the federal government. "Once it becomes pervasive in the public sector, the pressure will begin to develop in the private sector for similar benefits."

But 1980s Reaganism coincided with, and helped cause, a sharp decline in the power of the labour movement in the United States. Unions on both sides of the border weakened, the result of free-trade policies and the loss of industrial jobs to cheaper markets. Unionization rates, especially in the U.S., have hovered at the 10-per-cent mark for years now. Labour activists believe that media coverage of their movement is more sporadic and less sympathetic than in pre-Reagan days.

"Newspapers have responded to labour only when labour was disruptive enough to get attention," Gindin notes. "If the labour movement became militant again in challenging things, newspapers would have no choice but to cover these issues."

The COVID-19 pandemic – and the employer-employee chasm it sparked – brought labour coverage back to the forefront in *The Globe*. But long gone are the days when a publisher actively attempted to influence the outcome of a labour strike. Readers look for fairness and balance in *The Globe*, and it strives to deliver: covering the picket line, without crossing it.

Vanmala Subramaniam is future of work reporter at *The Globe and Mail*.

ABOVE: A small red dress, representing Indigenous children who died from abuse and neglect at Canada's residential schools, hangs on a cross in front of the former site of the Kamloops Indian Residential School in Kamloops, British Columbia, in June, 2021. (Melissa Tait/*The Globe and Mail*)

Ten:
Residential schools, *a* national disgrace

The Globe supported a policy of assimilation for Indigenous children for decades but had reversed itself by the 1980s |
Willow Fiddler

I came face to face with George Brown, or at least a bust of him, as I entered the executive offices of *The Globe and Mail*'s former Front Street headquarters in Toronto in 2015. I wasn't impressed. This was, after all, the man who founded the country's paper of record, a paper that had misrepresented my people throughout most of its history. I may have even scoffed at the sight of yet another white settler bronzed into a Canadian legacy.

I was a student in a journalism training program and had just learned about *The Globe*'s investigation into missing and murdered Indigenous women and girls. This was at a time when Conservative prime minister Stephen Harper was refusing to hold a national inquiry into those missing women and girls. The next day, when *The Globe* endorsed the Conservatives for re-election, the irony hit me hard.

If the role of the paper's editorial board is to be the voice of the paper and its proprietors, what responsibility does it bear for the mixed messages it sends when it comes to coverage of historical and continuing policies of assimilation against Indigenous people?

"To kill the Indian in the child." Harper used this phrase in 2008 when he apologized in the House of Commons on behalf of all Canadians for the abuse that generations of Indigenous children suffered at residential schools. The phrase, or one close to it, originated in the United States, to describe the philosophy of abuse of Native children at schools in that country.

The evil of those words spread across the continent as freely as the nations of Indigenous Peoples once travelled the lands. The words first appeared in *The Globe and Mail* in 1997, at a time when Canada's residential-school system was finally being outed as a horrific national disgrace.

From before Confederation until the 1990s, governments operated a system of schools across Canada that explicitly aimed, as Harper said in his apology, to "remove and isolate children from the influence of their homes, families, traditions and cultures, and to assimilate them into the dominant culture.

"Today, we recognize that this policy of assimilation was wrong, has caused great harm, and has no place in our country," he acknowledged. But a deep dive into *The Globe*'s archives reveals that, for well over a century, it had a place in this newspaper's pages.

Decade after decade, *The Globe* supported a policy of assimilation, a policy that the Truth and Reconciliation Commission later called cultural genocide. Pope Francis, who came to Canada in 2022 on a trip addressing the traumatic legacy of residential schools and colonization, told reporters that forced assimilation was genocide.

Management and senior editors of the paper were mostly indifferent to the suffering and abuse of Indigenous children at residential schools, even as journalists and critics, some of them writing for *The Globe*, chronicled that abuse.

From its earliest days, *The Globe* debated the "Indian question." While Brown was against "the policy of extermination," as an editorial referencing the Sioux raids in Minnesota made clear, the paper's call for "a rational treatment of ignorant and misguided savages who are scarcely more responsible for their actions than children" was far more telling.

The country's answer to that call came in the spring of 1879, when Ottawa's Privy Council was presented with a report from commissioner Nicholas Davin "on the advisableness of establishing Industrial Schools for the children of Indians and half-breeds." Davin, a settler born in Ireland, had been a *Globe* writer before founding *The Regina Leader* and becoming a lawyer. Basing his report on a study of industrial schools south of the border, Davin noted that they were the "principal feature of the policy known as that of 'aggressive civilization.'"

"The experience of the United States is the same as our own as far as the adult Indian is concerned. Little can be done with him," Davin declared. "The child . . . who goes to day school learns little, and what little he learns is soon forgotten, while his tastes are fashioned at home, and his inherited aversion to toil is in no way combated."

Davin recommended that the government contract with churches to run industrial boarding schools that would take Native children away from their families and communities and indoctrinate them in the Christian faith and settler values.

In 1883, Sir John A. Macdonald's government passed legislation authorizing the first three residential schools, based on Davin's recommendations.

Describing a residential school in Pennsylvania, U.S. Army officer Richard Pratt said, "All the Indian there is in the race should be dead. Kill the Indian in him, and save the man." An adaptation of that phrase, with "child" replacing "man," first appeared in a report to Canada's Royal Commission on Aboriginal Peoples in the 1990s.

Killing something has always meant killing something. How was it ever okay to think it wasn't?

In the following years and decades, industrial and residential boarding schools proliferated across the new Dominion, mostly in Northern Ontario and what are now the Prairie provinces. Catholic and Protestant churches administered the schools, which aimed to provide a basic English education, teach agricultural and farming skills, and instill the Christian faith, with the intent and hope of eradicating the Indian savage within. When it became clear that few Indigenous parents were willing to send their children to the schools, the government introduced legislation in 1920 to make attendance mandatory.

"I want to get rid of the Indian problem," Duncan Campbell Scott, the notorious deputy minister who oversaw the residential-school policy at its peak between 1913 and 1932, told a parliamentary committee. ". . . Our objective is to continue until there is not a single Indian in Canada that has not been absorbed into the body politic and there is no Indian question, and no Indian Department."

From the beginning, *The Globe* viewed the schools in a mostly positive light. In June 1880, the paper interviewed Reverend E.F. Wilson, who founded the Shingwauk Indian Residential School in Sault Ste. Marie, Ontario. He proudly explained the details of the five-year contracts they had for boys as young as eleven. "The first two years is devoted wholly to the school, in which are taught the elementary branches and some Latin," Wilson explained. "For the third year we hire the boy out to some mechanic, to whom we pay a small sum for teaching him his trade. In the fourth year the mechanic pays us $1 per week for the boy's services."

He boasted of how the schools had been able to gain the full support of the parents and families of the children in the district that spanned about five hundred kilometres from Sault Ste. Marie: "They sometimes would not hear of allowing their boys and girls to attend the school, while other parents would send a child for one or two years and take him away. This feeling is now all a thing of the past, and we have the hearty cooperation of all the Indians in our section."

Shingwauk sounded like a typical example of well-run institutions that offered enlightened and practical education for First Nations children. The opposite was true.

The schools were shoddily built, the teachers unqualified, the food substandard at best. Children became weakened and at risk of tuberculosis and other diseases. Over the decades, more than 150 schools took in more than 150,000 First Nation, Métis and Inuit children. The Truth and Reconciliation Commission said 4,100 children died while attending the schools, but the commission's chairman, Murray Sinclair, has since said the actual number could be more than 10,000.

The Globe was oblivious to the abuse, writing in 1887, ". . . after every Indian has thus had a farm assigned him, the residue sold and the proceeds held in trust by government will afford an ample fund for the instructors' schools and all other needful appliances, at the same time that the lands are thrown open to settlers. Can anyone doubt that this is the common sense solution of the Indian problem?"

By the 1890s, journalists were starting to report on the true conditions of the schools. In 1896, seventeen years after the Davin Report, a *Winnipeg Tribune* reporter toured St. Paul's industrial school in Middlechurch, Manitoba, calling it "one of the most villainously constructed buildings it would be possible to imagine, and it is a disgrace to the department."

In 1907, *The Globe* wrote about tuberculosis-related illnesses and deaths in residential schools, as outlined in a report from Peter Bryce, chief medical inspector to the Department of Indian Affairs. "Of a total of 1,537 pupils reported from 15 schools [. . .] 7 per cent are sick or in poor health and 24 per cent are reported dead," the report found. "In almost every instance the cause of death is given as tuberculosis." In one school, 69 per cent of former students had died, the report said.

Bryce went on to say that "under present circumstances about one-half of the children who are sent to the Duck Lake boarding school die before the age of 18, or very shortly afterward." He published a second report in 1909 recommending the government take over control of the schools from the churches.

But Scott suppressed Bryce's reports. Nothing was done.

If children weren't dying of disease, they were being abused by school officials. One 1934 article reveals how both First Nations parents and local townsfolk in Truro and Shubenacadie, Nova Scotia, were enraged when they learned a number of boys at a nearby residential school had been flogged after money had gone missing. The school's principal, Father J.P. Mackey, "did not consider the treatment unusually severe. The beatings had not been administered as punishment, he said, but to elicit information about the missing money."

Three years later, *The Globe* reported on the deaths of students at another school with the headline "Four boys die; find discipline is too severe."

There were other stories, here and there, over the years. In 1946, reporter Ralph Hyman wrote about an Anglican investigation of conditions in the schools. The buildings were fire traps and health hazards, the report concluded, and "reflect no credit on the Government of Canada which is responsible for them, or the Church which has put up with them." The report urged that the schools be rebuilt as quickly as possible.

What if a *Globe* editor had seized on that report and put a team of reporters on the story? What kind of influence could *The Globe* have had on the residential-school policy had it not been so prejudiced and neglectful in its editorials and news reports toward the Indigenous children and families that it wrote about – or, more accurately, failed to write about?

But a search of *The Globe*'s archives reveals the paper's discourse post-Confederation reflected colonial, white-supremacist values. Coverage mostly centred on solving the country's self-induced "Indian problem" and frustrations with any resistance encountered in the process.

And throughout it all, no Indigenous voices or perspectives. And certainly no Indigenous reporters or editors.

The Globe's centennial editorial in 1967 offered one of the first, albeit slight, indications the paper was starting to pay better attention to the many issues of assimilation and colonization facing Indigenous Peoples, in spite of the slanted and sporadic coverage it had afforded since before Confederation.

After quoting Prime Minister Lester Pearson's declaration that "Nobody need starve in Canada," the July 1 editorial rebutted: "Nobody need starve to death. But people do. Opportunities fumbled. The Indian and the Eskimo know how we have fumbled."

Yet biased and dismissive coverage was still taking place. Witness this headline from 1965: "Priest tells why he thinks Indians are not disadvantaged and backward."

In these years the effort to "kill the Indian in the child" migrated to child-welfare agencies, which removed an estimated twenty thousand Indigenous children from their parents in what became known as the Sixties Scoop. The children were put up for adoption, mostly to white Christian families across North America.

The Globe ran adoption advertisements that were blatantly racist, if unintentionally honest, in their attitude: "Sturdy little North American Indian . . . without any knowledge of his background," "a big boned, husky 3 year old Indian Protestant boy," "chubby Indian girl" and "Rose needs Roman Catholic parents."

But change was coming. A 1969 white paper from Indian Affairs minister Jean Chrétien recommended everything Scott had fought for: eliminating the Indian Act, selling off reserve lands to occupants, abandoning treaties. The backlash from the National Indian Brotherhood (which later became the Assembly of First Nations) and other First Nations forced the government into a full retreat.

Resource development in the 1960s and 1970s, including hydroelectricity projects and the proposed Mackenzie Valley pipeline, opened the floodgates of Indigenous activism, as First Nations leaders mobilized with increasing success to have their inherent and treaty rights – indeed their basic human and civil rights – acknowledged, respected and honoured. Because of their efforts, federal and provincial leaders were compelled, reluctantly, to recognize Indigenous rights in the 1982 Canada Act. Supreme Court rulings have increasingly affirmed those rights.

By the 1980s, *The Globe* had begun to grapple with what had gone on in the schools and why the paper had failed to properly report on it. This is around the time that the words "aboriginal" and "native" started being used instead of "Indian," and the paper began to include Indigenous sources in its coverage of historical events.

The 1990s would see the paper start to publish the hidden secrets residential school survivors had been long suppressing. In an October 1990 *Globe* article, Phil Fontaine – at the time grand chief of the Assembly of Manitoba Chiefs, later national chief of the Assembly of First Nations – for the first time publicly disclosed the physical and sexual abuse he had endured as a young boy at the Catholic-run Fort Alexander Residential School.

"I think what happened to me is what happened to a lot of people," Fontaine said. "It wasn't just sexual abuse, it was physical and psychological abuse. It was a violation."

By now, the paper was writing in horror of what had gone on. Take this editorial from January 8, 1998:

> Presumably because they viewed the children in their care as somehow less than human, authorities at all levels within the system failed to give them the care and protection to which they were entitled. Sexual and other forms of abuse took root and flourished. Unlike the cultural paternalism, this cannot be seen as an understandable but regrettable excess of the day. At no time has it been part of this country's values to allow the brutal exploitation of defenceless children in institutions charged with their care.

Except that this had been part of the country's values, had been part of the paper's values, for decades – to ignore the sufferings of Indigenous children and to ignore those who sounded the alarm.

Two decades after the Royal Commission on Aboriginal Peoples and several years after the Truth and Reconciliation Commission told us there were likely thousands of children buried at former residential school sites across the country, the Canadian public was finally opening its eyes as the first reports surfaced of unmarked graves at Kamloops in 2021 and numerous other former residential schools since. The schools not only tried to kill the Indian in the child. All too often, they killed the child.

When *Globe* staffers moved to new offices in 2016, Brown's bust moved with them. I haven't seen it though; I report from Northern Ontario.

I'm not sure what I would say to him if we ever did meet again. A lot of people are proud of Brown's contribution to this country. I'm not one of them.

Willow Fiddler is a reporter at *The Globe and Mail*, covering stories related to Indigenous Peoples and communities.

ABOVE: A crowd gathers in front of
The Globe and Mail building to get an
extra edition on September 3, 1939,
the day Britain and France declared
war on Germany. (*The Globe and Mail*)

Eleven: *At* war *with the* censors

During the Second World War, *The Globe* fought for the right to report on a military disaster | **David Parkinson**

C anada's first engagement of ground troops on a battlefield in the Second World War was a shocking, chilling disaster. In November 1941, Canada sent 1,975 troops to the then-British territory of Hong Kong to help deter the Japanese against a possible attack. By Christmas Day, when the British surrendered the colony to the overwhelming Japanese invasion force, nearly three hundred Canadians were dead and almost five hundred more were wounded. The rest were prisoners of war.

In the months that followed, evidence emerged that the Canadian troops had received minimal training and had arrived in Hong Kong without their vehicles or other equipment, which were delayed by logistical snafus. But the federal government's wartime censorship offices, the legally empowered gatekeepers of what Canadian newspapers could and couldn't say about the war, forbade the press from reporting the information.

Globe and Mail publisher George McCullagh, who had been tilting against the censors since early in the war, was now battering at the gates. At stake was the public's right to know the truth about one of Canada's biggest military tragedies. And a possible prison sentence for McCullagh if he dared to defy the censors.

"For several days, Mackenzie King's government seriously faced the prospect of sending the publisher of *The Globe and Mail* to prison," author Mark Bourrie wrote in *Big Men Fear Me*, his 2022 biography of McCullagh.

The standoff marked a turning point in the relationship between Canada's media and its government in wartime, a shift in the balance between the right to know and the duty to defend that had, in previous conflicts, tipped in favour of a secretive and controlling government. Newspapers had been a largely willing cog in the government's censorship and propaganda machinery that suppressed, edited and spun the facts on the nation's news pages in the name of national defence and patriotic duty.

But in the first global war of a truly mass-media era, *The Globe* was at the forefront of a new defiance of the government's censorship machinery. Its outrage grew into a national pushback against overreach by censors, restoring space for important debate of wartime political decisions in the nation's press.

The precedent for government censorship had been established in the First World War, when censors put an ever-tightening lid on any information considered "directly or indirectly useful to the enemy," as the law broadly defined it. That not only included things such as transportation of troops, movements of naval and air fleets, and equipment manufacturing and shipment, but extended to criticism of military leadership, strategy and wartime policy.

Most English-language publishers eagerly complied; they saw it as their patriotic duty to suppress information that was potentially helpful to the enemy while promoting public morale and support for the war. The French-language Quebec newspapers proved harder to contain, particularly around the issue of conscription: they opposed it as stridently as English Canada supported it.

The press-censorship system in both world wars was, nominally, voluntary. News outlets would decide for themselves whether a story, or a passage within it, danced on or over the line drawn by Ottawa's censorship regulations – and either self-censor or, if they were less sure, submit the text to censorship officers for a ruling. Most of the censors Ottawa hired were former newspapermen, who, the government hoped, could smooth over clashes with a collegial backslap over drinks at a local tavern.

But by the 1940s, publishers, reporters and editors proved much less pliable. Papers were increasingly willing to challenge censorship powers. None more so than *The Globe* and its young publisher, McCullagh.

The charismatic but emotionally fragile McCullagh – a high school dropout who made his fortune in mining stocks during the Depression – was just thirty-one years old when he took over *The Globe* and its competitor, *The Mail and Empire*, in 1936, merging them into *The Globe and Mail*. His new creation entered the Canadian media fray at the dawn of electronic media. Both private and public radio had blossomed in the 1930s. Newsreels were a staple of the country's movie theatres.

Newspapers still dominated the market, but many, including *The Globe*, had become stuck in an anachronistic rut. McCullagh was determined to revive his paper with a commitment to serious, modern, (relatively) non-partisan journalism, rooted in accurate and reliable reporting of the important issues of the day. He upgraded the quality and quantity of newsroom staff and focused on political and business coverage that remains the paper's foundation today.

One of that newsroom's stars was columnist Judith Robinson. The daughter of long-time *Toronto Telegram* editor John (Black Jack) Robinson, she was ferociously intelligent, deeply principled and wielded a rapier pen. She was among the earliest mainstream journalists in the English-speaking world to see through Adolf Hitler's smokescreen.

Robinson delivered her opinions with surgical wit. An example is her opening of a column in the fall of 1936, on the Nazi regime's indignance over the awarding of the Nobel Peace Prize to imprisoned German dissident Carl von Ossietzky: "Official Nazi objections to the bestowal . . . are quite Nazi. He shouldn't get a peace prize, Berlin says, because he is a pacifist."

In November 1938, when Hitler sent the Czechoslovakian government an ultimatum to hand over lands to Germany – just weeks after the Munich Agreement and Hitler's assurances that he had no interest in taking in "other nationalities" – Robinson's sarcasm was dripping: "It is sad for Herr Hitler. Who can doubt that it hurts him worse than it can hurt 850,000 Czechs, to have all those people he doesn't want cluttering up his Fatherland?"

Robinson could be just as critical of Canadian and Allied war preparations. She railed against British prime minister Neville Chamberlain and his pursuit of appeasement with the Nazis, to the displeasure of her bosses. Even as the paper grew less optimistic about the prospects for appeasement to succeed, its editorial board remained charitable toward Chamberlain – in contrast to the star columnist, who persistently ridiculed both the leader and his policy.

She was also a vociferous critic of Mackenzie King. "The Prime Minister has many admirers," she wrote, "but there is nothing in my record as a newspaper columnist to show that I am one of them." King was no fan of hers either; in his diary, he called Robinson "a writer whom I thoroughly dislike."

Early in the war, *The Globe* acknowledged the necessity of limits on press freedoms, at least in principle. "While the right to criticize is one of democracy's priceless privileges, self-imposed censorship in the name of patriotism is also a priceless privilege obtaining only in a democracy," a December 1939 editorial asserted.

But soon *The Globe* chafed at the restraints. Robinson and McCullagh were in the thick of it.

Through the fall of 1939 and into 1940, Robinson questioned the King government's wartime preparations, the weak supports for soldiers' families and the recruitment of unemployed and homeless men into service. She accused the government of providing inadequate training and equipment for Canadian soldiers. And when the censors took issue with her references to manufacturing and troop deployment plans or her criticisms of King's war policies, she went after the censors themselves.

"The war for liberty is only six months old, and already the system set up by a federal Liberal government can get away with liberty's murder," she wrote in the spring of 1940.

Robinson parted ways with *The Globe* not long after, following repeated clashes with senior editors over her relentless attacks. She and another outspoken *Globe* colleague, reporter and editorial writer Oakley Dalgleish, started a weekly paper, *The News*, which focused on Ottawa's wartime policies and strategies. King had the Royal Canadian Mounted Police tail both writers for a time in 1940, on the pretense that they were threats to national security.

When the weekly magazine *Saturday Night* broke the story of the RCMP surveillance in early 1941, *The Globe* was no longer in a mood to go with the government's flow. An editorial called the surveillance "beyond the bounds of what is right and proper" and accused authorities of trying to "intimidate writers who had been dissatisfied with and critical of the war effort of the Canadian government."

If McCullagh stood on the moral high ground, his footing was muddied. Although he had supported Ontario's Liberal premier Mitch Hepburn in the 1930s, he was now aligned with the Conservative Party and had political aspirations of his own – many believed he wanted to be prime minister some day. He certainly considered himself a king-maker and had become close friends with George Drew, leader of the Conservative opposition in the Ontario legislature and a fast-rising national Tory star.

McCullagh's relationship with Mackenzie King, a Liberal, was frosty. King confided to his diary that he believed McCullagh was part of a cabal of wealthy and powerful Toronto political and media elites who were out to destroy him. (He called them "a Nazi Fascist output with char-acteristics and methods comparable to those of Hitler.") King's paranoia aside, McCullagh was no political ally.

Drew frequently attacked King's wartime performance and had also taken up the censorship cause – often in op-eds and interviews in *The Globe*, which provided him a platform. He called the censorship system "a political machine for preventing effective correction of Mr. King's misstatements" and charged that the prime minister was trying to cre-ate "the machinery of a dictatorship."

McCullagh and Drew's censorship fight found its *cause célèbre* at Christmas of 1941, with the decimation of Canada's troops in Hong Kong. What had contributed to the death or capture of the entire two-thousand-strong Canadian force? The nation was grieving and wanted answers.

Under public and political pressure, King called a royal commission into the tragedy but ordered that its hearings be held behind closed doors. He appointed a sole commissioner, Lyman Duff, chief justice of the Supreme Court of Canada, who was also his friend and confidant.

The Duff commission report exonerated Canadian military and political officials. It issued no recommendations.

Drew, who had acted as the Opposition's counsel in the hearings, quickly labelled the report a whitewash. For the next several weeks, *The Globe* and Drew hammered away at the commission's conclusions and its secrecy. Their campaign culminated in mid-July when Drew wrote a thirty-two-page letter to King, outlining evidence of failures in leadership decisions, training and equipment leading up to the Hong

Kong tragedy. He sent copies to The Canadian Press wire service and the entire Parliamentary Press Gallery.

The censors, on King's direction, quashed any publication of the contents of the letter.

What followed was a torrent of outrage not only from *The Globe* but from newspapers from coast to coast. The censors were now dealing with a mountain of columns and editorials criticizing the government suppression of the Hong Kong issue.

On July 24, 1942, *The Globe* published a full page of editorials from newspapers across the country condemning the government's heavy-handed muzzling of press freedoms, under the all-caps headline: "GAG-GING PROCESS OF CENSORSHIP DRAWS PROTESTS ACROSS CANADA."

Meanwhile, McCullagh was weighing whether to defy censors' orders and publish the Drew letter. He asked Toronto regional censor Bert Perry point-blank what would happen if *The Globe* published. Perry told McCullagh that the paper could expect to be prosecuted and that he would face jail time.

While McCullagh was a bold personality who rarely shied from a good fight, he was also a recovered alcoholic who was prone to bouts of depression. Though we don't know for sure (McCullagh never wrote a memoir), he may have been self-aware enough to know he would not fare well in prison. *The Globe* continued to push the issue as far as it could without revealing Drew's arguments, but in the end, it didn't publish the letter. In fact, the missive remained under the cloak of government secrecy for years after the war had ended.

The Globe's decision to cede to the censors spared McCullagh a jail sentence, but it also spared top military and political decision-makers from a public airing of their mistakes.

Around the same time that Drew and *The Globe* were waging their censorship campaign, Harry Crerar – the army's chief of the general staff whose fingerprints were all over the Hong Kong calamity – was lobbying the British to give Canada a leading role in a key military operation. The

Brits agreed to place Canadians at the forefront of the raid on Dieppe in August 1942 – an even bigger military disaster than Hong Kong.

In his 2007 biography of Crerar, military strategist Paul Douglas Dickson noted that the Hong Kong controversy was on the general's mind during the planning for Dieppe. Perhaps Crerar might have been more circumspect in the lead-up to Dieppe had Hong Kong, and his role in it, received thorough scrutiny in the Canadian press.

Nevertheless, the showdown over Hong Kong was a watershed, and the government knew it. Afterward, censors were much more careful to stick to censorship that had a legitimate military objective and avoid clashes with the media over issues of political and public interest.

During the conscription crisis of 1944 – when King ordered that soldiers drafted for domestic duty be reassigned to the front lines – government censors pushed back against the military brass and the prime minister, who wanted to quash reporting on escalating protests among conscripts. The censors argued that the dispute was political at its root and that media should be left relatively free to cover it.

After the war, McCullagh expanded his newspaper empire, acquiring another cross-town rival, *The Telegram*, in 1948. Pierre Berton wrote in a 1949 *Maclean's* profile that "at 43, [McCullagh's] story is only half-told." But with health problems piling onto his psychological demons, McCullagh died, probably by suicide, in 1952. He was forty-seven.

By then, Dalgleish had become McCullagh's right-hand man, serving as *The Globe and Mail*'s editor-in-chief since 1948. He added the title of publisher in 1957, holding both jobs until his death in 1963.

Robinson revived her newspaper career in 1953, as *The Telegram*'s Ottawa columnist. She was still on the job when she died in 1961, at age sixty-four. She was the first woman to win a National Newspaper Award in news reporting, in 1953.

The Canadian military conducted a review of the censorship program in 1948 and decided against developing a new censorship plan for future conflicts. When Canada participated in the Korean War in the early 1950s, the government made no attempt to censor Canadian media, although the United Nations, which commanded the multi-national coalition sent to Korea, tried to clamp down on war reporters in the field.

Nearly seven decades after the Hong Kong affair, *Globe and Mail* reporters unravelling the Canadian military's role in the torture of detainees in the Afghanistan war were met not with censorship offices but with the stifling complexities of access to information requests and a sea of redacted documents.

"*The Globe* pushed harder than any other Canadian newspaper on the detainee story," says former *Globe* foreign correspondent Graeme Smith, whose investigations on the ground in Afghanistan helped blow the story open.

The paper's persistence led to military and parliamentary investigations, the public release of thousands of documents, and nearly brought down the government of Stephen Harper in 2009. Still, the final outcome contained regretful echoes of McCullagh's campaign: the scandal never received an open public inquiry.

"On balance, could we have pushed harder? Probably," Smith says. "The full story of what happened remains to be published."

David Parkinson is deputy head of newsroom development at *The Globe and Mail*.

ABOVE: Men and women repair a
broken dike in Haicheng County of
Fujian Province in the spring of 1960.
(Fred Nossal/*The Globe and Mail*)

Twelve: China's rising *through* Canadian eyes

The Globe was for years the only Western newspaper to maintain a presence in Beijing, but doing so wasn't easy | **Nathan VanderKlippe**

I n the final few days of June 1966, U.S. newspapers published photos of a nineteen-year-old Chinese man surrounded by officers in white uniforms who grasped his elbows and shoulders in restraint.

Yang Kuo-ching had been found guilty of knifing to death two foreigners. His subsequent execution by firing squad was "but one tiny facet of the convulsion that this nation of 700,000,000 is now going through," journalist David Oancia wrote of the show trial, held before a crowd of 1,300, which he witnessed and photographed.

Oancia's photos gave startling texture to the opening weeks of China's violent and cruel Cultural Revolution.

But what made Yang's trial especially notable was that Oancia was there at all. He was a reporter for *The Globe and Mail*, which for many years was the only Western newspaper to maintain a presence in the country, lending *The Globe* and its correspondents global importance.

The Peking bureau, as it was then known, provided a rare vantage point on what was then still a fresh-faced Communist regime. In the decades that followed, it has been Canada's most reliable window on China, bringing correspondents and readers into the midst of the country along its error-strewn march toward superpower status.

When Mao Zedong strode to power in 1949, he evicted much of the Western world from his newly minted Red China. The worst chapters in the country's modern history went unobserved by much of the outside world, including the Great Leap Forward, a failed economic and social campaign whose privations created a famine that killed many millions and drove some to cannibalism, and the violent gyrations of the Cultural Revolution that followed.

Communist China barred U.S. journalists, in particular, from its soil. It was not until 1978 that the Associated Press resumed its presence in China. Other U.S. journalists began to return the following year.

By then, *The Globe* could already boast decades of China coverage.

The newspaper's Beijing bureau was the creation of Oakley Dalgleish, the dashing *Globe* publisher whose fascination with the rising Communist establishment brought him to Soviet Moscow (where he interviewed Nikita Khrushchev) and then Beijing in the 1950s, where he struck a deal to install a correspondent in China.

The bureau became a springboard to reporting from across Asia, bringing *Globe* readers to Ulan Bator and Pyongyang, Bandar Seri Begawan and Dharamshala, Bangkok and Yangon.

But China has always been the central story. *Globe* journalists reported from the rubble of the devastating Tangshan earthquake;

from the birthplace of former leader Deng Xiaoping and the village where current president Xi Jinping once lived in a cave; from the hospital room where Mao's fat grandson endured forced dieting; from an illegal motorcycle market and prison factories; from inside the cloistered grounds of the Zhongnanhai leadership compound in Beijing; from the mosques, lamaseries and churches where some of the most brutal Chinese policies have gained expression; from the floodwaters of the Three Gorges Dam and the timeless landscapes of the Li River; from democracy protests and crackdowns; from the capital punishment execution grounds of Beijing and the harsh spotlights shining on prison-like re-education camps in Xinjiang.

The Globe's time in China brought with it major misses (understanding the country has never been simple; one correspondent wrongly predicted China would never demand sterilization to meet its reproductive targets), partial accounts of reality (it was only after leaving China for Hong Kong that a *Globe* correspondent documented food shortages so severe that calcium deficiency left toddlers unable to sit up) and journalistic triumphs (*Globe* correspondents were in the midst of young Chinese who publicly thirsted for democracy in the 1970s and then watched a decade later as tanks crushed those dreams around Tiananmen Square).

The Globe was there when millions of Red Guards gathered in Beijing when U.S. athletes arrived for ping-pong diplomacy, when Richard Nixon came to China, when Ottawa and Beijing consummated the restoration of diplomatic relations, when first Pierre and later Justin Trudeau were feted by the Chinese leadership, when shipments of Canadian wheat brought sustenance in time of famine and when Tim Hortons and Canada Goose built outlets to profit from the immense new wealth of Chinese consumers.

It all began with Dalgleish, an ardent advocate of official diplomatic recognition for Mao's China.

"There is no basis whatever for continuing to rope off China and make an enemy where, I am convinced, an enemy does not exist," he said upon his return from a 1958 visit in which he pleaded for a bureau in a meeting with Chen Yi, then China's foreign minister and vice-premier. A 1959 announcement about the opening of the Beijing bureau noted *The Globe*'s belief that "China might well hold the key to future peace."

In the 1950s, the paper was insatiably keen to witness what Mao had wrought. It dispatched London reporter William Kinmond on a 1957 trip to China that lasted nearly four months and took him on an 11,000-kilometre voyage from Hong Kong to the north and west of the country, before ending at Taipei. It was a preview of the decades to come, which saw *Globe* correspondents roaming the farthest reaches of the country.

Subsequent negotiations for the first resident *Globe* correspondent spanned nearly fourteen months. Chinese authorities rejected the newspaper's first two choices for the position.

Beijing wanted to ensure *The Globe*'s coverage was written by a naïf, unschooled in the country and less likely to see through its carefully constructed facades. "We learned that anyone who had experience in China (pre- or post-revolutionary), anyone with knowledge of the language (unless a Party nominee), was unlikely to be welcome," Dalgleish wrote later.

Even after securing agreement to make Australian Frederick Nossal the first *Globe* correspondent in 1959, the inaugural Beijing bureau lasted just six months. Chinese authorities refused to renew Nossal's visa, ensuring his expulsion just weeks after the arrival of his wife and four children, including five-year-old twins. Beijing could point to no specific reason, claiming only that his reports "had not been, in all respects, accurate."

It took nearly four years for China to allow another *Globe* correspondent to return. By then, Beijing was prepared to send one of its own to Canada.

China allowed *The Globe* into Beijing only on the condition that Ottawa open its own borders to a Chinese journalist. In July 1964, the New China News Agency – now better known as Xinhua – sent to Ottawa its inaugural Canadian correspondent, Pu Chao-min.

Pu cut an unusual figure in Canada. Ottawa required him to secure permission before leaving the capital, since *Globe* correspondents could not travel freely in China. He brought Canada into the Chinese press, filing articles about the spread of Maoist thought in Canada. Nonetheless, he received great warmth from *The Globe*, whose editors personally welcomed him.

"This was not just an ordinary journalist," John Fraser, *The Globe*'s Beijing bureau chief from 1977 to 1979, recalled years later. "This was the highest-ranking Chinese Communist Party member to be in North America."

It was not until many years later that a more detailed picture of Pu's full importance to Beijing came into focus.

Canadian security services identified him as an operative of the United Front, a shadowy and powerful organization dedicated to furthering the interests of the Chinese Communist Party. Even under RCMP surveillance, he occasionally managed to evade his followers, crossing the Ottawa River to hold meetings in the forests of Quebec, security sources told *The Globe* in 2000. China wanted Canada's nuclear-energy secrets, and it is believed Pu was charged with securing them.

In 1985, a University of Toronto engineering scholar was shocked to find a near-perfect replica of a Canadian research reactor in China.

Pu was only part of that effort. But had *The Globe* not struck a deal to go to China, it's doubtful he would have been in Canada.

For *The Globe*, the Beijing post was a coveted prize. In establishing the bureau, the newspaper also created a "Peking service" to distribute, and profit from, the unique coverage its correspondents provided. Users included *The New York Times*, the *Vancouver Sun*, the *London Daily Mail*, *Le Figaro* and other publications in the Netherlands, Finland, Germany and Australia.

In 1968, *Globe* correspondent Colin McCullough submitted photos of then-premier Zhou Enlai and other top political and military leaders, which he had snapped during a visit by an Albanian delegation to Beijing.

"Some of these Chinese leaders have seldom, if ever, been photographed for publication in the West," a *Globe* telegraph noted.

Three years later, *The New York Times* cabled Toronto with an all-capitals request, days before then-correspondent Norman Webster would cover one of the most important diplomatic breakthroughs of the twentieth century: "Anticipating Webster will photograph American pingpongists in Peking, would you rush us enlargements of his best pictures plus contact sheets?"

Webster sent out the pictures via Shanghai and Paris. "Hope it gets to you," he wrote the Toronto editors. "Should be first film out if it does."

Being witness to history came with its own struggles, particularly for writers more at ease behind a typewriter than a lens. Worse were the dirty tricks. "Although you may have to take plenty of duds to get a couple of good pictures, you run a good chance of getting nothing back from the developers but the duds," Webster lamented in early 1970. At least seven of his frames, he said, had "been deliberately washed out."

Photography, too, brought different people into the pages of *The Globe*. Many correspondents worked alongside spouses to both take pictures and document their reporting, including Fraser's wife, Elizabeth MacCallum. She received tiny-type credit for her images in the newspaper but recalls editors whose attitudes created a club of "angry Beijing wives." Some were themselves journalists. But their work in China was hobbled by the jealousies of a newspaper that coveted the work of its unique bureau. Editors bristled at the thought of competitors benefiting from the work of spouses *The Globe* had placed in China. "*The Globe and Mail* doesn't care about your wife," Fraser says an editor once told him.

From 1959 until today, *The Globe* has dispatched just one woman to China: Jan Wong, a one-time Maoist who was the newspaper's first Mandarin-speaking Beijing correspondent. By the time she arrived in the city for *The Globe* in 1988, the bureau had been open for nearly thirty years.

A few years earlier, Fraser had played a unique role in his reporting from a democracy wall that appeared in Beijing, when he forged an intensely personal connection to those who, for a time, gathered to imagine a different political future for their country.

Wong documented the devastating conclusion of that era, first from Tiananmen Square and then from a room in the Beijing Hotel, where she timed the long volleys of shots as soldiers gunned down students with copper-jacketed bullets and anti-aircraft machine guns. She watched as a man stood before a row of tanks, one of the most indelible images of modern China. After the shooting stopped, she set out to document its toll, interviewing two people who survived being run over by tanks – one with crushed legs, one with a mangled arm and an ear torn from his body – as well as soldiers who had shed their uniforms in shame and even a high-ranking general who made a remarkable admission. "Deng Xiaoping didn't handle it properly," he told her. "It was a mistake."

Wong's reporting benefited from her skill and curiosity but also from a growing Chinese openness to the outside world.

The first correspondents were constrained so tightly that they could not even access state media from provinces outside Beijing; they cultivated informants for their ability to deliver information on the going price of food. The requirement for permission to leave the capital was rescinded only ahead of the 2008 Olympics.

Today, the state finds its most intrusive expression in digital surveillance that monitors communication and cameras equipped with facial recognition that can frustrate attempts to conduct journalism undetected. Sneaking into rural China – such as *The Globe*'s efforts to document the mass internment of largely Muslim people in Xinjiang – has grown more difficult even as travel has grown easier on silken highways and space-age trains.

Being in China has nonetheless allowed correspondents to touch history in often unique ways. John Burns secured the chopsticks used by Richard Nixon during his history-making trip to China.

In 1976, after the death of Mao, *The Globe* sent to the Great Hall of the People a large wreath, draped in a ribbon inked with handwritten characters: "In memory of the great leader Chairman Mao."

"Under no circumstances publish this picture, but please send me one print of it," Ross Munro, the correspondent at the time, wrote in a note accompanying photos of the wreath, suggesting he recognized the delicate nature of commemorating a man who was both chief architect of Red China and head executioner of millions.

Through it all, the parsing of Chinese affairs has remained little changed. Indeed, a time-travelling correspondent from the 1950s would be startled by the familiarity of working in modern-day China: in the struggle against misunderstanding (one correspondent recounted a trip in which a local official was constantly addressed, in English, as the "Chief of Intercourse"); in the shadow-chasing hunt for information; in the reliance on local Chinese reporters whose personal risk-taking and vital contributions often went uncredited; and in the nights rendered sleepless by work in a time zone situated for maximum incompatibility.

The quotidian absurdities, too, have remained familiar. Allen Abel described in 1984 a day in the Beijing bureau:

6 a.m. – Awaken gently to murmur of construction men battering sewer pipe outside bedroom window. Check Telex machine for effusive praise from Toronto office. None.

10 a.m. – Housekeeper reports death of washing machine.

2 p.m. – Dispatch translator, housekeeper, driver in car to find part for washing machine.

3 p.m. – Press briefing by Information Department, Ministry of Foreign Affairs. Two hundred correspondents await announcement on Sino-Soviet relations, Vietnam border dispute, changes in Central Committee of Communist Party. Announcement: China to send fisheries delegation to Equatorial Guinea. End briefing.

4 p.m. – Staff returns from search. Good news: washing machine can be fixed. Bad news: toilet broken.

7:30 [p.m.] – Chinese secret contact phones. Speak in whispers. "The usual place." Meet secret contact. Secret contact wants new pair of tennis shoes.

10 p.m. – Spray cockroach killer down drains, under fridge, into closets, through rattan carpet. Check Telex machine for effusive praise from home office. Retire contritely.

It is, with only the most minor of alterations, an account that could have been written by generations of *Globe* correspondents.

Through those tangles of daily life, many *Globe* correspondents have won National Newspaper Awards for their reporting from Beijing, including Oancia, Webster (after whom the award is now named), Wong, Miro Cernetig, Geoffrey York, Mark MacKinnon and me.

But, nearly sixty-five years after the expulsion of Nossal, *The Globe* is once again without a correspondent in China. The paper's current Beijing bureau chief, James Griffiths, works from Hong Kong, unable to secure a visa as friction and suspicion fray relations between Canada and China.

History echoes.

After his departure, Nossal described the polite frigidity toward foreign correspondents from those he encountered, who treated them as "a quite unnecessary evil which had been imposed on them by sheer misfortune." It prompted a question for him: "Why did they allow reporters in at all?"

A quarter century later, Abel ruminated on the same, pondering the inscrutability of a posting whose importance has, since its inception, been wrapped in tangles of diplomatic messiness and journalistic ambition, between the kind embrace of the Chinese people and the iron dictates of the state that rules their lives.

"This is how it goes for the Peking bureau," Abel wrote in 1984, "feast and falsehood, light and shadow, a grasping at chimerical straws."

Nathan VanderKlippe is an international correspondent at *The Globe and Mail*.

ABOVE: Oakley Dalgleish, publisher of *The Globe and Mail*, 1957–1963. (Ashley & Crippen)

Thirteen:
Getting down *to* business

The one constant in *The Globe*'s 180-year history has been a drive to be essential to an audience that is passionate about business | **Andrew Willis**

"**Y**ou ruined my morning. And the morning of everyone I work with."

Not the feedback a Report on Business reporter wanted to hear after asking the head of one of the country's largest money managers – Len Racioppo, then-president of Jarislowsky Fraser Ltd. – what he thought of the reimagined *Globe and Mail* delivered to his office early on the morning of April 23, 2007.

Months of brainstorming, countless mock-ups and significant consulting fees went into the newspaper Racioppo just panned. The new business section, rolled out with a retooled ROB website that was chock-a-block with stock market data, represented *The Globe*'s latest, best attempt to retain its core readers, who treasured their daily paper, while staying relevant to an increasingly digital audience. A lot was riding on the redesign.

What exactly wrecked the money manager's morning? Racioppo, whose team managed $45-billion of clients' savings, explained that early each workday, Jarislowsky Fraser fund managers arrived at the Bay Street office, poured a coffee, gathered around the boardroom table and spread out the pages of the ROB containing the previous day's stock prices, currency and interest rates. While sipping from their mugs, some of the country's most influential investors would check what went up and what went down, looking for patterns and exchanging observations on the markets. Those early morning sessions were central to the firm's culture and "helped determine our activities during the day," he says now.

The reimagined Report on Business stripped much of the market data from the pages of the newspaper, moving it to a website featuring real-time stock moves, as opposed to yesterday's prices. In place of stock listings, the print edition of *The Globe* cleared space for additional articles from reporters strung across Canada, the United States and other foreign bureaus.

Sacrificed in the redesign were the neatly packaged, daily stock charts that served as touchstones in the lives of countless readers, including Racioppo. That triggered a brief moment of grousing from the fund manager, mirrored by angry e-mails from hundreds of subscribers. But within days, the outrage faded. Jarislowsky Fraser's morning gathering started featuring computer screens rather than a pulled-apart newspaper.

In 1844, *Globe* founder George Brown packaged a few stories into a section called "Financial Intelligence" that was delivered to Toronto's fledgling finance community – the country's commercial heart was in Montreal – and an equally small number of prosperous farmers surrounding the city. He also anticipated his readers' interest in national stories, and future bureaus in Calgary and Vancouver, by printing a "Western *Globe*" in 1845, from an office in London, Ontario, two hundred kilometres down the road.

The story of business journalism at *The Globe* is the story of Canada's economy moving, in fits and starts, from backwater colony to undersized but plucky global player. While the stand-alone Report on Business section that Racioppo tore apart each morning is a relatively recent creation – launched in 1962 – the concept of authoritative, timely coverage of Canadian commerce has always been among *The Globe*'s top priorities. Historically, the newspaper has dominated this market. Its ability to stay relevant to business readers, long after the last printing press goes silent, will be a crucial factor for the company's future. As Report on Business goes, so goes *The Globe*.

Reporters, by and large, see themselves as outsiders. When it comes to covering corporate CEOs, or premiers and prime ministers, the newspaper plays the role of watchdog or whistle-blower, sometimes scolding, occasionally cheeky, always aiming to serve the public interest.

The Globe's founders and several generations of owners would have snorted out their snuff at the suggestion that their newspaper served a public interest. One owned a newspaper, historically, to further one's political or business ambitions.

That was certainly the case with Brown, founder of the federal Liberal Party, elected politician and a Father of Confederation. He launched *The Globe* in the 1840s to boost his party and attack the Conservatives, led by the country's future prime minister, Sir John A. Macdonald. Owning *The Globe* proved an effective tool. The newspaper helped bring down Macdonald's Conservative government in 1873 over allegations of illegal fundraising, in what became known as the Pacific Scandal.

By the time the Depression took hold in the 1930s, *The Globe* was a blunt instrument for creating wealth. Publisher George McCullagh, who merged the Liberal-leaning *Globe* with the Conservative-backing *Mail and Empire* in 1936, used his position at the paper to help build a personal fortune from trading stocks and to forge political ties. In his 1992 history of *The Globe, Power and Influence,* author David Hayes described McCullagh as "a capitalist who believed that politics was just a subsidiary branch of business."

The Globe's business coverage got an even bigger boost from McCullagh's main financial backer, William Wright, who struck it rich as a prospector. When he decided to back McCullagh, Wright insisted on just one condition: expand the newspaper's business pages. "Anything that is of advantage to mining is of advantage to the country as a whole," Wright declared.

The seeds for what sprouted into the country's dominant business section were planted in 1948 when Oakley Dalgleish became *The Globe*'s editor. A native of small-town Canada – born in New Liskeard, Ontario, and raised in Moose Jaw – Dalgleish learned the business in part by reporting for London's Fleet Street papers before joining *The Globe* in 1934 as a reporter covering railways and hotels.

When Dalgleish took the wheel, the story of the Canadian economy was one of farms, fishing, forestry and the occasional mine. In 1940, manufacturing accounted for only one in four jobs. And a third of the population lived in rural settings – now, just one in ten Canadians are outside major cities.

As the postwar industrial boom kicked off, *The Globe* chronicled the transformation of both an economy and a society by covering the introduction of computers and advances in telecom. The newspaper provided context to the debut of Canada's first mainframe computer at the University of Toronto in 1949 by explaining: "It will be able to compute income taxes; to tell the trend of business at an electrified glance; to play a passable game of chess, and maybe even to forecast weather months in advance." *The Globe* reporter proved prescient on tech's coming role in commerce, if not the accuracy of weather predictions.

The Globe debuted a new stand-alone section: Report on Business. For a modern audience, accustomed to colour photos and graphics, the ROB's grey front page was a slog. It relied on data-driven stories – "TSE sets trading-value record" read one headline – anchored by a feature on a five-way merger among concrete producers. The only light touch was a photo of the latest French cruise ship, over the headline "Trouble for Queens," a reference to Britain's luxury liners.

In the 1960s, Canada's biggest business stories were in the auto sector, which took off after former prime minister Lester Pearson dropped by president Lyndon Johnson's Texas ranch in 1965 to sign the Auto Pact. In addition to covering the sector, the Report on Business pages became a forum where industry leaders fought battles for public opinion.

The first print run demonstrated ROB could help *The Globe* fulfill its long-held claim to being Canada's national newspaper, rather than one of many Toronto broadsheets. Dalgleish commissioned an extra edition printed on lightweight paper, which was loaded on to airplanes for delivery across the country on the day of publication. (The airmail network lasted until the 1980s, when *The Globe* began using satellite transmission to print across the country.)

Dalgleish initially published ROB on Tuesdays and Fridays, with plans to add more days if the launch was successful. ROB proved a huge hit with advertisers – by the 1970s, the section was winning 90 per cent of lucrative career ads – and justified being part of each daily edition.

The first stand-alone ROB in 1962 also featured on its front a blurb explaining *The Globe* had struck partnerships with foreign publishers, including the *Financial Times of London*, to ensure readers had access to breaking news from around the world. In the 1960s, foreign-owned companies controlled the domestic economy and Canadians were still working out their national identity. Running stories supplied by international outlets fit the spirit of the times.

The ROB spent the 1970s and early eighties broadening the concept of what counts as a business story. Editors established dedicated workplace and environmental beats and launched a Report on Technology. Business reporters worked in bureaus across the country, telling national stories through a regional lens.

Under editor Ian Carman, the section forged a reputation for being thorough and thoughtful, both admirable qualities, but dreadfully dull. Corporate earnings were dutifully covered; corporate personalities were largely ignored. "That huge societal changes had taken place by the early 1980s was scarcely evident in the pages of the ROB; it spoke almost exclusively to male executives and their princes in waiting," said Hayes. "The ROB failed to probe beneath the surface of business life in a systematic way, identifying long-term trends and providing analysis."

Somewhere in history, a brave priest pointed out the Bible might find wider readership if published in languages other than just Latin. In the same vein, Carman's successors, Tim Pritchard and Margaret Wente, pushed the newsroom to do something heretical: make coverage more interesting. Editors, and the advertising and subscription teams, wanted an ROB that appealed to a wide, if affluent, audience. Drawing on magazine-editing skills – honed in flashy, often CEO-focused features in the monthly *Report on Business* magazine, which debuted in 1984 – Wente pushed for stories featuring tension, you're-in-the-room insight and, most of all, personality.

"It helped that the 1980s saw the emergence of larger-than-life Canadian personalities like Robert Campeau and the Reichmann family, who made for compelling reading," says Wente. On her watch, business reporters became some of the highest-profile and highest-paid print journalists in the country, as *The Globe* and rivals waged a war for talent. "Before the 1980s, reporters were sent to the business section if they couldn't cut it on political or foreign coverage," says Wente. "ROB was considered a backwater."

Business leaders bridled at what for many was their first taste of critical coverage. The chairman of CIBC demanded a meeting with Wente, ROB editor, and the publisher of *The Globe* to complain about coverage of problems in the bank's loans to the Reichmanns' real estate company, Olympia and York. Early in the meeting, it became clear *Globe* reporters knew more about the secretive family's finances than the bank executive. The ROB continued to probe the Reichmann empire, and CIBC lost hundreds of millions of dollars when Olympia and York filed for bankruptcy in 1992.

Looking back on the era, Wente says the ROB made two significant shifts that successfully boosted readership: the section embraced investigative-style journalism and added personal finance coverage for do-it-yourself investors. "There was a spirited newsroom debate around offering readers advice on their investments, with a vocal faction saying we should avoid taking any responsibility for what people did with their money," she says.

Again, what was then radical is now traditional at *The Globe*. Personal finance columnists such as Rob Carrick and John Heinzl count among the platform's most-read writers. In 2022, ROB editor Gary Salewicz revamped the section by adding personal finance writers at the expense of one of the few remaining pages of stock charts. He received far fewer abusive e-mails than his predecessor.

The daily ROB faced its first real competitive challenge in 1988, when the *Financial Post* began publishing a daily tabloid, backed by its new parent, the *Toronto Sun* chain. The *Post* featured short news stories and spicy, pro-business columnists. In 1998, Conrad Black bought the *Post* and folded it into a right-leaning broadsheet, the *National Post*, aimed at dethroning *The Globe* as the country's first read.

The newspaper war served readers well and boosted the fortunes of business journalists. But by the end of the 1990s, it became clear the dailies were fighting the wrong battle. They faced an existential challenge from the internet. In 2000, *The Globe* launched globeandmail.com, an online version of the newspaper with a heavy emphasis on business content.

ROB reporters won countless awards for covering the tech disruption undermining the newspaper's business model. The rise and stunning falls of Nortel Networks and smartphone pioneer BlackBerry were covered in dramatic detail, as was the dot-com market crash at the beginning of a new century and the global financial crisis that began in 2007.

The Globe, like most print-based platforms, made early mistakes in rolling out an online strategy by allowing free access to content, on the theory digital advertising would pay the bills. As the sector matured, it became clear that search engines such as Google and social-media site Facebook were winning the bulk of digital ad dollars.

In the same 2007 *Globe* redesign that upset Jarislowsky Fraser's morning coffee routine, business editor John Stackhouse announced a shift in mindset: the online version of the ROB was on equal footing with the print edition. Again, in what seemed radical and is now commonplace, Stackhouse said the digital product and the morning paper were "not separate publications. They're run out of the same newsroom by the same journalists, using the best of the printed page and the Web."

Today's ROB, like the entire *Globe*, reaches the majority of readers as a digital product and earns the bulk of its revenues through payments from readers. Print subscribers have gone from reading Brown's few lines of Financial Intelligence to receiving e-mail alerts on stories from journalists who are increasingly digital natives. The ROB is going where readers and the country are headed, racing to stay relevant in a global economy, where the advantage belongs to those with the best access to information and news. That's a contest the ROB, and Canada, can win.

Andrew Willis is a columnist for Report on Business.

ABOVE: Ailsa Craig, left, and Aly
Drummond hug each other outside
the Legislative Building at Queen's
Park after the defeat of the Gay
Rights Bill (Bill 167) on June 9, 1994.
(Fred Lum/*The Globe and Mail*)

Fourteen:
A shift toward acceptance

The Globe helped to change the conversation on LGBTQ rights | **Rachel Giese**

To have been queer in Canada before the 1960s meant living in the shadows. You might have found your way to a spot frequented by others like you (a nightclub tucked away in a downtown hotel, a wooded area in a neighbourhood park). You might have recognized something of yourself in the works of James Baldwin, Gore Vidal and Djuna Barnes, or in dime-store pulp novels with titles like *Twilight Lovers* and *Women's Barracks*. You might have heard rumours about a certain confirmed bachelor uncle or spinster aunt. Or maybe you were part of one of the very small, very brave early groups of homophile activists, who came together in the 1950s to fight for dignity and respect.

In daily newspapers during the early Cold War era, you were all but invisible. Your existence had to be read between the lines: no acknowledgment of your culture, desire, love save for the occasional quote from a doctor on the pathology of homosexuality and its potential cures, or a police blotter report detailing raids on gay venues. You might have spotted a hint of gay sensibility in the arts pages – sections of newspapers then referred to as "the pansy patch" – but even that was sparing.

The Globe and Mail was no exception. Deep in the paper's library of print archives, in the files of pre-1969 coverage of gay issues, rests an envelope labelled "Homosexuals – Editorial. Previous to September 1969 See: Sex Perverts." In an essay from the 2017 history anthology *Any Other Way: How Toronto Got Queer*, Stephanie Chambers, one of the newspaper's researchers, writes of the pain that struck her coming across the file, noting "that those long-forgotten colleagues classified queerness in this way reveals much about their era."

There's a wealth of research suggesting that the way news media frame issues – from the approach of the storytelling and the selection of sources to the weight and space given to a subject – influences public attitudes and opinions. This effect can be even stronger if the audience's knowledge of, and direct experience with, the subject is limited.

And much of what Canadians knew about LGBTQ people in the early Cold War period they learned through lurid news coverage. This time of conformity and paranoia was ripe for media-fuelled moral panics about threats to the nuclear family, traditional values and national security. Nothing was more taboo in Canada than the acts committed by the deviants, degenerates and perverts, as they were portrayed in *The Globe*. No one was a more convenient scapegoat for society's real or perceived ills than the homosexual.

But even as news media reports influenced attitudes that led to a life sentence for one convicted homosexual and encouraged a purge of LGBTQ workers from the federal services, newspapers also started moving public opinion toward acceptance. As *The Globe* took up these stories, it helped to shift the conversation on LGBTQ rights, just as the movement for LGBTQ rights helped reshape the paper itself.

Here's what a reader might have learned about queerness as it was reported in *The Globe* in the years after the Second World War: a 1947 story by columnist John Verner McAree headlined "Scientific treatments for sex perverts" opens thus: "What are called sex crimes are increasing in Canada and the United States, and confronted with them the lynching spirit stirs itself." A 1963 interview with the leader of Toronto's morality squad is headlined "Degenerates parade, inspector says: blames lack of public disgust for growth of homosexuality." A year later, a news brief reported on police concerns that downtown bars that provided "a gathering place for homosexuals" offered "a chance for homosexuality to be spread by introduction." And another article from 1966 warned of undesirables in Toronto parks, the "exhibitionists, homosexuals, drunks, vandals and thugs."

In this period of silence and shame, there was scant attention or sympathy for those persecuted for their sexuality or gender identity. And it was within this silence that LGBTQ people in Canada faced the most virulent, state-sanctioned homophobia in the nation's history.

Beginning in the 1950s, the government of Canada instituted a policy to root out members of the armed forces, the RCMP and the federal public service who were suspected of being gay. Thousands were surveilled, harassed, interrogated and fired; thousands of careers, reputations and lives shattered.

At the same time, police staked out cruising spots to entrap men seeking sex with other men, oftentimes going undercover as a potential connection. Once caught, these men might be taken somewhere remote and beaten up, arrested on charges of gross indecency or buggery and have their names publicized – thousands more careers, reputations and lives shattered.

Then came the prosecution of Everett George Klippert. Arrested in Calgary in 1960, the bus driver confessed to eighteen counts of gross indecency and served four years in prison. In 1965, after confessing to similar acts in the Northwest Territories, he was declared a dangerous sexual offender – in effect a life sentence – which the Supreme Court upheld two years later.

But if Klippert's sentence marked the peak, or nadir, of the persecution of homosexuals in Canada, it also marked the beginning of change.

Even by the standards of the time, Klippert's sentence was seen as cruel and excessive. "It's ridiculous that any man . . . would be put into jail because they are affected by [a] social disease," Liberal MP Bud Orange, who represented Klippert's riding, told the House of Commons. "I hope the ridiculousness of this situation forces the government to make a move in this regard." A December 12, 1967, editorial in *The Globe* argued that "homosexual acts committed privately between consenting adults should not be a crime, just as fornication between consenting adults is not a crime." What's more, the state's responsibility "should be to legislate rules for a well-ordered society. It has no right or duty to creep into the bedrooms of the nation."

Justice minister Pierre Trudeau cribbed that last bit – "there's no place for the state in the bedrooms of the nation," he told the press – when he introduced a sweeping omnibus crime bill one week later that, among other reforms, decriminalized sex in private between two men over the age of twenty-one. (Lawmakers at the time were seemingly oblivious to the existence of queer women, who were absent in laws and in public discussions.) The bill became law under Trudeau, who was by then prime minister, two years later.

In arguing for partial decriminalization, the paper may have been influenced by an earlier battle against police overreach waged by its editor Richard Doyle. A freethinker who embraced the old newspaper adage about afflicting the comfortable and comforting the afflicted, Doyle challenged the paper's long-standing establishment biases.

In a 1964 editorial, he took aim at proposed Ontario legislation that would have empowered police to summon any person for questioning in secret, deprive them of legal advice and hold them indefinitely if they refused to respond to questioning. "For the public good," the editorial argued, Ontario "proposes to trample upon the Magna Carta, Habeas Corpus, the Canadian Bill of Rights and the Rule of Law." The bill was withdrawn. Three years later, the paper was advocating for the partial decriminalization of homosexual acts.

The same year the decriminalization bill passed, continuing police raids at the Stonewall Inn and other gay bars in New York provoked hundreds of protesters to take to the streets in an uprising now viewed as the genesis of the modern LGBTQ rights movement. Support and advocacy groups, as well as annual Pride Day celebrations marking the Stonewall uprising, soon sprang up throughout the U.S. and Canada.

In 1971, two hundred people gathered on Parliament Hill in Ottawa for the "We Demand" rally, the first large-scale LGBTQ rights demonstration in Canada. One of the group's concerns was that the law decriminalizing only sexual acts in private between two men over the age of twenty-one might lead to greater persecution of other forms of gay sex. The escalating raids of bathhouses in the decade that followed proved them right. Also in 1971, *The Body Politic*, a provocative gay liberation magazine, arrived in Toronto, providing a voice for the community. Part of the community, anyway – its publishing collective was made up almost entirely of white gay men.

The Globe's coverage of LGBTQ issues in the 1970s was marked by guarded encouragement and support for some gay rights. The paper covered individual cases of discrimination relatively sympathetically, such as the 1975 firing of horse-racing steward John Damien, who lost his job for being gay. Language changed too. Gone were "perverts" and "degenerates." Instead the paper standardized the use of the more neutral "homosexual."

Ed Jackson, a long-time Toronto LGBTQ activist and organizer, credits Doyle's influence and the presence of gay reporters – such as film critic Jay Scott and dance critic Lawrence O'Toole – for helping to shape the paper's stand on homosexuality at this time, especially as the LGBTQ rights movement was becoming more empowered. "Having gay staff might not have necessarily led to more open coverage," Jackson says, "but I do think it had a dampening effect on publishing the egregiously homophobic stories that ran in the past."

However, sociologist and author Gary Kinsman notes that *The Globe*, while broadening its coverage on queer issues in those years and later, misunderstood the broader context of the queer movement. "What often happens with the mainstream media is that the struggles that lead up to particular events are not covered," Kinsman says, and then one person's experience "is covered as an isolated event or like something that just fell from the sky."

The Globe's more open, though still imperfect, approach was already apparent in the paper's coverage of the Toronto bathhouse raids in February 1981, when in a co-ordinated crackdown at four establishments, police taunted and brutalized patrons and arrested 286 men for being found in a common bawdy house. It was one of the largest mass arrests in Canadian history. *The Globe* extensively covered the raids and the mass protests that followed – one story took readers on an intimate tour of a bathhouse, even alluding to what occurs inside (not exactly common news fare at the time) – while an editorial railed against the "heavy hand of the law," noting that there had never been similar raids on other private clubs or on heterosexual bawdy houses in the city. "This flinging of an army against the homosexuals," the paper argued, "is more like the bully-boy tactics of a Latin American republic attacking church and lay reformers than of anything that has a place in Canada."

Just as gay-rights activists were fighting for greater acceptance, and receiving at least partial acceptance in the pages of *The Globe*, news reports in the early 1980s began warning of the sudden rise of a rare form of cancer called Kaposi sarcoma and other opportunistic infections among gay men with mysteriously compromised immune systems. HIV-AIDS had arrived.

As *The Globe* struggled to cover the crisis, its treatment of LGBTQ issues began to transform. Increasingly, feature stories about HIV-AIDS focused on the voices of real people grappling with the ravages of the disease, not just the voices of medical experts. Early on, the illness was referred to as "the gay plague" and people who had been infected with the virus were labelled "diseased," yet the paper did cover HIV-AIDS as both a health crisis and as a political issue.

In 1983, Yves Lavigne's story "Gays afraid AIDS spells repression" looked at rising homophobic sentiment and quoted activists, including Jackson, about fears that gay sex would be stigmatized through moralistic public-health campaigns. "There are groups who would like to use this as a means of controlling the gay community and denying us our civil rights," he warned.

Yet even as greater numbers of LGBTQ people were coming out publicly, fighting for – and winning – further rights and protections, the systematic purging of suspected LGBTQ people from the armed forces, the RCMP and the federal civil service continued, largely in silence under the guise of national security. Michelle Douglas, an officer with the Special Investigations Unit in the Canadian Forces, finally outed the military when she sued after being honourably discharged in 1989 because of her sexuality. "There weren't that many openly lesbian women at the time willing to have their name attached to something that was deemed a landmark case," Douglas says. *The Globe* and other media treated her case sympathetically. "I think there was genuine shock among some journalists and most Canadians that this had unfolded, that this was still going on."

Douglas never had her day in court. In 1992, the military settled, and the Federal Court of Canada ruled that the Canadian Forces could no longer ban LGBTQ people from serving in the military. The decade that followed saw a cascade of further legal and political victories: protections for domestic partners, adoption rights and marriage equality.

Unfinished business remained, however. An older generation of queer people had unresolved trauma; a younger generation was largely unaware of their elders' past battles. On November 28, 2017, after years of community activism and in the wake of a series of *Globe* stories about

Klippert and about the persecution of public servants – which had prompted a class-action lawsuit – Prime Minister Justin Trudeau rose in the House of Commons to formally apologize for the federal government's role in "the systemic oppression, criminalization, and violence against the lesbian, gay, bisexual, transgender, queer, and two-spirit communities."

"When a prime minister rises to apologize for the actions of past governments," wrote *The Globe*'s John Ibbitson, "he or she is saying not that we are better than that now, but that we should have been better than that then. That even then, voices were warning that this was wrong, but we ignored those voices and so people suffered. In that apology, we promise to listen to voices who warn us today of injustice: against women, against racial minorities, against sexual minorities."

But battles for rights and recognition remain, particularly for those who are transgender or non-binary. Trudeau put forward legislation prohibiting discrimination against trans people, which Parliament passed in 2017. In response to support for trans rights and protections, many on the right have returned to stoking moral panic over the safety of children, falsely claiming that trans activists are psychologically manipulating, chemically dosing and surgically mutilating confused children.

In the midst of this debate, *The Globe* has spoken out in defence of trans rights. As a June 2023 editorial put it: "Almost 60 years ago, when committing a homosexual act was a serious felony in Canada, this newspaper declared, in support of a bill to decriminalize such acts, that the state 'has no right or duty to creep into the bedrooms of the nation,' and Pierre Trudeau, then minister of justice, famously rephrased that declaration as 'there's no place for the state in the bedrooms of the nation.'

"Now, a new struggle to protect the rights of LGBTQ Canadians is emerging. And this newspaper wishes to be just as emphatic today as we were then: The state has both a right and a duty to protect sexual and gender minorities across this nation."

We are a long way from the dark, furtive days and cruel language of the 1950s. But LGBTQ rights are never permanent ones; there are people who would claw back what has been gained. All of us, including this newspaper, have a duty to protect the vulnerable, however they identify and whomever they love.

Rachel Giese is a deputy national editor at *The Globe and Mail*.

ABOVE: *Globe and Mail* sports columnist Dick Beddoes eats his column, shredded into a bowl of borscht, in Toronto on September 3, 1972, after Russia beat Canada in Game One of the Canada-Russia Summit Series. (Tibor Kolley/ *The Globe and Mail*)

Fifteen: *The necessity of excess*

Sportswriters are encouraged to go big, which is why they can get so much wrong | Cathal Kelly

Ahead of the 1972 Summit Series, *Globe and Mail* sports columnist Dick Beddoes promised to eat his column if the Soviets beat Canada: "If the Russians win one game, I will eat this column shredded at high noon in a bowl of borscht on the front steps of the Russian embassy."

Montreal Star columnist John Robertson made the same promise but came at it from the opposite direction. He pledged to eat his column if the Soviets lost.

So Beddoes splashed the columnistic pot. If the Soviet Union won the series, he'd also eat his signature accessory – his hat. Beddoes was famous for the hats. These weren't porkpie jobs. They were garishly coloured, deeply unfashionable, cartoonishly wide-brimmed fedoras. We're talking multiple square feet of felt. No man, however robust, could eat one of those hats and live.

It was an eight-game series. Not a best of eight, but eight games total. Beddoes wasn't making a bet. He was leveraging a guaranteed loss.

Canada was wiped out 7–3 in the first game. Beddoes's game-over mea culpa was so ornately over the top (for example, "The Northern Lights are dimmer than a mole's boudoir in a Siberian salt mine at midnight") that he must have been working on it for days before puck drop.

The next day, Beddoes went to the Hyatt Regency in Montreal, where the Russians were staying. While a writer from Pravda tore the column up and placed the pieces in the bowl, Beddoes squatted on the ground and slurped his borscht. A couple of grinning Soviet players loomed in the background.

Guess what? There were cameras there. And giddy coverage by other outlets. And a chance to write another column about the previous column and then a couple of columns after that. This was excellent content back when people still called such shenanigans regular life. No hat was ever mentioned again.

Beddoes had a wonderfully broad and comedic way of writing. But if you had to reduce all those columns to their essence, it's a guy sitting on his haunches eating paper in order to amuse his readers.

When one of Beddoes's *Globe* predecessors, Jim Coleman, retired from the paper in 1950, he blamed the daily pressure. Coleman was emblematic of a certain sort of mid-century sportswriter. A hearty, jocular man's man. A leftover from the Hemingway ideal of a commentator who not only taught but did. Coleman's trick was burying his machismo in self-deprecation.

In reflecting on his choice to leave, Coleman talked about the "sword hanging from the ceiling" inside *The Globe*'s newsroom. "Any daily columnist can tell you about the sword," Coleman wrote later.

"As soon as one is completed, the scribe heaves a couple of deep breaths and begins to worry about the next day's chore. Like the simple, but perilous business of staying alive, writing a daily column is a job that ends only once."

This is good stuff. It's a guy who writes about other guys running around in their pyjamas for a living telling you that what he does isn't just important, it's existential. This is the kind of thing sportswriters do – "Ha ha, what we do is ridiculous. But it's also, ha ha, more important than space exploration. Ha ha."

This tradition of bluster is unique to just one corner of the newsroom. It begins with a couple of basic principles.

First, sports writing is not important and everyone knows it. I don't know how it goes at your job, but at ours, someone else is always doing something way more important than whatever you're doing. Down the hallway, someone is blowing the lid off government corruption. Two aisles over, someone else is writing a touching human story that will change the way the country thinks about a given issue. What are you doing? Trying to figure out who's starting in net on Saturday night. This inherent triviality encourages wild excess.

That's the second principle of sports writing – don't be afraid to be big; don't be afraid to be wrong. The Sports section is the only one in the newspaper where it is not only possible to be incorrect, but encouraged. You could guess right, but it's more amusing if you're usually wrong. It's certainly more fun to write. That's what Beddoes was doing. Being big by being wrong. And it worked. Of course, anyone can be wrong on the regular. The trick is doing it with panache.

The Globe's first, and possibly most often wrong, sports columnist was Francis Nelson. He gave himself the job after being named The Globe's sports editor in 1888. A man of tremendous energy, Nelson didn't just write and edit sports, he also played them. All of them. He grew continentally famous later in life as a horse-racing impresario. When he died on a steamer in the Panama Canal, one paper said of him that "no man was better known in Canada."

Like any good sports columnist, Nelson had a lot of strong opinions on things about which he knew relatively little. He delivered them in a rat-a-tat-tat style in a garrulous, impossibly long regular entry entitled "Jack at Play." At the time, the fashion was to treat the Sports pages as agate – a long list of results. Nelson instead used them as a pulpit to hector his readers, with a few results thrown in.

Among the things Nelson held in esteem: the spirit of amateurism, anything that happened in the only place that really mattered (that is, England), lacrosse. Things Nelson did not esteem: the Olympics, anything that happened in Quebec, professional hockey.

He spent years trying to take down the NHL (then called the NHA), calling the people who ran it "parasites" and those who wrote about it their "promoters." In 1915 he wrote: "Other newspapers may if they choose donate the greater part of their sporting pages to free advertising for a commercial enterprise with a sporting side, but *The Globe* does not see the light that way."

In 1913, Nelson wrote off the sport in Toronto, since the audience "knew little of real hockey." He also rubbished the new five-a-side "mongrel" version of the sport. His complaint? "Rapid scoring." The Toronto Maple Leafs would be founded four years later, so the scoring part would eventually take care of itself. Did Toronto ever figure out real hockey? Based on recent history, no. It's one of the few predictions Nelson got right.

What else didn't Nelson like?

Curveballs (1914): "The comment of English papers on baseball as demonstrated by the Chicago-New York exhibition displays many varied views of the game, but on one point there is absolute unanimity. The critics were not so simple as to be taken in by any stories about the curve, drop and 'fade-away' deliveries of the pitchers. They knew that it was contrary to the *laws of nature* for a man to influence the course of the ball after it had left his hand."

The laws of nature, eh?

Women in sport (1908): "Modern women are exceedingly keen on sport. The more violent the sport, the better they enjoy it. This is excellent from the hygienic point of view, but it has also its drawbacks. The sportswoman loses much of the grace and charm inherent in womanhood, and mentally she often lacks refinement."

Eeeesh.

The natural world (1912): "It is probable that the King's bag in the Nepal hunting ground constitutes a record in big game shooting, says an English correspondent. Thirty tigers, and thirteen rhinos, in a little more than a week is certainly a wonderful achievement. But it is to be remembered that his majesty is one of the finest shots, with a rifle or a gun, now living."

By 2009, there would be 121 tigers in all of Nepal.

Fair to say that if a couple of "Jack at Play" columns were reprinted in *The Globe* today, there would be a torch-wielding mob outside the building by midmorning.

Sportswriters don't mind upsetting people, but never too much. It's one thing for them to love to hate you. It's another if they plain hate you. Robertson of *The Montreal Star* used to say he wanted his correspondence to be at least 80-per-cent negative. (There's only one way to keep the ratio that high, and it isn't pristine intellectual integrity. For those who seek blanket approval, it works the other way round as well.)

Mid-twentiethth century, sports writing was moving away from the "hygienic" Nelson model to a new prognosticating model. Suddenly, everyone was an odds picker. It's safer that way. Better to guess the score wrong than to misjudge shifts in social mores.

Some newspapers do hard sports. Through its hiring choices, *The Globe* held sports at some remove, viewing them with a sense of ironic detachment. The mid to late twentieth century lineup was all-star, all the time. Beddoes, Scott Young, Trent Frayne, Allen Abel, Christie Blatchford, Stephen Brunt. If you have cared about sports in Canada during that time, you know these names.

What linked them all was a literary approach and a sense of humour. There is nothing in the world more deadly serious than a hockey writer faced with a goalie crisis. They care more about it than the team or the goalies. *The Globe*'s sports ethos avoided this sort of parody.

This is what happens when you work with people whose journalism really matters. It gives you a freeing sense of perspective. Important human stories that just happened to involve sports would also be told. But in *The Globe*'s Sports section, the writing always led the way.

Of course, there were still plenty of bad predictions, too numerous to recount here. If it could be guessed wrong, it was. The philosophy was best summed up by Frayne in the late 1980s, when the pick 'em wave was ebbing. In one of those columns plucked from nothing on a day when the sword was hanging closer than usual, Frayne went off on the practice of guessing results: "The only guy I know who handled this assignment was author Scott Young who, back in the days when writing a *Globe and Mail* column, made 4,739 selections during a brilliant career. As he himself noted, Right, 4,739; Wrong, 0; Pct. 1.000."

You still have to guess. No one wants to read "Blues play Reds tomorrow, hard to say what will happen." But don't hector. Don't guarantee unless you already know what you're doing once your guarantee disintegrates. People had learned that much since Nelson's time.

Though she did it for only a short while, Blatchford remains the iconic modern *Globe* sportswriter. That is in part because she got out of the Sports section as soon as she could. She had more important things to write about. An unabashed fan of the men and women who do it, but not of sports in general, Blatch wrote everything with a small curl of the lip.

Here she is on covering the only event she kept coming back to throughout her career as a big shot: "An Olympics is that occasion, every two years, wherein the profoundly unknowledgeable and often profoundly unfit affect expertise in such things as biathlon, skeleton and moguls and then presume to judge the performance of those who do the actual competing."

A good sportswriter is always advancing. Never retreat. If you're dead wrong, advance at a trot. Blatch lived that credo.

Thirty years after it happened, another *Globe* great, William Houston, went back and relived the Summit Series from the perspective of the sportswriters who were there. His view – never specifically laid out but hinted at everywhere – was that they'd shamed themselves. They couldn't help but get tangled in the flag and act the fools.

Coleman, who one supposes missed the sword and had gone back to sports writing, recalled standing in the press box and pumping his fist at Soviet leader Leonid Brezhnev after Paul Henderson's goal to win the series for Canada. In his memoir, he described the feeling as "delirium."

That's what sportswriters must avoid at all costs. You are not a fan. You aren't part of the team. You're not getting a playoff bonus. Though it is beyond your capacity to do so, you're there to explain what it's like and to critique. Since you can't do that authoritatively, try to have some fun with it.

Sports hates fun. Sports is always trying to drag things back to a fascistic impression that it really is us versus them, and that all of this actually matters. When things were going really wrong in that series, Frayne got caught in an elevator with Alan Eagleson. Eagleson, the Richelieu of Canadian sport, asked what he'd thought of the game they'd both just watched. Recounting the exchange to Houston, Frayne said something complimentary about Soviet puck handling.

"You must be a fucking Communist," Eagleson replied.

"All I said was their passing knocked me out," Frayne said.

"We lost, you know."

"Yeah, I know we lost."

"We lost and you're telling me you liked their passing?"

"Yeah, well, I certainly liked their passing."

"Anyone who thinks like you has to be a fucking Communist."

Frayne said the exchange left him "astonished." But what's astonishing is how Frayne remembered the back-and-forth. Listen to those beats. That is real conversation. No embellishments. Whether it is a verbatim recounting doesn't matter. It's the way people actually talk, so it sounds true.

If the Sports section is great – and who's anyone from the paper to say that? – that's why. Because it was a home to writers like Frayne. People who understood you could get it wrong, but you couldn't be boring or pedestrian or false while you did so.

In this one section alone, being right is overrated. And so's being wrong. Being willing to eat your hat is what sets you apart.

Cathal Kelly is sports columnist at *The Globe and Mail*.

ABOVE: A woman watches a group
of children climbing a path in
Africville, Nova Scotia, ca. 1965.
(Bob Brooks/Nova Scotia Archives)

Sixteen:
Remembering Africville, *the* razing *and the* racism

The Globe was an active participant in shaping the narrative around the historically Black community | **Dakshana Bascaramurty**

Beatrice Wilkins's childhood home was steps from the Bedford Basin at the tip of the Halifax peninsula. She remembers spending summers fishing for eels, lobsters and mussels and playing hopscotch and double dutch with the neighbourhood kids. Gifted with an angelic voice, Wilkins loved to sing at church on Sunday and in school concerts. At the annual Christmas show, the audience had a chance to clap for the singer they liked most, and year after year, the applause for Wilkins was deafening.

Growing up in the historically Black community of Africville was comfortable, she recalls. "You could knock on anybody's door when you came home from school if you were hungry," says the septuagenarian, now living in Dartmouth, Nova Scotia. "The community was more than accepting – they were nurturers."

At the time of Wilkins's upbringing in the 1950s and 1960s, *The Globe and Mail* had a different way of describing Africville: "a wretched black ghetto," "often awash with piles of rotting garbage," "a Negro slum." There was no acknowledgment of the bonds between family and neighbours that were so central to Wilkins's childhood recollections. In 1967, on Canada's one hundredth birthday, the newspaper sent a columnist and photographer to capital cities across the country and published their dispatches in a special centenary edition. While in Halifax, a *Globe* writer chronicled his time in Africville as if he were on safari, visiting a primitive civilization:

My fellow Canadians, it is strange to bump along the waterfront over tracks and through potholes until, near the city dump, you come on a place of shacks on a hillside where the children run for shelter when they even see a car slow down. We got lots of pictures of them fleeing from us, pushing old bicycles and ruined baby carriages used as playthings, scuttling like scared squirrels while their mothers rapped on windows and urged them to run faster – lots of those pictures, but only one of children stock still, a second before they broke and ran. But Halifax is trying. Many people of Africville have been induced to move to bright public housing. The old ones generally refuse. All that can be done is to wait until they die off.

At the time, there was little room for nuance or introspection in the government's pursuit of the liberal welfare state, which was greatly aided by the mainstream media. Under the banner of progressivism, Canada was on a mission to clear out so-called ghettos and liberate their residents from poverty, but without taking responsibility for how the state had contributed to the historical injustices that had created those communities in the first place. And they, as well as the press, gave residents little voice during this process.

Perhaps nowhere in Canada was this seen more starkly than in Africville, where between 1964 and 1967, about four hundred residents were displaced from the twelve-acre settlement that had been an established Black community with a rich history and culture for more than a century. *The Globe* was an active participant in shaping the narrative around Africville and justifying its razing.

In the decades after Africville was cleared out, the politics of the time changed and so did the way *The Globe* wrote about the community. For the most part, this shift – in which former residents were interviewed and given agency, where the relocation project and the decades of neglect of the community that preceded it were described as racist – only occurred in the pages of the newspaper after a political shift among the country's white establishment. But by then, so much had been lost.

The history of Black settlement in Canada began in the mid-eighteenth century, when British and American settlers brought hundreds of enslaved Africans to Nova Scotia. The Black people who built much of Halifax lived on the northeast tip of the peninsula, in what later became known as Africville. By the mid-1800s, Africville was an established Black settlement made up of Africans who had escaped slavery in Jamaica (known as "Maroons"), refugees from the War of 1812 and formerly enslaved people whose families had been in Canada for decades or longer. They made a living fishing and farming. By 1849 they had built a church, and by 1883 they had a school.

Remember Africville, a 1991 documentary by filmmaker Shelagh Mackenzie, features CBC interviews with former residents, footage from a 1989 conference about Africville, as well as photographs and home movies shot by community members. Those personal images, in particular, offer a counternarrative to how Africville was understood by most Canadians. They depict detached homes, much like the ones that dotted the rest of the Halifax peninsula, painted in vibrant colours. Women in sunglasses show off tailored dresses before heading to church services. Children play baseball together. Bare-torsoed men flex and grin for the camera before taking a dip in the Bedford Basin.

But throughout the 1950s and 1960s, *The Globe*'s coverage of Africville drew mostly from the perspectives of officials – politicians, bureaucrats, social workers – rather than the residents themselves. The joys of Africville's residents, their culture and motivations and bonds, were never explored.

In the first half of the twentieth century, local government made clear that Africville was not considered an official part of the city, denying it many of the basic services offered to other residents, such as running water and garbage pickup and, later, paved roads and electricity. It also built a railway extension that cut through the community; residents who lived beside the tracks could stick their arms out their windows and touch the high-speed trains as they zoomed by.

When a French ship carrying munitions and a Norwegian ship carrying humanitarian supplies collided near Halifax in 1917, the resulting blast destroyed much of the city's north end – as well as Africville situated above it. The damaged swaths of Halifax were rebuilt, but Africville did not see much of the federal funding.

In *Remember Africville*, residents candidly describe the ways in which neglect of their community turned to negligence. "Our folks went to the city to find out about the roads, the lights and the garbage and what's the use? It made no difference," said resident Leon Steed during a video interview conducted in the late 1960s. "If the city had took care of this place instead of neglecting it, it would've been a lot better than what it is today."

Because ambulances would not come to Africville, Wilkins's mother had to deliver one of her own children – Wilkins's youngest sibling – herself at home. She cut the baby's umbilical cord, carried the newborn out of their house on Forrester Street, flagged down a police car that was patrolling the city dump and got a lift to the hospital – just in time to deliver the placenta.

There was an incentive for the state to contribute to Africville's decay by withholding municipal services: it helped frame the bulldozing of the community and relocation of residents as acts of liberation. *The Globe*'s coverage bolstered that argument, with quotations from provincial politicians who said razing Africville would "bring about a great transformation" and news pieces based more on conjecture than on facts.

In one 1959 story, for example, a *Globe* reporter describes youth who allegedly threw stones at a freight train that passed through Africville as part of the community's "bad element" and speculates they did so to protest the replacement of coal-fired engines with diesel locomotives. He alleges that "Negro juveniles" stole from coal trains to fuel their homes, but there are no interviews with the youth or any other residents of Africville. Nor is there an acknowledgment of how the municipality failed to provide electricity to the community.

Other stories from that era discuss how Halifax employers and landlords didn't want to give jobs or housing to Africville residents because of their perceived lack of hygiene. But those stories don't ascribe any responsibility to the City of Halifax for the polluting industries placed in or beside the community – an open-pit dump, a fertilizer plant, an abattoir and a prison – or the lack of running water in homes.

Laying this groundwork in the years leading up to the razing of Africville was key to selling the public on the idea of slum clearance as "urban renewal," explains University of British Columbia historian Tina Loo. "There's this notion of 'modern cities don't have slums, they don't have racial segregation,'" she says.

In the U.S., racial segregation was rampant and seen as "the bogeyman," she says. The civil rights movement there was met with violent resistance by the state. White liberal Canadians liked to think of themselves as part of a more humane society, one where integration was the goal, even if it was a process navigated clumsily and against the wishes of Africville's residents.

Of course, the relocation efforts weren't just about "rescuing" residents of Africville but about the city acquiring an extremely valuable parcel of land, as a *Globe* journalist wrote in a 1962 story: "Roughly bounded by the Halifax shipyards, the harbor and several industrial developments on what used to be the city dump, Africville would be valuable for factory buildings as well as for construction of an express highway now in preliminary planning stages."

Speaking at the 1989 conference on Africville, Reverend Donald Skeir agreed: "This was prime land. That was important land. That kind of land was not for Black people."

It's not like there weren't critics of these processes at the time. Jane Jacobs famously critiqued slum clearance in her seminal 1961 work *The Death and Life of Great American Cities*, condemning the ways in which people like those who lived in Africville were "pushed about, expropriated, and uprooted much as if they were the subjects of a conquering power." She pointed out there was an irony to municipalities trying to clear slums in the name of urban renewal, when the housing projects they moved residents into only "became worse centers of delinquency, vandalism and general social hopelessness."

Indeed, Wilkins's family was moved into a housing project in Mulgrave Park, while many close neighbours and family friends were relocated to Uniacke Square, another project. Others scattered to communities farther away, outside central Halifax. The wide-open fields of Africville that provided spaces for children to play were replaced by concrete. Residents who previously lived in mortgage-free homes went on welfare for the first time to pay their new housing costs. After the relocation, the only chances Wilkins had to reconvene with the community were at Sunday services at Seaview United Baptist Church in Africville, until that, too, was bulldozed.

Laura Howe, speaking at the 1989 conference, described how her teenage son came home in the middle of the night and told her the church was gone: "That was done in the early hours of the morning. It seemed to me such a cruel thing to do to a church."

In an editorial published at the end of 1968, *The Globe* cites the dissolution of Africville as evidence of triumph: "Neither Africville nor the segregation remains. As we passed into the more socially conscious era of the 1960s, Nova Scotia began its earnest plodding along the path toward civil rights."

If razing Africville and dispersing its residents around Nova Scotia was meant to paint over an embarrassing chapter in Canadian history, it wasn't long before chips began to appear on the surface of this attempt at "renewal." In 1968, the Black Panthers arrived in Halifax and began empowering former residents to speak up about the injustices they'd faced. A pivotal meeting took place among Black Nova Scotians, who formed the political organization the Black United Front, which gave them a powerful voice.

By the early 1970s, the Africville relocation project had been transformed from "a symbol of civic and humanitarian progress to a symbol of Black consciousness and white racism," wrote Richard Bobier in a 1995 academic paper. He credits this shift in part to a change in the broader political climate across the continent, a rise in class consciousness and the emergence of the "New Left" – sociologists who explored power relations and gave voice to the laypeople they studied rather than speaking on their behalf.

That shift can be tracked in the pages of *The Globe*, where, in 1972, a story was boldly headlined "Africville relocation called a social failure." In tone and sourcing, it veered dramatically from the newspaper's previous coverage of Africville. But critically, it was based on a report that had been commissioned by the province and authored by academics at Dalhousie University that criticized, in detail, the way the relocation was carried out. The story gave Black people a voice, but it was through these academics.

The report polled former residents about their experience, finding that 73 per cent missed their lives in Africville "very much." Of those surveyed, 95 per cent said the city gained the most from the relocation and they gained the least. The report quoted Black leaders who described the relocation as "racial warfare" and took a sharply critical lens to the way city officials broke their promises to former residents regarding financial assistance and other supports.

By the 1980s and 1990s, the language *The Globe* used to describe Africville had evolved. Earlier in the century, reporters had described the place as a slum or shantytown; later, they attributed those descriptions to city council or planners at the time. As respected human-rights groups and academics acknowledged the ways in which residents had been failed by the state, and politicians offered mea culpas, *The Globe* quoted them. Most importantly, the paper began including voices of the residents themselves.

In 1989, Halifax correspondent Kevin Cox attended the same conference featured in *Remember Africville*. He quoted several former residents about the discrimination they faced and the struggles they still battled because of the relocation.

"My strongest memory is of my grandmother crying; she didn't want to leave and she was never happy after she left," said Irvine Carvery, president of the Africville Genealogy Society. "The relocation took five years minimum from the lives of the older ones."

Cox also included comments from Skeir, who was critical of the Africville relocation planners. "[They] overlooked the fact that black people are human beings," he said. "We can think and we can feel and there is no place like home no matter what condition it may be in."

Notably, Cox didn't seek rebuttals or counternarratives from officials – a major turn in the narrative of Africville as portrayed in the pages of the paper.

Later, in a 1990 story about a touring exhibition on Africville, *The Globe*'s Stephen Godfrey wrote about the "racist attitudes toward Halifax blacks" in Africville and described the media having "signalled a change in attitude toward Africville." He even shares an unsavoury quote from the *Toronto Star* to illustrate his point – but never calls out his own paper for its failings.

As a former resident of Africville, Wilkins was pleased to see the media eventually change its tune but wondered why none were brave enough to give her family or neighbours a voice when Africville still existed, when it could have been saved.

"They were people on the bandwagon trying to right a wrong," she says. "They left us in a foreign land, basically. They took us from what we knew. We don't know how we would've flourished in our community."

Dakshana Bascaramurty is a reporter at *The Globe and Mail*, focusing on race and ethnicity issues. She is based in Halifax.

ABOVE: A *Globe* office worker holds
baskets of mail received from
children wanting to enroll in a
children's safety club, March 18, 1928.
(John H. Boyd/*The Globe and Mail*)

Seventeen: Special deliveries

To letter writers and their editors, the resilience of the form feels as essential as journalism itself | **Cliff Lee**

Former federal cabinet minister Lloyd Axworthy has worn many hats during his long career in politics and academia. In 1964, however, he was but a young Winnipegger who had recently completed a graduate degree in politics at Princeton University and was looking forward to coming home. Unfortunately, he wasn't having much luck landing suitable work in Canada.

So, when he read *The Globe and Mail*'s lead editorial on April 13, which lamented the brain drain of Canadian talent to the south, something stirred in him. "While Canada bleats out its anguish over the desertion of many of its talented citizens, it might pause to consider the cases of unrequited love, of which I am sure mine is not alone," he wrote in a letter to the editor that the paper published about a week later.

Before the pervasiveness of social media and online commentary, a letter to the editor was one of the few ways that ordinary citizens and public figures alike could prominently voice an opinion on the news of the day, even if one was a then-unknown young Canadian, thousands of kilometres away at school in New Jersey.

As former letters editor Jack Kapica crystallizes in the introduction of the book *Shocked and Appalled: A Century of Letters to* The Globe and Mail, published in 1985, "the letters page of a newspaper must be a forum dedicated to its readers, a page where their opinion can be heard, their honour defended, their spleens spilled." (The phrase "shocked and appalled" has become a fond shorthand for letter writers and *Globe* editors, used as a knowing wink to exaggerated indignation.)

Amid the instantaneous connectivity of modern life, letters persist. They are a bulwark against the volatility of online conversation, which can be enlightening and respectful but is oftentimes knee-jerk and inflammatory despite the best efforts of those tasked with its moderation. Letters are a bastion of civility and consideration appreciated by readers, even as they have evolved from physical mail to faxes for a blip to e-mails.

There may be a future when they cease to exist, finally succumbing to digital disruption. But for letter writers and letters editors, who together form a delicate ecosystem, the resilience of the form feels as essential as journalism itself.

Letters are, by the nature of journalism, edited. *The Globe* carefully curates and publishes as many as a dozen of them each day from the hundreds that readers send.

As letters editor for more than a decade from 1979, Kapica read about a quarter million letters of every conceivable type, particularly during his eighteen months of archival research for the book.

What he found true then remains true today. "History plays a part in the letters page only as it is manifest in the readers' minds," Kapica wrote. While wars and other strife rage around the world, letter writers are often more concerned with the daily rhythms of domestic affairs, whether the author is a prominent figure or general reader.

Here, a chronological sampling of Canadian preoccupations through the years:

January 25, 1889: A.M. Taylor of Toronto fretted over the identity and culture of a nascent nation, proclaiming that "there is not a Canadian literature because there is no Canada. The Dominion has not yet cast aside its swaddling clothes and evinced the courage to announce its own majority."

August 16, 1902: A pseudonymous writer from Hamilton ("Civis") wonders about the dangers of electricity, still limited then, and its potential effects on the Canadian climate: "Our men of science should collect facts and inform us as to the future consequences of unlimited production of electricity and using it as power."

November 24, 1926: Amid the debate over prohibition in Ontario, former Alberta MLA Nellie L. McClung asked, "Is it all right for a country to produce drinkers and drunkards if it is done legally, and the Government receives a rake-off?"

May 4, 1929: *The Globe*'s coverage of the news could excite readers' ire or admiration – or both. S. Stuart Crouch of Toronto concludes, "For your narrow, bigoted, religious opinions and editorials, and for your fanatical personal attacks on those you dislike . . . I despise *The Globe*, and am frequently tempted to stop taking it, but for the sake of accurate news I enclose renewal cheque for six dollars."

March 26, 1945: As the Second World War stretched on, readers such as Beecher Parkhouse of Fergus, Ontario, found ways to stay positive:

"I guess the war must be going pretty well for our side. We have not been called on for a Day of Prayer for some time."

October 24, 1970: Poet Irving Layton took stock of a dark chapter in Canadian history. "It's to the great credit of Canadians that they've decided their lives and liberty are safer with Pierre Trudeau than with the degenerates of the FLQ and bleeding heart liblabs who . . . haven't a clue to what's rising up to smash them."

August 16, 1973: Writer (and frequent traveller) Pierre Berton relayed that "I have just emerged from my umpteenth experience at Terminal 2 – one which has again reduced me to a stage of helpless rage." ("Berton would never stop," Kapica remembers. "You had to go off and yell at him to stop.")

February 11, 1977: Former Nova Scotia premier and federal Progressive Conservative leader Robert Stanfield defended his honour after a columnist wrote that "he has the reputation among his friends of being the worst driver this side of Hull." Stanfield considered "suing *The Globe and Mail* and Geoffrey Stevens for several millions of dollars, and I most certainly will if his irresponsible comment should cause an increase in my insurance rates."

February 7, 1980: On economic inequality, author Robertson Davies wondered "if the poverty level is anything under $10,000 a year, above what line may we place wealth? In my novelist's innocence, I thought it might be $100,000 a year. Where does it truly begin?"

There are also letter-writing giants such as Eugene Forsey, a former senator and constitutional expert who, having written some eight hundred letters to various publications over his lifetime, is the subject of his own academic compendium from 2000, *The Sound of One Voice: Eugene Forsey and His Letters to the Press.*

"The moment you saw the name Eugene Forsey," Kapica recalls, you knew you had a contender. "The guy required no grammatical correction, no spelling or anything like that. The man was very educated."

Forsey's letters appeared in *The Globe* roughly three hundred times. His high dudgeon could entertain in a single sentence, such as a one-liner from July 27, 1967, three days after the French president's infamous declaration of "Vive le Québec libre!" Forsey was not impressed: "General de Gaulle and Quebec Premier Daniel Johnson appear to believe that Quebec is Canada's Sudetenland."

He was further at his best when bringing his encyclopedic knowledge of government and country to bear on the pages of *The Globe*. On February 10, 1977, he was particularly vexed by an article that suggested a fully decentralized Canada with ten separate tax systems. But even while taking the contributors to task for omitting the issues of provincial equalization and economic imbalances, his serious concerns were tempered by the acerbic wit that made him so popular with readers. In this case, he even broke out in song: "With glowing hearts we've seen arise / Ten Norths, nor strong nor free / But we'll stand on guard, O Canada!"

(*The Globe*'s appreciation for the original poetry and prose of letter writers waxes and wanes; at the time of this writing, it is very much on the wane.)

Forsey published his first letter to *The Globe* in 1948; his last was in December 1990, just months before his death. His final grievance took on a familiar topic: "Some months ago there was talk of privatizing the Post Office. Now it's the CBC."

While Forsey's letter-writing record isn't likely to be surpassed, one man who became a prolific letter writer in his own right has been a favourite of *Globe* readers since 1991. That's when James Stewart, who first appeared in *The Globe* in 1990 defending the pugnacity of hockey, published his first letter using his three initials: J.D.M. Stewart. A history teacher who has published "probably around 250" letters by his own count (the number is difficult to nail down in *The Globe*'s archives), Stewart has mastered what Kapica calls whimsy. "No one – not even the editor of *The Globe and Mail* – can take relentless earnestness forever," Kapica noted.

Because of his knowledge of quotations and his humour, Stewart's musings have often appeared as the kicker on the letters page. He also understands the latter-day letter-writing art of brevity: "A lot of people spend seventy-five words clearing their throat before they get to their point. You just can't do that," Stewart says, adding that "humour is always great."

Put that all together and a honed letter writer might submit what Stewart successfully had published on November 2, 2006: "I would just like to remind the good U.S. ambassador of Canada's sovereignty over the Arctic by quoting former prime minister Brian Mulroney, who said of the area: 'We own it. Lock, stock and iceberg.'"

Stewart's popularity and frequency on the letters page soon invited detractors. Eventually, one frustrated letter writer suggested *The Globe* would surely publish any letter, no questions asked, if it was signed "J.D.M. Stewart." From there, it was determined that regular contributors would be limited to every two weeks. Today, like many other daily publications, *The Globe* tries to limit writers to every four weeks.

The form of letters has always changed along with the country. Today they bear little relation to what graced *The Globe* at its founding in 1844: from anonymous, gossip-laden dispatches that made up most news before and after Confederation, to full pages of letters on single topics by the end of that century (a Christian populace was invested in the issue of trolleys operating on the Sabbath, for example).

In the early 1900s, *The Globe* tried to tame the epistolary overflow by breaking letters into column filler wherever they could fit. By 1910, reader opposition forced the singular return of letters to the editorial section, where they have resided on the printed page ever since.

That real estate is now at a premium. A single epic missive of yore could take up the entire space allotted for modern-day letters, where writers are today limited to 150 words. In 1991, such constraints were met with consternation by a researcher, who filed a complaint with the Ontario Press Council after *The Globe* declined to help reduce his 1,200-word letter to size. The complaint was dismissed.

There were still other developments: letters to correct the record, often cheeky correspondence that relishes in the thrill of being right, became the purview of the public editor, rechristened the standards editor in 2023; preposterous pseudonyms such as "Fidelis" and "Veritas" gave way to real names, first in 1930 on divisive letters about religion, then on all letters by 1940; the preponderance of letter-writing public figures plummeted in recent decades with the advent of a dedicated op-ed section. Lloyd Axworthy is a frequent contributor.

As the institution of letters continues to evolve with the times, it would be fair to ask: What next? A pessimist may hold the view that its stubborn resilience is generational and tied to an aging population of boomers, the main demographic for printed periodicals. An informal survey of more than two hundred of *The Globe*'s most frequent letter writers conducted for this essay bears that out: the majority of respondents were fifty-plus, many of them retired; more than a few were in their nineties.

But their reasons for writing give less credence to the form of letters and more to the importance of journalism and the act of engaging with it meaningfully. "Writing letters puts me in the habit of being an active reader, and possibly a more active citizen," says Chester Fedoruk, a contributor from Toronto who counts more than fifty published letters in *The Globe* since 2016. "Putting myself on the spot to develop a point of view – to get beyond my initial ignorance, confusion, support, disagreement, indignation and resentment – often requires additional reading and research (a purposeful mission for a retiree). The excitement of reading and writing letters makes me feel part of the Canadian conversation: imperfect, iterative, open-ended, balancing passion and respect and striving for both rigour and humour."

It remains to be seen if there will be a generational shift in those active citizens who write letters. For now, the journalists who edit them will continue their publication as long as they are still sent by the hundreds. And, at least, there has been succession among their – our – ranks that provides reasons for optimism.

As of this writing, Elliot Kaufman, a twentysomething Canadian, is the letters editor at *The Wall Street Journal* in New York. Like the fortysomething writer of this essay, he inherited the position from a highly regarded colleague who retired after more than a decade on the job. His childhood claim to fame: at age nine, publishing a letter in the *National Post* that called for the privatization of the Canadian Wheat Board. He got his wish when it was dissolved in 2015.

"In a way, letters are free from some of the drawbacks of debate in a way that social media isn't," he says of his youthful hobby turned professional preoccupation. "In a debate, you can make a point and an audience can applaud. That's bias. Let people come to their own decisions. If you want a pure exchange of views, I think the letters section is still the way to get that at its best."

Others also see a strong digital future for letters, acting as a complement to online comments rather than a contrast. *The Globe*, for its part, links to online versions of the daily letters offering at the bottom of every article, where subscribers post and read comments. And in 2019, the newsroom began to publish additional letters online on Sundays (a day when there is no printed paper), owing to the sizable number of worthy submissions left over by the end of the week. It's become a popular feature on a quieter publishing day.

At *The Telegraph*, letters editor Orlando Bird (who took the baton from a colleague who held the role for nearly two decades) has experimented with a letters-focused newsletter to attract new audiences. "It can be seen as part of this wider rise of reader-generated content. Audiences do expect to be more part of the conversation now, rather than just listening to columnists and so on," says Bird, adding that letters differ from social media. "It's curated, it's edited. There's accountability. At its best, it's the opposite of an echo chamber."

The future of letters to the editor, like the future of news, will boil down to age and engaging new readers – and writers. Stewart, the history teacher and prolific letter writer, is doing his part to foster the medium's next generation, urging his students to craft letters as a way to learn the value of reasoning and pithiness in one's writing. He offers one more important piece of advice to young, aspiring letter writers: "Don't be afraid to say 'Ashley Smith, Grade 9 student.' Because papers love to run the odd letter when it's by a kid. Right?"

Who knows: maybe that's how *The Globe*'s future letters editor gets their start.

Cliff Lee is letters editor at *The Globe and Mail*.

ABOVE: First national edition of *The Globe and Mail* transmitted by satellite, October 23, 1980. In Montreal, publisher Roy Megarry holds up the negative of the front page. (Dennis Robinson/*The Globe and Mail*)

Eighteen:
The great transformer – *and* disruptor

From the electric telegraph to artificial intelligence, technology has helped *The Globe* draw a national audience | **Temur Durrani**

G eorge Brown, who founded *The Globe* in 1844, always wanted a national audience for his paper. He envisioned a country that would stretch beyond the united colonies of Upper and Lower Canada (present-day Ontario and Quebec) and Atlantic Canada to include the vast lands to their north and west. To spread this message, he turned to new technologies that were revolutionizing Victorian society.

About two months after publishing *The Globe*'s first edition using a hand press that printed two hundred copies an hour, Brown travelled to New York. There, he bought a rotary press from famed inventor Richard March Hoe that could produce 1,250 copies an hour. The state-of-the-art press transformed *The Globe*'s reach, allowing the weekly to start publishing twice every week by 1846 and daily by 1853.

But he didn't stop there. After the electric telegraph arrived in Toronto, Brown signed a deal with one of his rivals, the *British Colonist*, to share the cost of a telegraph service from New York. The new technology was a game changer. Before the telegraph, most news travelled at the speed of sail or horse and rider. Now, it could be transmitted almost instantly. Brown later secured access to a second line from Montreal.

Brown also took advantage of improved roads and the new railway to deliver the paper into the southwestern communities that had then represented the limit of colonial settlement in Upper Canada.

His obsession with technology made perfect sense. Canada, even before Confederation, was such a large land and so thinly populated that any newspaper seeking to be national in scope needed to grasp any invention that solved the problems of distance and time.

All of this was expensive, but the investments paid off. By Confederation, *The Globe*'s circulation had surpassed that of any other newspaper in British North America – reaching fifteen thousand people, as of 1868, more than half of whom were outside the paper's home in Toronto.

Brown established a template that future publishers have followed: exploit new technology to establish and expand *The Globe*'s reach across the nation and around the world. More than once, this formula saved the paper.

Over the years, *The Globe* has celebrated several technological feats. The newspaper brought readers the first photograph wired to Canada on December 9, 1936. (The photo was of Wallis Simpson. King Edward VIII's decision to abdicate the throne to marry her dominated the news for weeks.) *The Globe* was the first subscriber to Bell's new mobile telephone service, introduced in 1947, decades before the arrival of cellphones. (We predicted, somewhat prematurely, that "the day is rapidly approaching when Mr. Motorist will pick up a telephone receiver in his car and tell his wife that he is caught in a traffic jam on Avenue Road and won't be driving into his garage for another seven minutes.")

But when Roy Megarry arrived as publisher in 1978, he didn't like what he saw. *The Globe* was shipping its six national editions across the country by air or post, which was costly and inefficient. Editors had to manually lay out, proof and adjust pages with new stories for each edition – an old-school approach that Megarry found infuriating.

More significantly, *The Globe*'s circulation was flatlining at around 300,000. It faced stiff competition in its primary market of Toronto; 60 per cent of the paper's readers in the city also read the *Toronto Star*, which had lower ad rates and a much higher daily circulation of 500,000. The new *Toronto Sun*, launched after the demise of *The Toronto Telegram*, was also attracting readers.

Megarry believed he had the answer to all these problems. *The Globe* could increase its circulation and justify higher ad rates by escaping the limits of the Toronto market and becoming a truly national newspaper. And the way to do that, he bluntly told the paper's owners, was to invest in computer technology to deliver the paper by satellite.

"*The Globe* could never become the *Star* in Toronto," says John Stackhouse, former editor-in-chief of *The Globe*. "And so, with the satellite, suddenly we were able to sell in Canada's other biggest cities."

When the Thomson family acquired the paper in 1980, they embraced the idea. On October 23, 1980, *The Globe and Mail* was delivered for the first time across the country through microwave signals flashed by a satellite high above the Pacific Ocean to printing plants from the furthest corner of the Maritimes to the edge of the West Coast – "one giant leap," the newspaper declared on its front page.

The shift transformed the paper's business model. Before the satellite, in 1978, *The Globe*'s daily circulation outside Ontario was about twelve thousand customers. By 1992, it had reached 120,000.

"Thank you for saving *The Globe*," owner Kenneth Thomson told Megarry at the publisher's retirement dinner in 1992. The paper that year had reached a record-breaking $37-million in profit.

"*The Globe* will need saving again, and again," Megarry predicted in reply. He was right.

In 1999, Edward Greenspon, then executive editor, approached publisher Phillip Crawley about establishing a news website for *The Globe and Mail*. The timing was tough: *The Globe* was embroiled in a newspaper war with the *National Post*, and that battle required management's full attention.

The Globe had a static website at the time, created by Globe Information Services (GIS), which displayed high-level data and insights. It launched earlier than other webpages and had been a hit with techies, but the resource was not useful for a broader audience.

"What if the web posed an equal threat to *The Globe* as the newspaper war?" Greenspon recalls pondering. "What if we were losing out by not getting into the game and launching an internet-based breaking news service?"

In February 2000, Crawley gave the green light for a news site that depended on GIS and newsroom collaboration. The next one hundred days were a frenzy. Greenspon travelled to newsrooms across the U.S., attended conferences and investigated best practices. He received advice on how to staff the website, which articles to post right away and which to hold on to. He also learned about the dangers of letting stories be too long.

Some marketers wondered whether *The Globe* was too old and stuffy a brand for the internet. Maybe it should use a different name, as some other publications had done. Greenspon and Crawley paid no heed. The paper intended to use its brand to expand its reach through the web.

Globeandmail.com launched on June 19, 2000. A team of seventeen web journalists repackaged content from the newspaper and updated readers with fast-breaking news. When terrorists flew airplanes into the

World Trade Center and the Pentagon on September 11, 2001, readers were glued to the website for the latest updates. When the federal Liberals chose a new leader in December 2006, a team of *Globe* writers filed incessantly to the web. When an earthquake shook Ottawa in June 2010, with people fleeing and buildings swaying, *The Globe* had a photo and a story online before any other news source.

But there was pushback, much of it from the newsroom itself. Some *Globe* journalists saw the website as a threat. Reporters did not want to share their work, considering it to be cannibalizing their journalism. Digital journalists were dubbed "bloggers" or "renegades," and those words were not compliments. Eventually, however, all but the worst Luddites accepted that the medium didn't matter; what mattered was preserving the paper's integrity. "Everyone simply had to get on board," Greenspon says.

While globeandmail.com took steps to establish itself as a news website, elsewhere, another group of *Globe* staff were building a new online business.

That group, led by digital pioneer Lib Gibson, eventually became Globe Interactive, with its own offices on King Street in Toronto. Over the course of seven years, the team launched a stream of successful products that gave *The Globe* a reputation for digital innovation and boosted the bottom line of the business.

GlobeFund, launched in October 1997, enabled users to track, rank and filter mutual fund data, revolutionizing access. GlobeInvestor allowed users to track their stock movements multiple times per day, instead of waiting for the paper to deliver the previous day's data.

Gibson and Crawley persuaded their bosses to shift *Globe* careers advertising online, through what became Workopolis in January 1999. It was a bold move, given that the founding partners were two long-time print rivals, *The Globe* and the *Toronto Star*. But it worked: Workopolis rapidly became Canada's top jobs site, and *La Presse* soon joined. Within a few years, Workopolis was contributing half of *The Globe*'s profits. (In 2006, *The Globe* sold its 40-per-cent stake in Workopolis to its Torstar partner.) GlobeInvestorGold, a subscription site delivering real-time stock quotes without a twenty-minute delay, opened up another revenue stream for *The Globe*.

Nevertheless, despite all of these innovations, a harsh new truth had emerged: while the internet offered many opportunities, it also posed a lethal threat to every newspaper, including *The Globe*.

From the very beginning of the internet, most news content was free – and readers assumed it would remain that way.

Publishers debated how to monetize the huge readership they were reaching on the web. Could advertising, which sustained the print edition, support the digital product? Was the answer to charge for a digital subscription and introduce online paywalls?

While owners dithered, walls caved in. Many city papers found that classified ads evaporated with the arrival of Craigslist in the early 2000s, though *The Globe* was less affected. Then tech giant Google and the fast-rising social-media platform Facebook hollowed out much of the digital ad revenue that remained. Smartphones replaced desktops, laptops and tablets as the primary venue for reading news. How could you make money displaying news content on a phone?

Too often, newspaper owners in Canada and the U.S. responded with layoffs and cuts, leading to poorer-quality journalism and diminishing readership. Newspapers started closing down. The *Guelph Mercury*. The *Halifax Daily News*. The *Cambridge Reporter*. The *Prince Rupert Daily News*. Dozens of other weeklies and dailies.

To avoid such a fate, *The Globe* had to act fast. In 2010, the paper relaunched its print edition with new state-of-the-art presses and glossy stock for some pages. In 2012, the newspaper announced the rollout of its digital subscription package, providing free online access to print subscribers and allowing online-only readers access to ten free articles a month.

Then, in 2015, *The Globe* turned to artificial intelligence. A proprietary system named Sophi helped predict which content was most valuable to readers, in turn helping maximize digital subscription revenue.

Sophi became a vital tool in *The Globe*'s editorial process, allowing editors to determine, through extensive analytics, what kind of content audiences value and are willing to pay for. In August 2023, *The Globe* sold Sophi to Mather Economics, a global subscription and revenue management company.

While Sophi has been important, it is only a tool. Major investigations remain part of the paper's mandate, regardless of analytics, as they have since *The Globe* first detailed widespread abuse at the Kingston Penitentiary in the 1840s. Whether it is probing the struggle of thalidomide survivors as they age, the underreporting of sexual assaults by police, Chinese interference in Canadian elections or government efforts to suppress information, the mandate of the paper remains to investigate and report.

Artificial intelligence is expected by many to change nearly every facet of society, with both investors and developers salivating at its potential. The perils of this new technology are equally plain: deepfake videos and photos of politicians, or even songs mimicking celebrities, are running rampant.

For journalism, AI stands as both a threat and an opportunity. Disinformation and misinformation are becoming more extensive and harder to detect, even as public trust in Canadian news declines – by 40 per cent in Canada between 2016 and 2023, according to a Reuters poll.

The Globe has developed guidelines to harness this technology while preventing errors and abuses. The new rules include close scrutiny of AI-generated research and data, a prohibition on AI-generated writing for publication and alerting readers to any AI-generated visuals.

Still, other challenges remain. Will digital subscriptions grow to the level needed to preserve the core functions of the newsroom and the bureaus across the country and around the world? Can supplementary revenue streams help the bottom line without distracting from the core mission of the organization? *The Globe* is a newspaper and site that also hosts luxury cruises, while renting out an event space at its Toronto headquarters for weddings and conferences.

For 180 years, this newspaper has used every tool at its disposal to explain what is happening and why it matters to readers across this vast land. We don't plan to stop.

Temur Durrani is a national reporter, based in Winnipeg, at *The Globe and Mail*.

ABOVE: *Globe* reporter June Callwood
at the closing of the old section of
Toronto's Don Jail, January 1, 1978.
(Tibor Kolley/*The Globe and Mail*)

A Turkish policeman stands over the body of a little boy lying face down in the surf on a beach near the resort town of Bodrum, Turkey – one of at least 12 Syrian refugees who perished trying to reach the Greek island of Kos. On Wednesday, Turkish media identified the drowned boy as three-year-old Aylan Kurdi, whose five-year-old brother died on the same boat. Reports said he was from the northern Syrian town of Kobani near the Turkish border, the scene of heavy fighting between Islamic State insurgents and Kurdish forces a few months ago. REUTERS

A moral crisis › In a world filled with graphic horrors, the Western media have become increasingly squeamish about showing what war, famine or death actually look like. There is an understandable fear of upsetting the audience, and a well-founded reluctance to be seen making a market out of the suffering of others. But some upsetting images demand to be seen, precisely because they are a true representation of reality. They show us the world as it is, its cruelties exposed, and not the world as we would wish it to be. And by the shock to our eyes, our conscience may be stirred. FULL EDITORIAL, PAGE 10

The scale of the problem
A look at the swelling numbers that define the harrowing scope of the migrant crisis
FOLIO, PAGES 6-7

A call for compassion
Rather than sealing themselves off, affluent countries should give more to alleviate suffering
COMMENT, PAGE 12

---

7 73552 00004 9   3 6

FEDERAL ELECTION 2015

Liberals planning to repeal balanced budget law

BILL CURRY OTTAWA

Justin Trudeau's Liberals are planning, if elected, to scrap a law entrenching federal balanced budgets in order to run deficits to finance a spike in infrastructure spending.

The party confirmed its policy on the Conservative legislation after recently making the contentious deficit-boosting pledge the centrepiece of its campaign in the run-up to the Oct. 19 vote, drawing criticism from both the Conservatives and the NDP.

The issue of whether to balance the books is shaping up as a key dividing line in the federal campaign.

Liberal candidate John McCallum said the Conservative balanced-budget law needs to be replaced.

"If we have to get rid of a gimmick to do what is right, then it's what we would have to do," he said Wednesday in an interview with The Globe and Mail. "We do not think this is a serious piece of legislation and so we are determined to implement our plan."

The NDP isn't going that far, insisting it has no plans to drop the law even though it opposes it – and may have to live by it – should the party form government and the current fiscal year's books slip into deficit.
Liberals, Page 4

POLICE

Ontario moves to allow chiefs to dock suspended officers' pay

PATRICK WHITE

The Ontario government is close to hammering out a new law that would grant police chiefs the power to halt pay for suspended officers, which currently costs municipalities about $6.4-million a year and exacts a toll on public trust in local law enforcement.

Currently, Ontario is the sole province mandating police forces to maintain pay for any suspended officers, even those facing charges. Chiefs can revoke a suspended officer's salary only if the officer is sentenced to prison.

But that outlier status is set to change under a provincial push to reform the Police Services Act that follows the revelation one officer, who was paid hundreds of thousands of dollars during his suspension, boasted he was enjoying the time off.

"I think we've come 80 per cent of the way towards a solution," said Joe Couto, director of government relations for the Ontario Association of Chiefs of Police, which has been working directly with the province on reforms.
Police, Page 8

The September 3, 2015, front page of *The Globe and Mail* showing the dead body of two-year-old Alan Kurdi included an excerpt from that day's editorial about why the paper chose to use the photo. The caption, provided by a wire service, included mistakes in his age and the spelling of his name – information that was later corrected by his aunt, who lives in Canada.

TOP: Then-president Donald Trump extends his hand to prime minister Justin Trudeau during a meeting in the White House on February 13, 2017. Some commentators incorrectly stated that Trudeau refused to shake Trump's hand, but Trudeau reached out his hand a moment later. (Kevin Dietsch/Pool/ Bloomberg)

BOTTOM: Former prime minister Pierre Trudeau pirouettes at Buckingham Palace on May 7, 1977. For years, the woman walking away was identified as Queen Elizabeth when in fact it was Princess Margaret. (Doug Ball/The Canadian Press)

Progressive Conservative leader Robert Stanfield grimaces
as he drops a football while campaigning in North Bay,
Ontario, on May 30, 1974. There were numerous photos
of Stanfield successfully catching the ball, but *The Globe*
published the image of the fumble. Many believe the
photo had an impact on the election, which Stanfield lost.
(Doug Ball/The Canadian Press)

OPPOSITE: *Globe and Mail* reporter Paul Koring, who visited the Iraqi city of Halabja shortly after a gas attack by president Saddam Hussein's forces in March 1988, photographed the bodies of a man and baby near a step on a main street of the city. (Paul Koring/*The Globe and Mail*))

TOP: Kids play in Halabja, Iraq, in the mid-1990s on the same step where years earlier reporter Paul Koring had documented civilian deaths from the Iraqi gas attack. "In this horrific, God-awful place, there was a new generation," Koring says. (Paul Koring)

BOTTOM: This graphic illustrates how *Globe and Mail* photo editors were able to verify that the location of the two photos by Paul Koring was the same. The brick pattern from the March 1988 photo after the gas attack (1) matches perfectly with the wall from the later image (2). (Murat Yukselir/*The Globe and Mail*)

TOP: How photographs appear can depend on the choices made by the photographer and the editor. Photographer Fred Lum took care, as an outsider, to portray Northern life with sensitivity as he photographed Maria Noolook and her daughter Adelynn from Rankin Inlet, Nunavut, on October 20, 2022. (Fred Lum/*The Globe and Mail*)

BOTTOM: Christy Clark, the first woman elected premier of British Columbia, introduces her new executive council during a ceremony in Vancouver on June 7, 2013. The paper chose an image that focused on her legs, which upset some readers. (John Lehmann/*The Globe and Mail*)

ABOVE: Soldiers from the Armed Forces of the Democratic Republic of the Congo detain two suspected M23 rebels near Rutshuru on August 16, 2022. The Geneva Conventions, which dictate the treatment of prisoners of war, factored into a debate about whether to run the photo of the captured soldiers. *The Globe* published the image. (Goran Tomasevic/ *The Globe and Mail*)

LEFT: A photo shows the body of William Poole after he was shot by police in 1945. The line midway through the image shows where editors cropped out the bleeding corpse. (*The Globe and Mail*)

The Globe and Mail's front page on May 8, 1945, VE (Victory in Europe) Day. The paper today would never permit a staged photo such as this one, which was taken in a studio in Toronto, not on the battlefield. (The Globe and Mail)

Nineteen:
The power gap *through the* decades

Women who worked at *The Globe* often watched the world take new shape while it remained unchanged in the newsroom | **Elizabeth Renzetti**

P erhaps no one on the editing desk saw the irony. In February 1976, *The Globe and Mail* profiled Maureen McTeer, the wife of the new Progressive Conservative leader Joe Clark. She was a law student and a feminist – though not, as *The Globe*'s reporter was careful to point out, a strident one.

"Maureen McTeer won't disappear in Clark's shadow," read the headline on the profile. She was determined to have her own views, her own career, her own name. At least that was the plan, but *The Globe* was not playing along: "Mrs. Clark – who has kept her maiden name . . ." The story referred to her throughout as "Mrs. Clark."

A flame war, 1970s style, broke out on *The Globe*'s normally sedate letters page. Peppery missives denounced Ms. McTeer's convention-flouting – but more readers supported her. "Don't you think it's time *The Globe and Mail* came of age and recognized that women's choices are our own to make and not yours to restrict?" wrote Rosemary Billings of Ottawa, who pointedly did not include her husband's name.

One important group of women agreed that yes, indeed, it was time *The Globe* grew up. And that call was coming from inside the building: a number of female *Globe* journalists were incensed enough to write a petition to management demanding that the paper call the opposition leader's wife by the name she chose.

Sylvia Stead, who joined *The Globe* as a summer student in 1974 and retired in 2023 as the newspaper's public editor, remembers signing the petition: "Women in the newsroom were very unhappy about that and said, 'Women have the right to their own name.'"

It was not the first or last time that turbulent social currents would rock the comfortable *Globe* boat. During the periods of second- and third-wave feminism, roughly from the 1950s to the present, women who worked at the newspaper were put in the uncomfortable position of watching the world take new shape out the window, while it remained stubbornly unchanging inside. They were witnessing, and writing about, the seismic transformations taking place as women fought for legal, social and political rights. At the same time, they were arguing for equality in their own careers in a business that did not always adapt to change at the speed of light.

For example, despite the petition, *The Globe* did not adopt the honorific Ms. until 1984 – eight years after the *Oxford English Dictionary* recognized it, but two years before *The New York Times* took it up. Unfortunately, the recognition of Ms. came too late for *The Globe*'s reporting on the important work of the Royal Commission on the Status of Women, created by Prime Minister Lester Pearson in 1967.

Doris Ogilvie, a distinguished judge and panel commissioner, was described this way in the paper: "Mrs. Ogilvie, formerly Doris Dyer of Halifax, is a dentist's wife with four teenage daughters. She is also a law graduate." And the commission was headed by Anne Francis, who used that name professionally but was referred to in the announcement establishing the commission as "Mrs. John Bird."

Decades earlier, the women's pages had been created as an advertising-friendly cocoon of recipes, sob stories and distractions from the unladylike harshness of a cruel world. *The Globe* and *The Toronto Mail* newspapers learned early that publishing women writers was good business – especially if they didn't have to be paid as well as men. One of the most popular columnists in the country in the late nineteenth century was *The Toronto Mail*'s Kit Coleman, a dispenser of advice and pithy aperçus in her Woman's Kingdom (she also became the first accredited female war correspondent while covering the Spanish-American War in Cuba). The journalist-adventuress also made for good copy: readers of *The Globe* eagerly awaited the dispatches of Alice Freeman, writing under the pen name Faith Fenton, as she reported on the gold rush in Yukon Territory.

Though famous, these women were anomalies, and poorly paid anomalies at that. Only thirty-five women were listed as journalists in the Canadian census of 1891, according to Carole Gerson's *Canadian Women in Print, 1750–1918*. A male journalist in Ontario in the late nineteenth century could hope to make $550 a year, while a woman would be lucky to take home $300. (The fight for equal compensation would continue at *The Globe*, and other newsrooms, until today.) Women also had to fight to write about serious topics, which were seen as the proper real estate of men.

Battles for women's suffrage raged on the streets and in parliaments, and they were echoed on the letters page, often among women readers and cloaked in early twentieth-century ideas about the proper sphere of feminine influence. "Is there any vocation or walk of life where women are not showing daily they are as able as men?" wrote A Woman Who Pays Taxes in 1908. A reader who gave her name only as Nelly countered: "A thoughtful, intelligent, loving woman who loves her family and her home will exercise a long and far-reaching influence that a suffragette can never possess."

By the time the Second World War and its labour shortages rolled around, notions of where women belonged began conveniently to shift. The newsroom's floodgates opened and young women with a taste for adventure (if not for luxurious living) poured in. In the early 1940s, a spirited teenager named June Callwood found a job as a reporter at *The Globe*, where, according to David Hayes's 1992 history of the paper, *Power and Influence*, owner George McCullagh "used to chase her around the newsroom, because, as she would later recall, 'he collected virgins, which I was at the time.'"

Callwood started out writing stories about women's participation in the war effort, such as one from 1943 that appeared under the headline "Airwomen accorded praise by once-skeptical airmen." Decades later, after a career reporting on social issues, she was awarded the Order of Canada, an honour also given to another *Globe* trailblazer, medical reporter Joan Hollobon.

Hollobon's illustrious career took off when she replaced the male medical reporter, who took a one-year sabbatical in 1959 and came back as the science reporter. She covered the medical beat for the next twenty-six years, breaking stories about everything from surgical mistakes to disease outbreaks. Hollobon's career began at a time when it was unusual to see female reporters covering "hard" beats and also at a time that allowed memorable leads like this one from 1959, about a weight-loss study: "Sad news for weak-willed fatties," she wrote, a sentence that would probably cause an editor to faint today.

While the paper was only lightly populated with women, each one shone ferociously bright. There was Jean Howarth, "empress of the editorial board," as Hayes described her, "a gnomish figure with an acid tongue," and Kay Kritzwiser, an influential feature writer and art critic, whose charms were summed up by Richard Doyle, a former editor of *The Globe*, in his memoir *Hurly-Burly*: "The lady knows how to bat an eyelash, swivel a hip, show off an ankle or arch an eyebrow." Maybe there was a reason women struggled to find a place in the newsroom after all.

Christie Blatchford's career would take her to all of Toronto's major daily newspapers, but she started at *The Globe*, with her first story appearing in January 1973, when she was still at journalism school. Already she possessed that ineffable quality called "voice," as she wrote about a shabby hotel and strip club where "a fellow with too much time on his hands can find himself in time-consuming arguments that mean nothing when they're over."

Blatchford joined *The Globe*'s sports department as a columnist that year. Like many female journalists of the time, she cultivated a tough and witty exterior, preferring to laugh off the everyday sexism she encountered. But in her first book, *Spectator Sports*, she offered a more introspective reason for leaving *The Globe* for the *Toronto Star* in 1977: "I was also, I think now, a little lonely; being one of a handful of women writers was always interesting, but after a few years it was also isolating and unnerving."

This was the dichotomy for *The Globe*'s women journalists in those decades: they were grateful for opportunities, often given to them when they were quite young, but also desperate for female mentorship and leadership. "When I started, it was a real male bastion, there were very few women in the newsroom," says Gwen Smith, who joined *The Globe* in the early 1980s as a copy editor and made a rapid ascent through the ranks. She was the paper's national editor when she was still in her twenties and later became deputy managing editor. When she left after a decade, "there were a lot more women at *The Globe*."

Some of that hiring was done by progressive-minded men like managing editor Geoffrey Stevens, but the snowball really picked up speed when women like Smith and deputy managing editor Shirley Sharzer made a concerted effort to diversify the newsroom. This diversity, of course, was limited to gender; racialized journalists continued to be dramatically under-represented well into the twenty-first century.

In this way, the atmosphere for women at *The Globe* continued to reflect the world outside: still chilly, but growing warmer. Editorials appeared in favour of increasing access to abortion, legalizing divorce and equalizing pay. But there remained a suspicion about the political enterprise of feminism and how it might turn otherwise nice girls into gorgons. As one *Globe* reporter wrote in a profile of a women's rights activist in 1970, "Justly or not, there is an image printed on the minds of men and women of what women's liberationists are like – strident, shrill, emotional and paranoid hawk-faced females who go around burning bras and trying to wear pants."

It bears noting that the activist in that profile was fighting to return to her job as a university researcher after her maternity leave – a struggle that was mirrored in *The Globe* newsroom, where it was not uncommon for women to return post-childbirth to find they'd been reassigned to different beats or even new sections of the newspaper.

It became the work of female journalists to turn the page on women's-lib stereotypes. "Dispelling the myth of feminists as monsters" was the headline on a column by Adele Freedman, who was soon to make her mark as *The Globe*'s architecture critic. In the 1980s, Linda Hossie's unofficial beat was "women's issues," and she wrote stories – some of them irritatingly unresolved to this day – about pay equity and discrimination against Indigenous women. She left the Toronto newsroom to become one of the paper's first female foreign correspondents (in Latin America) and was soon followed in the correspondent ranks by Jan Wong in China, Isabel Vincent in Brazil and Stephanie Nolen in several bureaus around the world.

But even as the news pages were grappling with the rise of women in the workforce, and bowing to that pesky honorific Ms., the manpower on the masthead – and it was almost exclusively man-powered – failed to see the need for corresponding progress at *The Globe* itself.

"We were busy writing daycare stories and pay-equity stories," says Vivian Smith, who was the national beats editor and a feature writer in the 1980s. "But the managers didn't look around the newsroom and think that they needed to change as well."

The irritation built up until it was ready to blow. A group of women began to organize what they called "femfests" – raucous, sometimes-boozy gatherings where they could share their irritations and triumphs, trade war stories and discuss how to achieve a fairer newsroom through collective action. It was solidarity with a side of sauvignon.

The femfests were a place to vent about sleazy behaviour, like the senior editor who asked a female journalist to sit on his lap while discussing her news plans, or the other senior editor who called across a room to a reporter: "Hey, are you pregnant? Your boobs look bigger."

As Gwen Smith and others pointed out, though, the casual sexism of the newsroom was just one part of a brusque culture that also rewarded resourcefulness and ambition. A young woman could rise quickly through the ranks, get fascinating assignments and run large departments. When Chrystia Freeland was in her early thirties, with no hint yet of the success she'd find in federal politics, she became *The Globe*'s deputy editor. Depending on where you stood, Freeland's energy was either bracing or shrivelling. "In a buttoned-down environment like *The Globe*, she was a curiosity," Leah McLaren, who worked for Freeland, wrote in a profile in *Chatelaine*. "As a manager, Freeland quickly developed a reputation for being demanding. She brimmed with energy and new ideas at a paper then primarily known for its unwavering resistance to change."

Not everyone enjoyed the winds of change, as the women at the femfests discovered when they began to demand more systemic transformation. At one point, they pushed for the company to conduct a survey of daycare possibilities for the newsroom. In the end, the majority of *Globe* staff did not want toddlers anywhere near the building, and a human resources executive told them they could have a daycare when she could bring her cat to work.

Working through their union, women at *The Globe* also fought for maternity pay top-ups and won better compensation for parents in a series of contracts beginning in 1992. The issue of women being reassigned when they returned from maternity leaves continued to be a problem, though, with one reporter yanked from her beats twice (once for each baby).

Pay equity, of course, was another major challenge, although it was not taken up as a cause until the past decade, when union representatives studied newsroom wages and discovered that "a substantial pay gap exists between male and female employees." The issue continues to be a contentious one at contract-negotiating time, as the union pushes for *The Globe* to study and improve wage equity – not just between genders but for racialized journalists as well.

With the pay-equity issue, the tension between what women at *The Globe* write about and what they experience in their own careers continues. One of the newspaper's most resonant investigations in recent years was Power Gap, a series of articles about income discrepancy in Canada by staff journalists Robyn Doolittle, Chen Wang and Tavia Grant. "For women in the workplace," they wrote, "progress has stalled. By almost every metric, they continue to lag generations behind men."

The Power Gap series examined vast chasms in influence and income in various fields – law, business, medicine, academia, public service. But the very newspaper in which it ran – and which continues to run important stories and opinion pieces about gender inequality – has never had a woman in the very top positions of editorial leadership, as either publisher or editor-in-chief.

There's a famous phrase that former prime minister Kim Campbell has said: if you're not at the table, you're on the menu. Over the years, *The Globe and Mail*'s leadership table has become more inclusive, providing a richer experience for staff and readers alike. But the best seats, at the head of the table, still remain out of reach.

Elizabeth Renzetti is an author and former columnist at *The Globe and Mail*.

ABOVE: Thousands of Montrealers march in the St. Jean Baptiste parade, June 25, 1990, carrying Quebec flags and signs advocating for independence. (Paul Chiasson/ The Canadian Press)

Twenty: *The* not-so-quiet revolution

Perhaps no other topic has consumed editors at *The Globe* as much as the question of Quebec's place within Canada | **Konrad Yakabuski**

T he short, unhappy life of the Meech Lake Accord ended on June 23, 1990, sparking an intractable question that gnaws at us still: Who killed Meech?

All we know for sure is that if the accord's death could not be definitively pinned on the actions of a single person or party, *The Globe and Mail* emerged as an unintentional accessory in its demise. Though its editorials had been strongly supportive of the federal-provincial pact aimed at bringing Quebec into the 1982 Constitution, a front-page scoop on Prime Minister Brian Mulroney's controversial strategy to corral three recalcitrant premiers into signing on to Meech before a critical deadline created a national uproar. Meech never had a chance after that. What followed was a lost decade of existential angst that nearly spelled the end of Canada itself.

The 1987 accord – so named for the Gatineau Park retreat where Mulroney and all ten premiers had reached a deal to address Quebec's constitutional demands – was initially hailed as a historic triumph, a rare show of unity in the federation that would end years of constitutional bickering and deliver a death knell to the separatist cause.

But the months leading up to the June 1990 deadline for provincial legislatures to ratify the accord were filled with acrid debate. Opponents said the accord would mean the end of Canada as they had known it; supporters warned its demise would mean the end of Canada, period.

By the spring of 1990, Newfoundland, Manitoba and New Brunswick had still not ratified Meech. Mulroney made a last-ditch effort to avert a constitutional crisis by gathering the premiers in Ottawa in early June. After marathon talks, they reached a deal to pass Meech in exchange for a promise of future Senate reform. An ebullient Mulroney called *Globe* editor-in-chief William Thorsell to tout his achievement; Thorsell persuaded him to grant the paper an exclusive interview about "these historic meetings," as he called them in a 2022 memoir.

For *The Globe*, the timing could not have been better. Under Thorsell, the paper had embarked on an ambitious redesign and had set June 12, 1990, as the relaunch date. With Mulroney's interview in the bag, Thorsell was "delighted that we were fortuitously headed for a scoop about a critical national issue under our new nameplate on an auspicious day."

Thorsell had no prior inkling of the firestorm that the front-page story that appeared below the fold that Tuesday morning would unleash. In it, Mulroney confided to Ottawa correspondents Susan Delacourt and Graham Fraser that he had chosen to "roll the dice" (the quote was later clarified to be "roll all the dice") in summoning the premiers to eleventh-hour talks to save Meech, rather than meeting with them weeks earlier. His comments suggested he had made a conscious decision to gamble with the country's future. On seeing the story, Newfoundland premier Clyde Wells was furious: "It gives the impression we're being manipulated."

Before the story appeared, Wells, Manitoba premier Gary Filmon and New Brunswick's Frank McKenna had agreed to put Meech to a vote in their respective legislatures before the deadline. After the story ran, only McKenna made good on his promise. Meech died on Saturday the 23rd. The following day hundreds of thousands of Quebeckers marched in Montreal's St. Jean Baptiste Day parade, the theme of which – *Notre vrai pays, c'est le Québec* – set the political tone for years to come.

The debate over Meech exposed once again the fault line on which Canada had teetered since the pre-Confederation era. Perhaps no other topic has consumed editors at *The Globe and Mail*, or filled its national news pages, as much as the question of Quebec's place within Canada.

Its hand in Meech's death notwithstanding, *The Globe* has typically strongly defended accommodating Quebec's differences within the federation. Early *Globe* editors drew a line when it came to matters of allegiance to Britain, as did later ones on questions touching language rights and religious freedom. But most of the time, keeping Canada together – and out of the hands of the Americans – required letting Quebec be Quebec, the editors argued.

It didn't start out that way, however.

At its founding in 1844, the paper was hostile toward French Canada's cultural and religious protectionism. Founder George Brown's devotion to the twin political causes of representation by population – which would have left French-speaking Canada East with fewer seats in the legislative assembly than English-speaking Canada West – and his opposition to state funding for Catholic schools pitted him against Quebec's powerful clergy and their ally, Tory leader Sir John A. Macdonald. "There can be no permanent peace in Canada till every vestige of church dominancy is swept away," Brown wrote categorically in the autumn of 1850.

But by 1863, Brown had become a skilled and seasoned politician and had come around to accepting Quebec's distinctness as a necessary condition of Confederation. "It is true that the [French] show at this moment considerable dread that as the English population outnumbers them, attempts may be made to proscribe their religion, language and laws," Brown wrote in an editorial that year. "It is possible that we need to reassure them on this point, to give them such guarantees as they may desire that their peculiar interests shall not be touched upon." On that basis, Brown and Macdonald found common cause to launch the talks that ended in Confederation and the British North America Act of 1867.

For the next century, *Globe* editors remained sensitive to Quebec's "peculiar interests," with notable exceptions. The paper's Loyalist bent asserted itself during two world wars, as it backed conscription in 1917 and 1942 over fierce opposition in Quebec. And *The Globe* saw Quebec premier Maurice Duplessis, who ruled the province through a mixture of fear and coercion, as such a scourge that it became the first non-Quebec newspaper to open a Quebec City bureau in 1954. After Duplessis's 1959 death and the election of a reformist Liberal government in 1960, *The Globe*'s editors rejoiced that "the voters of Quebec have rebelled against the Union Nationale corruption and elected the Liberals, who have promised a thorough house-cleaning." It marked the beginning of a new era that would forever change the province, and Canada.

In 1963, *Globe* reporter Anne MacDermot first wrote of the "not-so-quiet revolution" sweeping Quebec society. Soon after, the term "quiet revolution" was appropriated by Québécois analysts. *La Révolution tranquille* marked the rise of a new political consciousness, underlined by French president Charles de Gaulle's infamous "Vive le Québec libre" declaration from the balcony of Montreal City Hall in 1967.

The Quiet Revolution took a dark turn in October 1970 when Marxist *indépendantistes* belonging to the Front de libération du Québec kidnapped British trade commissioner James Cross at his home in Westmount. Five days later, the FLQ abducted and later killed Quebec deputy premier Pierre Laporte. On October 16, Pierre Trudeau invoked the War Measures Act.

The Globe's editorial the following day questioned, without condemning, whether the crisis warranted the suspension of basic civil rights and limits on press freedoms the act permitted: "Only if we can believe that the Government has evidence that the FLQ is sufficiently armed to escalate the violence that it has spawned for seven years now, only if we can believe that it is virulent enough to infect other areas of society, only then can the Government's assumption of incredible powers be tolerated." The Trudeau government, *The Globe* concluded, had not produced such evidence. (The government negotiated Cross's release on December 4 by granting several FLQ members safe passage to Cuba; all returned to Canada within a decade and served only short prison sentences.)

In November 1976, Quebec elected a new premier, the charismatic founder of the separatist Parti Québécois, René Lévesque. The following year, the PQ introduced Bill 101, legislation that made French the sole language of the province's legislature, courts and workplace. It limited access to English-language public schools and banned the use of English on outdoor commercial signs. Anglophones began leaving the province in droves; so did the corporate head offices. "The Parti Québécois has made many businesses feel insecure, has put their profits under threat, with its language law and its intention to take Quebec out of Canada," *The Globe* wrote in an editorial.

Still, in 1980, on the eve of the first Quebec referendum on sovereignty, *The Globe*'s editorial board insisted a No victory could not mean business as usual: "It should be recognized by Canadians outside Quebec that when we urge the people of Quebec to vote no, we are committing ourselves to the negotiation of change, real and possibly wrenching change, in the structure of Confederation as we know it." The No side won, handily.

In 1981, the PQ vowed to fight Trudeau's efforts to unilaterally patriate the BNA Act. But an alliance of Lévesque and seven other premiers opposed to patriation collapsed at a November first ministers' conference in Ottawa. The federal government and nine provinces excluding Quebec agreed to patriate the BNA Act and include a new Charter of Rights. In April 1982, Queen Elizabeth proclaimed the new Constitution in a ceremony on Parliament Hill.

The Globe editorial page provided a mixed assessment: "What was accomplished was considerable. At least we finally moved as a federal state. Some of us argued that we had laboured and produced a typical Canadian compromise. It was nothing of the sort. It was an angry settlement, arrived at in the worst way to effect abiding change. It involved methods that, if indulged in often, would leave us in danger of ceasing to be a country."

Campaigning in 1984, Mulroney promised to bring Quebec into the 1982 Constitution "with honour and enthusiasm." His Tories swept Quebec, and the Meech Lake Accord was struck on April 30, 1987. "[The] accord is a progressive, supple, sometimes wisely ambiguous document that is well-suited in most of its provisions to Canada in modern times," the paper argued in a March 23, 1990, editorial. It is with some irony, then, that *The Globe*'s front-page scoop on June 12 dealt the perhaps fatal blow to Meech.

Affronted by the accord's demise, then–Quebec premier Robert Bourassa launched and strongly supported a commission that called for a provincewide referendum on either sovereignty or a new constitutional offer from the rest of Canada by October 1992. In response, Mulroney and constitutional affairs minister Joe Clark gathered with the non-Quebec premiers to formulate a new offer to Quebec, which became known as the Charlottetown Accord.

Bourassa decided to hold a referendum on this modified version of Meech, which included additional guarantees of self-government for Indigenous Canadians and the promise of a Triple-E (equal, elected and effective) Senate. Mulroney opted for a referendum in the rest of Canada.

The Yes campaign got off to a terrible start after *The Globe*'s Quebec City correspondent Rhéal Séguin obtained the transcript of a telephone conversation between two of Bourassa's top constitutional advisers. According to Séguin's September 16 front-page scoop, André Tremblay told Diane Wilhelmy that Bourassa had "never wanted a referendum on sovereignty" and had "caved in" to pressure from other premiers to sign on to the Charlottetown Accord.

Once again, *The Globe*'s news and editorial pages were at odds with each other on the critical national-unity file. "The Charlottetown accord maintains a rational balance between individual rights 'guaranteed' in the Charter, and the recognitions of Quebec and the aboriginal peoples," the paper editorialized on October 22. "The history of Canada was made by saying Yes to compatriots of different kinds within a single state. Yes then; Yes still." Four days later, Canadians voted No to Charlottetown.

In 1994, the PQ returned to power with a majority government under Jacques Parizeau, with a second referendum on sovereignty set for October 30, 1995. After early campaign polls showed the No side with a large lead, sovereigntist strategists persuaded a reluctant Parizeau to take a backseat to the charismatic Bloc Québécois leader Lucien Bouchard, a gifted orator who a year earlier had survived a near-fatal bout of flesh-eating disease that claimed his left leg.

"His presence electrifies Yes supporters in packed halls," *Globe* columnist Jeffrey Simpson wrote of Bouchard on October 12. "He, more than the other secessionist leaders, can reach ordinary francophone Quebeckers, summoning their Volksgeist in a supreme collective act of 'national affirmation' that will, once and for all, enable Quebec to meet the rest of Canada equal to equal, face to face, people to people."

Jean Chrétien had refused to make concessions to Quebec. Only days before the vote, with the No side faltering, the prime minister relented in a televised address to the country: "We must recognize that Quebec's language, its culture and institutions make it a distinct society. And no constitutional change that affects the powers of Quebec should ever be made without the consent of Quebeckers."

The referendum results rattled Canada to its core. The No side eked out a razor-thin victory of 50.6 per cent, besting the Yes side by a mere 54,000 votes. "No longer will Quebeckers, especially francophone Quebeckers, accept the federation status quo," Séguin wrote. "Without major reforms, Canada's crisis seems certain to continue."

The Globe's lead editorial on the result was categoric: "Whatever the method, change must come, as the Prime Minister and other leading federalists promised explicitly during the campaign that it would."

Chrétien's post-referendum approach to Quebec was more stick than carrot. Bouchard, who had replaced Parizeau as premier, insisted Quebec could unilaterally declare independence if the Yes side won a simple majority in a future referendum. The Chrétien government asked the Supreme Court of Canada to settle the matter. In 1998, it ruled that international law did not confer on Quebec a right to secede unilaterally, but that Ottawa and the other provinces would be required to negotiate Quebec's secession if a "clear majority" of Quebeckers voted yes to "a clear question" on sovereignty.

Chrétien moved to entrench the court's ruling in the 1999 Clarity Act, a provocative move that many federalists feared would generate a backlash in Quebec. Simpson summed up Ottawa's strategy: "If you cannot woo Quebeckers, as Mr. Chrétien has failed to do, then trap them . . . He has produced a straitjacket from which the secessionists cannot escape."

Chrétien's tactic appeared to work; the sovereignty movement entered a period of decline. The 2018 election of the Coalition Avenir Québec, under former PQ cabinet minister François Legault, saw the province revert to an earlier form of nationalist affirmation reminiscent of the Duplessis era with a modern, secular twist. Like Duplessis, Legault has sought more autonomy for Quebec within Canada and governs the province in open defiance of federal norms.

In 2019, the CAQ approach yielded Bill 21, which prohibits public employees in a position of authority, including teachers, from wearing religious symbols. The CAQ sought to shield the law from a court chal-lenge by pre-emptively invoking the notwithstanding clause embedded in the 1982 Charter.

In keeping with its pluralist view, *The Globe* called the secularism law a denial of Quebec's own history of accommodation, embodied in the 1774 Quebec Act that recognized the religious freedom of the colo-ny's Catholic majority: "Simply by accepting that people of different religions can nevertheless forge a shared identity, practising different faiths yet united in the same respect for the law and at the same love of country – what a radical, beautiful idea – Canada became possible."

The CAQ's use of the notwithstanding clause for a second time, adopting Bill 96 to strengthen French-language protections in 2022, drew a stiffer rebuke from *The Globe*. "It was always assumed that, if Quebec ever left Canada, it could only happen through the front door . . . Canada needs to recognize that the current government of Quebec is trying to tiptoe out the back door," stated a May 25, 2022, editorial. "It is doing so by poking ever larger holes in Canada's constitutional order, which protects fundamental rights, and replacing it with a parallel regime where the executive can curb rights and meddle in people's lives with little to no judicial oversight." This sounds like something a young George Brown might have written himself.

Whenever possible, *The Globe* has advocated for the accommodation of Quebec's differences within the federation. It has not always been easy to square this circle in Charter-era Canada.

Konrad Yakabuski is a columnist at *The Globe and Mail*, based in Montreal.

ABOVE: *Globe and Mail* film critic
Jay Scott, circa 1993. (Fred Lum/
The Globe and Mail)

Twenty-One:
Great Scott

Jay Scott changed how Canadians consumed, talked about and processed culture
| **Barry Hertz**

I f you worked in the Canadian film industry in the 1970s, eighties or nineties, you probably had a Jay Scott story. Perhaps you were there when he held a riotous party inside a hotel room at Toronto's Park Plaza, keeping neighbour critic Roger Ebert up all night and prompting phone call after phone call to the front desk pleading for quiet. Maybe you were there when he arrived at a Cannes party in nothing but a Speedo. Or you might have been stargazing outside a row of limos, delighted to see actress Liza Minelli step out, her arms locked with none other than . . . Jay Scott, film critic for *The Globe and Mail*.

But for every Jay Scott story, there are a hundred more Jay Scott reviews – intensely insightful, playfully experimental and relentlessly entertaining master classes in arts journalism that opened up entire worlds to readers. Over the course of his sixteen-year career at *The Globe*, Scott changed how Canadians consumed, talked about and processed culture.

But before Scott could do any of that – before he could introduce North American audiences to the brilliance of filmmakers such as Germany's Rainer Werner Fassbinder, champion such emerging Canadian voices as Denys Arcand and David Cronenberg, become a passionate advocate for queer storytellers or predict how the blockbuster machine would one day rule the Earth – a young man named Jeffrey Scott Beaven had to figure out how to get the hell out of Albuquerque, New Mexico.

Beaven was born October 4, 1949, in Lincoln, Nebraska, the only son of Muriel, a high-school English teacher, and Bruce, an insurance salesman. Both parents were Seventh-Day Adventists who didn't own a television and believed cinema was a sin. Still, they took the boy to see his first movie, the Marlon Brando comedy *The Teahouse of the August Moon*, when he was seven.

"I got really excited by it and have vivid memories of it," Scott (as he later became known professionally) recalled during a 1985 radio interview. "Then I got sent to a few Disney movies, and I remember Bambi's mother dying, which was particularly traumatic."

Aside from sneaking into a double bill of *Dracula* and *The Thing That Couldn't Die* when he was eight ("It caused me nightmares for months, but I loved it") and a showing of *Ben-Hur* with his parents at age eleven ("I thought it was the greatest thing I had ever come across"), Scott would not see another film until late into his high-school career in Albuquerque, where the family had relocated.

After enduring a tumultuous adolescence – his parents divorced when he was sixteen, his father dying by suicide shortly thereafter – Scott propelled himself into the arts. He studied art history at New College in

Sarasota, Florida, before focusing on acting at the University of New Mexico, where he also edited his campus newspaper's arts section. At last, people with a range of tastes and philosophies surrounded him; he was, as he would later say, "liberated."

Well, almost. Scott was not yet out of the closet, and in 1968, he married Mary Bloom, whom he met while in Sarasota. One year later, the couple packed their bags for Toronto, where Scott got a job writing for a construction-trade paper, the *Daily Commercial News*. Depending on whom you ask, the move north was an act of draft dodging, a career-motivated leap of faith or something more ineffable.

"I think he wanted to get out of Dodge. Albuquerque was a tough town, it was rough for him there," recalls Helga Stephenson, Scott's close friend and the long-time head of Toronto's Festival of Festivals (before it was called the Toronto International Film Festival). "He was kind of a lost boy."

The couple's emigration did not immediately take, though; the pair moved back to New Mexico in 1972. Scott joined the *Albuquerque Journal* as an investigative reporter, writing film reviews on the side.

Wanting a break from the grind of news, Scott answered an ad for *The Calgary Albertan*, which was seeking an arts reporter. Back in Canada, he quickly made his mark, winning a 1975 National Newspaper Award for a review of *The Alberta Cowboy Show* by Toronto's Theatre Passe Muraille only a few months into his new job. The honour caught the eye of *The Globe*'s editor-in-chief, Richard Doyle, who hired the young star as a features reporter in 1977.

Now twenty-eight years old, Jeffrey Scott Beaven was reborn, in byline form, as "Jay Scott."

Initially, Scott wrote a daily *Globe* column called "FYI," a high-low mix of gossip and news. A year later, he moved over to the arts desk to cover film. While the paper boasted a decent history of film critics – starting with Roly Young in the 1930s through to Martin Knelman in the seventies – movies were a tertiary concern. The arts section was internally known as "M&D" – music and drama – derogatorily dubbed "the pansy patch." However, Scott and a fresh batch of twentysomething writers and editors had an eye toward changing that.

"I won't demean Jay's predecessors by saying it was like high-school book review writing, but it was much more traditional, without his flair and creativity and unexpectedness," says Karen York, who joined *The Globe* a year before Scott and would soon become his editor.

"In terms of *Globe* style, it was quite grey up till that point, very reportorial," says Liam Lacey, who started on *The Globe*'s arts desk as a music writer two years after Scott. "Jay played around, he experimented, he had fun – he had opening graphs that were sixty words long. He threw around allusions. It was sexy, not in the range of what newspapers were doing."

Scott wrote film reviews in the form of dialogues (Woody Allen's *Interiors* was critiqued via a discussion between a tragedian and a comic); fictional first-person monologues (Sidney Lumet's *The Morning After* was dissected with an imagined confession from Jane Fonda's heroine); and even multiple-choice questionnaires (Was Frank Marshall's *Arachnophobia* a: a rip-off of *The Birds*, but not as scary; b: a rip-off of *Tremors*, but not as funny; c: a rip-off of *Gremlins*, but not as clever; or d: a rip-off of *Poltergeist*, but not as gross? The answer: all of the above.)

When Scott loved a film, his reviews were invitations to broaden sensibilities and curiosities. On Francis Ford Coppola's *Apocalypse Now*: "When it was all over, when the audience had applauded desultorily, too devastated and perhaps too heartbroken and certainly too depressed to summon the bravos that were demanded, Coppola's $30-million Vietnam War movie would dissolve in the mind into one long, fluid camera movement, a movie fabricated from a single operatic take to a single operatic purpose, a movie commencing with the mundane and ending with the monstrous, a movie made with the swiftness, the silence, the subtlety – and the savagery – of a spear thrown home to the centre of the heart."

When Scott loathed a film, his reviews were puckishly sour suckerpunches, enthusiastic exhortations to join the well-deserved pile-on.

On Frank Perry's *Mommie Dearest*: "What appears to be one of the worst movies this year – it was hissed at an invitational screening this week – *Mommie Dearest* might be a consciously subversive satire of hype, the American dream, the nuclear family, gossip-mongering and the movies themselves (no one ever goes out a door without pausing at the threshold to make a curtain speech), all filmed in the style of a Joan Crawford vehicle. Then again, it might be a hoot 'n' holler stinker, more dirty fun than mud wrestling."

Scott loved art-house dramas as much as he did glossy blockbusters. Margarethe von Trotta's "near masterpiece" *Marianne and Juliane* was as worthy of serious conversation as James Cameron's "efficient, cold-blooded" *The Terminator*. Movies were just one of Scott's obsessions though. He was a social animal, as eager to see things as he was to be seen. He devoured, and wrote about, books, music, visual art and restaurants. Scott ushered in a sea change at the paper, becoming as much of a star as those he was writing about.

As Scott's profile rose – he published two books, hosted his own show on TVOntario and won two more NNAS – every newspaper and magazine was desperate to find its own Jay Scott. Rival critics were eager to rise to his level, without wholly ripping him off.

"I couldn't read him before I wrote my own review. Whatever I was struggling to write about in the back of my head would be in the front of his head," recalls Brian D. Johnson, long-time film critic and arts writer for *Maclean's* magazine. "One thing I stole from him quite consciously was that by the time that you got to the second graph of his review, you would know what was singular, groundbreaking or new about this film – why it mattered for somebody who didn't even go to the movies."

Outside Canadian journalism, things were also changing. Hollywood's easy riders and raging bulls – Coppola, Martin Scorsese, William Friedkin, Robert Altman, Peter Bogdanovich – were stripping the facade off the American dream and taking the real pulse of Western culture. Their roguish work required an equally rebellious strain of analysis and critique.

"Jay was part of a new wave of criticism, like Pauline Kael at *The New Yorker*, who sought to mix true intellect with what was going on in film," says Harlan Jacobson, the long-time editor of *Film Comment* who would meet up with Scott at Cannes and Toronto. "There was an understanding with Jay that a movie was the opening salvo for a conversation about an important topic to the culture at large."

In 1980, Scott and his wife divorced. Scott soon found a long-term romantic partner in Gene Corby, a schoolteacher. Yet he did not exactly broadcast his sexuality, at least not to his co-workers or readers.

"He was sociable and witty, but I don't know how many people in the office were as knowledgeable about his background," says William Thorsell, *The Globe*'s editor-in-chief from 1989 through 1999. "Because we were gay newsroom brothers in a sense, he would confide in a way with me and not others."

According to Cheryl Thibedeau, Corby's niece, Scott felt he also had to put his personal life to the side while operating inside the Hollywood machine.

"One time he interviewed Mel Gibson, he actually had him over to his house for lunch, and he invited me. But he asked me, 'Do you really want to meet a homophobic, misogynistic man?' No, as it turned out, I didn't," Thibedeau recalls.

Scott was a vocal champion of emerging gay filmmakers, particularly Fassbinder and a young Pedro Almodóvar. And when he felt that homophobia was being weaponized on screen, he was ferocious: "Everybody connected with *Basic Instinct* should be spanked and put to bed without supper, but on the basis of the evidence at hand in this sadomasochistic disaster, they might enjoy it."

The latter half of Scott's *Globe* career represented a remarkable run of criticism that knew no borders, geographical or metaphorical. Just as he helped establish Toronto's Festival of Festivals as an international destination, Scott brought the global cinema of Cannes back to Canadian readers.

"Everyone knew that Jay liked to party at Cannes, but there was a moment where you'd be at a party with him and then he was gone, returning to his hotel to write reviews until dawn, then back at morning screenings," says Bonnie Voland, a film marketing and publicity veteran. "It'd be 'Oh my God, I just saw you two hours ago, how did you write that review just now?'"

Whether out of Cannes or Toronto, industry gatekeepers from every corner of the world knew that Scott could make or break movies, careers, companies and lives.

"Jay was one of those barometers – he had a feel for the moment in time, the culture, the audience," says Tom Bernard, co-founder of New York–based Sony Pictures Classics. "He put movies on the map that no one else did; he was always on the edge, discovering new works."

One such discovery was *Diva*, director Jean-Jacques Beineix's operatic thriller that flopped when first released in France in the spring of 1981. After *Diva* had its North American premiere at Toronto's Festival of Festivals that fall, Scott hailed it as "the most impressive debut from a French director since Godard's *Breathless*." Distributors were suddenly fighting with each other to secure *Diva*'s North American rights.

"Jay's run was the only time since I've been making films where what a Canadian critic said had influence with critics elsewhere, as opposed to the other way around," says Canadian mega-producer Robert Lantos, whose 1991 drama *Black Robe* became a Canadian box-office sensation in no small part due to Scott's rave review ("a technical achievement of the highest order"). Scott's opinion was so highly coveted that Lantos cooked up a private arrangement between them.

"I would show him a film I had produced first before anyone else in the world saw it, and in exchange for that priority, if he didn't like the film, he would agree not to write about it until everyone else did," Lantos explains. "But if he did like the film, Jay would write about it before anyone else, with my blessing. He had influence over any other Canadian critic and beyond our borders too."

When Corby died of AIDS-related illness in 1989, it shook Scott deeply. "My uncle died a terrible AIDS death, and Jay didn't ever want to go like that," Thibedeau recalls. Scott himself tested HIV-positive in 1986 and by 1991 would become noticeably thin and weak. Although his pace slowed, he never stopped writing, even attending Cannes in the spring of 1993, when it was a struggle to walk the Croisette. Two months later, Scott died of AIDS-related complications.

His funeral was as unorthodox as his writing. Arranged by Stephenson and Thorsell, Scott's ceremony was held at the Timothy Eaton Memorial Church in Toronto, but as per his instructions, there would be no Christian liturgy. There was, however, a boom box blasting Bette Midler's "Wind Beneath My Wings."

Listing *The Globe*'s arts and culture writers who picked up Scott's legacy – John Allemang, John Bentley Mays, John Haslett Cuff, Joanne Kates, Johanna Schneller and Stephen Godfrey (who died suddenly the same year as Scott) – threatens to require a separate chapter. Liam Lacey and Rick Groen would immediately continue to cover and expand the paper's film coverage, albeit with Groen confessing that he was "admiring and intimidated and foolish enough to steal from Jay shamelessly."

In the decades since Scott's death, wave after wave of disruptive change has rocked both the journalism and film industries. As traditional print advertising crashes, arts writing is the first beat chucked overboard to save costs. Although there are now more outlets than ever offering film reviews online, only a small handful of writers can claim to make livings as full-time critics.

As for the movie business, it would likely feel both disorienting and familiar to Scott were he alive today. The streaming wars, the crash of theatrical exhibition and the overreliance on uber-franchises might seem apocalyptic to any cinema lover who remembers the 1970s. Yet Scott was all too aware of the direction that things were heading.

In his 1993 review of Steven Spielberg's *Jurassic Park*, one of his last bylines before he died, Scott laid out a vision of the future: "Some day, scientists will pick through the fossilized remains of Hollywood. They will find *Jurassic Park*. They will screen it. They will use it to reconstruct life eons ago, when directors and producers roamed, if not ruled, the Earth. Citing the film as evidence, the scientists will release their conclusions: Movies died out because they got too big for their pea-sized brains. The scientists will have a name for the extinct species: Cinesaurus."

Barry Hertz is film editor at *The Globe and Mail*.

ABOVE: Peepeelee and Joe Arlooktoo in their
Kimmirut, Nunavut, home on October 12, 2021.
(Pat Kane/*The Globe and Mail*)

Twenty-Two:
The true North

The Globe once portrayed the region almost as a colonial playground but now includes northern Indigenous voices
| **Patrick White**

I
n the opening lines of her 2022 feature "No place to grow old," health reporter Kelly Grant invites readers into a living room in Nunavut. There are purple curtains, a flower-covered cross hanging over an easy chair and an elderly Inuit couple, Joe and Peepeelee Arlooktoo. The couple want to stay in their beloved hamlet of Kimmirut. But Joe's advancing dementia and diabetes require constant professional care that's unavailable in the territory.

The Arlooktoos faced the same excruciating decision confronting many Nunavut families: keep their ill elders at home with inadequate help, or ship them to the alien world of the south to live out their final years. The Arlooktoos chose to keep Joe in Kimmirut. "It's important for the kids and grandchildren and great grandchildren to know that he is their grandpa," Peepeelee told her. "I want them to know where they come from."

Grant wrote the piece as part of a year-long series on why Nunavut has some of the country's worst health outcomes. She succeeds precisely where the paper has, historically, so often failed. Her work brims with northern voices. She eschews hoary Arctic clichés. She implores governments to do better for a population that remains woefully underserved.

It's a sharp contrast from the early years of *The Globe*, when writers used terms like "savage" and "heathen" to describe the Dene, Inuit, Innu and Cree peoples of the North – if they bothered to mention them at all. Northern Indigenous voices really didn't factor into the paper's coverage until the 1960s and seventies, when the excessive encroachment of oil and mining companies sparked an organized resistance. Prior to that, a casual *Globe* reader could be excused for viewing the North as a colonial playground for brave white adventurers.

"I guess you have to remember the spirit of that particular time, but it still riles me reading those stories," says Deborah Kigjugalik Webster, an anthropologist and curator of heritage collections for the government of Nunavut. "There will be an account of how great a northern patrol or expedition was, with no mention of the people – the northerners – who actually helped them get there."

Sir John Franklin was the first of these near-mythological characters to preoccupy *The Globe*'s coverage of the North. When his 1845 expedition to find the Northwest Passage failed to re-emerge, the paper lapsed into copy suitable for the *National Enquirer*. One story featured a clairvoyant in Calcutta who claimed to have seen Franklin during a hypnotic trance; another speculated that he'd sailed into Symmes Hole, a theoretical opening in the poles leading to the Earth's interior.

The first sensible explanation of Franklin's fate came in 1854, when Scottish surgeon and explorer John Rae met some Inuit families who spoke of ships crushed in the ice and a starving crew who resorted to cannibalism before perishing. The finding that these mariners of high station had descended into madness made Rae one of the most unpopular men in Victorian England; Charles Dickens mocked him and *The Globe* referred to him as a "charlatan." The Inuit role would be relegated to the margins of the Franklin caper until 2014, when a Canadian team finally located his ships based largely on clues from Inuit oral histories.

Those early editions of *The Globe* were fixated on another northern prize, this one directly from the mind of the paper's proprietor. George Brown had long pressed for an end to the Hudson's Bay Company's trading monopoly over Rupert's Land and the North-Western Territory, which stretched to the Rocky Mountains in the West and the Arctic Ocean in the North. And he wasn't afraid to use the paper as his political bullhorn. "The idea of confining Canada within her present bounds, in order that the Company may have its hunting grounds and trading posts unmolested, is too preposterous to be long persisted in," noted one 1856 article. Fourteen years later, Brown would get his wish. It was likely the first time *The Globe*'s influence had shaped the North, but certainly not the last.

The transaction put Canada in control of a remote western region known as the Klondike. On August 17, 1896, three people from Tagish First Nation – Keish (Skookum Jim Mason), Káa Goox (Dawson Charlie) and Shaaw Tlá (Kate Carmack) – along with Carmack's American husband, George – found gold there on Rabbit Creek.

The news took time to travel. *The Globe* caught gold fever a full year later: on a single day, July 28, 1897, the paper ran ten articles on the Klondike, stoking interest in a gold rush that would eventually attract tens of thousands of prospectors. "The world has never produced its equal before," stated one miner in an article titled "Letters from the Klondike." Another said gold was so common in the region "it seems almost as cheap as sawdust."

The influx of wealth-seekers tested Canada's commitment to the region. One August 1897 story suggested American miners were conspiring to claim the region for the U.S. "Before I left there was a strong feeling that the Stars and Stripes should float over the Klondike gold fields," said an American prospector. *The Globe* called on Canada to boost the government's presence in the area. Ottawa obliged, flooding the area with North-West Mounted Police.

The northern incursion had dire effects: epidemics of measles and tuberculosis ravaged Indigenous populations. Around this time, *The Globe* started to report on colonialism's toll but played up the growing role of alcohol in Inuit deaths. "The liquor obtained by Esquimaux was the cause of many murders among them, not a season passing without two or three during their drunken bouts," a 1903 dispatch stated in a disapproving tone. "The numbers of Esquimaux are decreasing very fast." Only later does the story mention that measles, not booze, was killing off entire Inuit encampments.

This arrogant approach to northern welfare would continue for decades. At the dawn of the Depression, one front-page story predicted "ultimate extinction" for six thousand Indigenous northerners due to "the spread of civilization." It was a typical article of the age, blaming Indigenous Peoples for dire circumstances created by settlers: "Measles, whooping cough, chickenpox, grippe and other ailments he gets from the white man himself, and yet he is most happy in his company."

Until the 1930s, the paper relied almost entirely upon wire services and southern-based reporters for Arctic coverage. In 1938, it sent columnist Norman Winston on a dream assignment: a two-month, thirteen-thousand-kilometre trip across northern Canada to file sixty thousand words in the form of daily letters. It was, and possibly remains, the lengthiest and most ambitious *Globe* assignment in the North. He spent most of his time in the company of white professionals and miners, offering a few brief descriptions of the Inuit. "They giggled and bobbed, standing around me in a circle and smoking cigarettes, while I asked them questions about the caribou migrations," he wrote. "They gave me the information seriously and politely, but kept right on grinning as though the white race were the greatest joke on Earth – and undoubtedly we are."

Along the shores of Great Bear Lake, Winston became enamoured with a silver, radium and uranium mine called Eldorado and the wealth that one hundred miners seemed to be pulling from the ground. He saw Eldorado, and the Arctic riches it symbolized, as Canada's path out of the Depression: "By opening a new frontier to city people it will help prevent, in Canada, the malignant growth of class hatred, the congestion of idle population, the tissue-destroying sickness of politics, from which the world is suffering today."

The Eldorado mine shut down two years later. It would eventually play a world-changing role – just not the one Winston envisaged. The government surreptitiously reopened the mine in 1943 to supply the Manhattan Project, America's atomic bomb development program. The bombs dropped on Hiroshima and Nagasaki were built, in part, with Eldorado ore.

A moral reckoning would come much later. In 1998, *Globe* reporter Anne McIlroy travelled to the surrounding community and found a cancer cluster among Dene men who'd worked as ore carriers at the mine. Their town, Deline, had come to be known as "the village of widows."

During and after the Second World War, the country rallied around calls from Winston and others to develop the North, to buttress the economy and to maintain Canadian sovereignty in the region. The completion of the Alaska Highway in 1942, which *The Globe* had long supported, along with construction of weather stations and Distant Early Warning radar outposts in the fifties, introduced the building blocks of Western society – telephone lines, pipelines, generators, prefab buildings. The government encouraged Indigenous groups to settle down in government-built houses, attend government-built residential schools and take government welfare. The societal costs of this cultural whiplash are still accruing.

In 1958, Prime Minister John Diefenbaker promised to institute his *Globe*-endorsed "Northern Vision," which involved heavy investment in transportation and communication that would spark a new era of prosperity. By the 1960s, however, it was becoming clear that while postwar government spending had changed Indigenous life in the North, it had not necessarily improved it. Through the sixties and seventies, that tension erupted into the pages of *The Globe* as a new generation of Arctic leaders sought to restore self-determination to northern peoples.

Perhaps the most sensational example landed on the front page of September 30, 1968, when an Inuvialuit university student, Mary Carpenter, accused Ottawa of turning northern peoples into "a servant class people, or slaves, take your choice." Speaking to the Indian-Eskimo Association of Canada, she said a government oil development scheme, Panarctic Oils, had only served to exploit northern land while employing fewer than ten Indigenous men.

"I don't wish to alarm you," she said in her speech, "but the facts are that the federal Government is doing exactly to my people, the Eskimos, what the whites have done to the Negroes of the United States." She went on to accuse the news media of falling for Ottawa's line that "the rape of the North is good for the Eskimo people."

Hers was one of many rallying cries for northern self-determination that led to the formation of Indigenous-led advocacy groups, such as Inuit Tapiriit Kanatami, Indian Brotherhood of Northwest Territories and the Council for Yukon Indians. In the 1970s, the groups fiercely opposed plans to build an oil and gas pipeline from the Arctic Ocean south to Alberta, forcing Ottawa to strike the Mackenzie Valley Pipeline inquiry under Justice Thomas Berger.

Berger would recommend putting people ahead of pipelines, calling for a ten-year moratorium on oil and gas development until northern land claims were settled. *The Globe*'s Martin O'Malley chronicled Berger's efforts to include Indigenous groups in the proceedings and bring the inquiry to every community the development would affect. "The North is the battleground of just about every cause there is today:

environment, development, pollution, nationalism, socialism, capitalism, energy," he wrote.

The inquiry would mark a turning point in the country's perception of the North, and the paper's coverage of the region. The usage of "Inuit" gradually overtook the word "Eskimo." Datelines from northern communities increased sharply throughout the 1970s and eighties. Indigenous northerners slowly moved to the centre of a story long dominated by white southerners.

By the 1980s and nineties, land claims came to dominate *The Globe*'s northern coverage. *Globe* writers detailed backroom political manoeuvrings along with the hopes and fears of northerners. "Nunavut's not going to change anything for the better: it'll be the same old world with the same old problems, probably bigger problems," one Inuk, Levi Palituq, told writer Scott Feschuk in 1994, a year after the settlement of the Nunavut Land Claims, which laid the groundwork for the creation of Nunavut in 1999.

At the same time, the land in question was changing. Environment reporter Martin Mittelstaedt wrote some of the first stories on polar bears starving because of melting ice conditions. Science writer Alanna Mitchell wrote an eight-thousand-word piece explaining the dire effects of climate change in the North. "The rivers began running and the lakes melting and all of a sudden, the ice fishing and the geese hunting was over," Rosemarie Kuptana of Sachs Harbour, Northwest Territories, told Mitchell in 2000, when the usual month-long spring melt, a time of bountiful hunting and fishing, had taken place in just two days.

The big thaw was also drawing increasing international marine traffic to the Northwest Passage, reigniting questions around Canada's hold on the region. "Canada has a choice when it comes to defending our sovereignty over the Arctic," said then–prime minister Stephen Harper in 2007. "We either use it or lose it." His definition of using the Arctic mainly involved the military: he wanted new icebreakers, five hundred troops based in Iqaluit, a deep-water port on the northern tip of Baffin Island and frequent Far North military exercises.

A few years later, I was among a group of journalists and dignitaries flown in to observe one of these exercises at Canadian Forces Station Alert. During the trip, *The Globe* dutifully reported on Canada's partnership with a Danish military dog-sled team, a record-breaking military dive and a successful test of cutting-edge thermal underwear. But nowhere in the paper's coverage – my coverage – was there mention of the people who inhabited the territory. It was an unfortunate lapse into *The Globe* of old. Here, in 2010, we were repeating the same sin of omission.

On the return flight, I sat next to future governor-general Mary Simon, then-president of Inuit Tapiriit Kanatami. She doubted the prime minister's promises and bristled at his "use it or lose it" philosophy that seemed to overlook a few millennia of Inuit use and occupation.

Her skepticism was well-founded. In a 2014 story, *Globe* reporter Steven Chase found that Harper's vision was a calculated policy decision, designed more to get southern votes than improve northern lives. At the proposed deep-water port, Chase found just a fuel depot and a rusty, sinking dock.

Simon and other northerners have long asked reporters to start writing stories about northern people, rather than prop up popular southern myths, especially those spouted by high-ranking politicians. We haven't always honoured the request but, after 180 years, *The Globe*'s recent coverage is placing greater emphasis on northern voices describing northern life.

No longer is the North a setting for Victorian adventure talks, its people relegated to cameo appearances. *The Globe* has no dedicated northern correspondent. It can't supply continuous coverage of local issues. But it can, as Grant demonstrated, invite readers inside northern living rooms to hash out big northern issues. Her work marks a high point in the history of *The Globe*'s northern coverage.

Patrick White is a reporter at *The Globe and Mail*, writing mainly on reconciliation and justice issues.

Twenty-Three:
The perfect shot

Decisions around what photos run in *The Globe* have been influenced by changing cultural values – and the always looming deadline | **Erin Anderssen**

At first light on March 23, 1988, *Globe and Mail* foreign correspondent Paul Koring stepped off a helicopter outside Halabja, Iraq, and into the scene of a nightmare. Once home to sixty thousand people, the city was now silent but for the artillery fire echoing from a valley a kilometre away. The buildings were battered by gunfire and bombs. At every corner, Koring saw death, the result of a gas attack ordered five days earlier by then-president Saddam Hussein against his own people, after Kurdish rebels seized the city. The bloated bodies of women, children and elderly citizens lay on the ground, as if they had fallen where they stood. A crowd of corpses rested in the dirt by a stone wall. An old man slumped in a doorway, half-embracing a baby.

The trip had been rushed. A dozen or so journalists piled into two helicopters flown from Tehran and were left to wander the streets of Halabja. Koring, working as both writer and photographer, had half a roll of film in his Pentax Spotmatic camera – eighteen exposures to record evidence of a war crime for Canadians back home. "I could have taken two thousand pictures," he says, "and not duplicated a body."

He snapped pictures carefully and tried not to dwell on the fact that their ride had flown off, with no guarantee of returning. By the time the helicopters came back, it was nearly dark and Koring, his film spent, was hiding in a ditch with several other journalists and a dying goat.

He had his story. But taking the pictures was one challenge. Getting them in the paper was another.

Over many decades, the decisions around what photos run in *The Globe* have been influenced by technology, changing cultural values, editorial responsibility and, of course, the always looming deadline. Especially for crime and conflict photography, the line between what editors decide a reader needs to see and what not to show them has shifted back and forth. What might be cropped in 1948 could have run columns wide on the front page in 1975, and perhaps not at all in 2023. Images merit careful consideration: someone opening *The Globe* at the breakfast table could stop at the headline. But the most powerful photos cannot be unseen.

In the years before Photoshop and deepfakes turned us all into visual skeptics, photos were seen as objective reality. A writer could make stuff up, but a newspaper photographer captured what was truly there, or so many people thought.

Of course, as *The Globe*'s historical preponderance of photos of middle-aged white men clearly shows, pictures are just as good as words at embellishing certain people and communities and disappearing others.

A newspaper reader never sees the photo not taken. They see the image that a journalist in a war zone snaps before his handlers arrive or his film runs out. The ones an editor decides readers can digest over breakfast at the kitchen table. The photo that's picked from a finite pile, burned in a darkroom, cropped on a light table, debated in a newsroom, defined by a headline, described by a cutline.

The war photographer who has to count exposures and wait for a darkroom will never capture the same scene as a peer who can catch a dozen frames per second and see them instantly on a screen. A white male photographer will not approach subjects with the same perspective as a female or Indigenous or Black colleague. Different editors will make different judgment calls. Readers will experience the image differently.

"Photography is the product of humans, not machines," says Thierry Gervais, a professor at the School of Image Arts at Toronto Metropolitan University. "It can only be historically anchored."

In the early twentieth century, as art historians Sarah Bassnett and Sarah Parsons write in their 2023 book, *Photography in Canada: 1839-1989,* pictures influenced how Canadians understood the country and the world.

An illustrated insert in a 1910 Saturday *Globe,* headlined "Types of new Canadians," showed immigrants at work and school, in keeping with the paper's economic leanings, Bassnett says.

"*The Globe* was trying to convince its readers that a kind of benevolence towards new immigrants was their responsibility," she says. "That's what's so fascinating about photographs. They're emotional and persuasive, and yet there's this sense that they're real."

The images that began to fill the pages of *The Globe* focused on industry and politics – men in suits shaking hands in Parliament or on the steps of newly opened factories. *The Globe* hired its first full-time photographer, John H. Boyd, in 1922, but many of the paper's pictures were little more than glowing advertisements provided by companies themselves.

The Globe has long relied on wire photographers and freelancers for foreign coverage, including during the Second World War. This likely explains the choice of photo that ran above the fold on the front page on May 8, 1945, the morning of Germany's official surrender. "This is victory," the headline trumpets.

In the photo, an unidentified Canadian soldier holds his helmet over his heart, his eyes looking off in the distance, his face and hands smeared with dirt as if he'd crawled out of a trench on the front lines.

Only inside, on page 3, does the reader learn that the man in the picture is Wilfred Nottelman, a soldier recently returned from overseas, who was found at the local YMCA and posed over a two hour-photo session at a Toronto studio down the street from *The Globe* newsroom. The brief paragraph offers no details of his service or background, no quotes from the subject himself.

He was chosen, the blurb explains, because "his features lend themselves best to the concept of a characteristic Canadian soldier." The front page has long hung in a frame in the Toronto newsroom. For *Globe* photo editors, it is a classic reminder of what never to do.

Deadlines and resources put a soldier in a studio in 1945; three years later, editors were prepared to crop the truth out of a *Globe* photo to protect readers' sensibilities. While interrupting a break-in at the Toronto Florist Co-operative, police fatally shot the robber, William Poole. *The Globe*'s photographer arrived at the crime scene in time to capture the full story. But what readers saw in the paper was the black safe and an overturned bottle in a warehouse room. The photo was cropped in half and airbrushed, erasing the sprawled and bleeding body of the burglar.

Roger Hargreaves, curator at the Archive of Modern Conflict, oversaw Cutline, a 2016 exhibit taken from twenty thousand *Globe* archive photographs donated to the National Gallery of Canada. Compared with the artful photo alterations of other publications, which might actually paint a face to change the expression, Hargreaves says that *Globe* editors in the 1940s to 1960s were "very restrained" in their edits. "They might enhance an eyebrow, but they wouldn't raise an eyebrow to change the expression."

They were, however, still far more liberal with cuts and cropping than the modern photo desk would permit. Moe Doiron, a former *Globe* photo editor, remembers going through the newspaper's photo archives from the 1950s and sixties and finding prints where people had been cut out with scissors, or two photos that had been glued together to make a single image. "We found many more fake pictures before there were computers," Doiron says. Now rules prohibiting that kind of image doctoring is "built into our Code of Conduct."

Having the near-unlimited ability to alter pictures afforded by modern technology led professional photographers and newsrooms to set clear guidelines. At *The Globe*, photos must not be digitally altered beyond minor corrections, such as removing dust or scratches, and photo illustrations must be clearly labelled for the reader.

Even using respected wire sources, a photo editor needs to be careful. Doiron describes a picture that went viral online that appeared to show Prime Minister Justin Trudeau rejecting a handshake from then-president Donald Trump during a visit to Washington.

"That just didn't happen," Doiron says. He compared pictures to the scene broadcast on TV. "It was just one second of one person being quicker to put their hand out than the other."

History is full of famous pictures that captured a single moment and became the story. For years, an infamous photo of then–prime minister Pierre Trudeau performing a cheeky pirouette at Buckingham Palace in 1977 was said to show the Queen walking away, bolstering its symbolism as a rejection of royal deference. Yet, as Canadian Press photographer Doug Ball later confirmed, the photograph actually showed Princess Margaret walking away.

Three years earlier, Ball snapped an iconic image that is often said to have altered history after it was published in *The Globe* – an action shot of Progressive Conservative leader Robert Stanfield fumbling a football. Ball explains he had taken a roll of thirty-six frames, including the candidate catching and throwing the ball with staff during a campaign stop in North Bay, Ontario. A photo editor picked the fumble for the front page. The next day, Ball says, veteran political reporter Charles Lynch sat down in front of him on the Conservative bus and announced, "Trudeau just won the election." The picture was not the sole explanation, but Lynch was right about his election call.

It's hard to imagine the twenty-first-century *Globe* reader letting this kind of editorial choice pass without comment – as Sylvia Stead learned during her tenure as public editor from 2012 until she retired in 2023. Stead had her own experience with subjective photo choices. In her first summer at the paper in the mid-1970s, she wrote a story about the controversy around a nude beach in Toronto ("Nudes scare families," the headline read). While the story says the swimmers were "mostly men" – Stead sheepishly admits she failed to recognize the spot as a gay beach – the paper ran a photo of an unnamed topless woman in the water.

That kind of editorial decision, says Stead, would have prompted a blistering reaction from contemporary readers, who have easy e-mail access to send both compliments and complaints.

Readers are especially vocal around issues of gender and race. One reader called out *The Globe* for a 2013 picture that focused on then–B.C. premier Christie Clark's legs while she spoke at a podium. That same winter another counted up the faces that appeared in a Saturday edition of *The Globe* and found that only two weren't white. "This seems ridiculous, and certainly doesn't reflect the Canadian population," the reader wrote.

Along with others, Stead began tracking gender and race in the paper's photos, breaking it down into statistics over several years, showing progress as concerted efforts in the newsroom addressed the issue of diversity.

Today, says Liz Sullivan, the paper's deputy visuals editor, photo decisions are framed against a new understanding of trauma, a higher bar for privacy and the care taken not to exploit people who cannot give their permission to be photographed. A photo, especially one on the front page, no longer remains on a printed page, crumpled and tossed the next day. Whatever images *The Globe* publishes now wander the internet, given legitimacy by the newspaper brand.

Sometimes, however, *Globe* editors decide the reader shouldn't have the choice to look away.

In 2015, a two-year-old boy named Alan Kurdi drowned with his mother and brother while crossing the Mediterranean Sea. His family were Syrian refugees trying to flee to Europe by boat. While other newspapers chose to run an image that showed a rescuer carrying the partially obscured body, *The Globe* decided to run an image taken by a Turkish photographer that showed the little boy's body on the beach, his face turned toward the camera.

"I am simply appalled at the front cover of *The Globe and Mail*," one reader tweeted. "Who publishes pictures of dead bodies nowadays? A child, at that?"

But *Globe* editors held their ground. An editorial explaining the decision acknowledged that Western media had become "increasingly squeamish" about showing the horrors of war and famine. "There is an understandable fear of upsetting the audience, and a well-founded reluctance to be seen making a market out of the suffering of others," the editorial said. "But some upsetting images demand to be seen. They show us the world as it is, its cruelties exposed, and not the world as we would wish it to be."

The picture, published in the middle of a federal election, prompted a public debate about the plight of refugees, as well as an outpouring of donations from Canadians. As Jonathan Rose, a Queen's University professor of politics, wrote in an online essay at the time, the unforgettable photo was far more persuasive than any logical argument or statistics. "It's not about the image," he wrote. "It's what the image does to you."

After landing in the dark in Tehran, Koring and *Washington Post* reporter Patrick Tyler found an old Telex machine in a cement factory and filed their stories. When Koring returned to London, he developed the photos. "I wired them over," he says, "and then we had this argument." Was he certain, an editor asked him, that the picture of the man and the baby had not been posed before he arrived? In the horror of Halabja, Koring argued, that wasn't likely.

Were the pictures too graphic to run? "Shocking photos of man's inhumanity against man shouldn't be suppressed. If it makes people lose their dinner, tough," Koring believes. In the end, *The Globe* ran the picture of the man and baby on the lower right-hand corner of the front page of an inside section a week later, accompanied by a longer feature piece on the gas attack. But the worst ones, Koring says, never appeared.

Would *The Globe* run the picture from Halabja today? It is a decision the paper would consider very carefully, Sullivan says. These are daily conversations, she says, that are informed by history, framed by modern-day values, focused by journalistic rigour and informed by the trauma a photo might inflict on some readers.

The Geneva Conventions, which dictate the treatment of prisoners of war, factor into a debate about whether to run a photo of captured M23 militia soldiers in the back of a truck in the eastern region of Democratic Republic of Congo. A picture of a rescue from a crumbled building after an earthquake in Morocco is selected so it doesn't show covered bodies lined up on the street. In Nunavut, a place long subject to pictorial stereotypes, *Globe* photographer Fred Lum considers what images tell the story of overcrowded housing without violating the privacy of the family who allowed a reporter and photographer into their home.

One afternoon in the mid-nineties, Koring returned to Halabja. He found what he believes to be the same doorstep where the man and the baby had died half a dozen years earlier and snapped an image. In the picture, a boy in a brown shirt and a girl with a pink barrette in her hair are raising their arms above their heads, smiling at the camera.

"In this horrific, God-awful place, there was a new generation," he says. That picture never ran in *The Globe*. That picture the photographer took for himself.

Erin Anderssen is a feature writer at *The Globe and Mail*, based in Ottawa.

ABOVE, LEFT TO RIGHT:
Paul Bernardo in April 1994.
Karla Homolka in July 1993.
(Frank Gunn/The Canadian Press)

Twenty-Four: Crime *and* punishment

As a national paper, *The Globe* focuses on institutional justice and this country's legal systems | **Omar El Akkad**

What was then the longest murder trial in Canadian history almost ended with the conviction of an innocent man. In April 1985, police arrested Guy Paul Morin and charged him with the rape and murder of his nine-year-old neighbour, Christine Jessop, whose skeletal remains were found three months after she disappeared from her home in Queensville, Ontario. A nearly decade-long criminal proceeding followed, marked by cascading incompetence and bias – doctored police notes, missing evidence, viable suspects ignored, key testimony withheld.

In January 1995 – after Morin had already been tried, acquitted, tried again and convicted – a DNA test fully cleared the man police were so convinced had done it. But by then, many Canadians had been made aware of just how sloppy investigators had been, largely because of the work of a single *Globe and Mail* reporter: Kirk Makin. Over the course of hundreds of articles (and, eventually, a book), Makin painstakingly detailed the flaws in the case, shifting public opinion to an extent that arguably changed the story's outcome. (In 2020, DNA evidence proved Makin right again when it helped investigators identify the killer – a friend of the Jessop family who took his own life in 2015.)

Makin's work provides a textbook example of often-glamourless crime and justice reporting, a beat that offers perhaps the clearest insight into a newspaper's inner workings. No other area of coverage has so frequent and thorough a convergence of journalism's most challenging issues: unreliable and often conflicting information, massive asymmetries of power and the visceral human reaction to violence. It is precisely because of these challenges that crime and justice reporting can become such a clarifying prism through which to view and understand a newspaper – its strengths, blind spots and the diversity (or lack thereof) of the people who write, edit and decide what's worth covering.

One of the defining features of *The Globe*'s crime coverage, almost since the paper's inception, has been a focus on the relationship between crime and institutional justice. The country's national paper believes it has a duty to examine not only the details of individual wrongdoing but how a nation's legal systems address that wrongdoing. *The Globe*'s crime reporting has led to some of the finest journalism the paper has ever produced – stories that launched national inquiries and helped get innocent people acquitted. But it is also behind some of the paper's failings.

In 1846, just two years after *The Globe*'s creation, founder George Brown was already using the pages of his nascent newspaper to call out institutional failings in the justice system. He detailed horrific conditions at Kingston Penitentiary, where even children were routinely whipped or put in solitary confinement. In 1848, Brown headed a commission on prison reform, whose recommendations included banning excessive corporal punishment and hiring professional inspectors.

Decades later, *The Globe* took issue with a different aspect of prisoners' rights, perhaps with less success. In the summer of 1935, officials granted early parole to notorious bank robber Norman "Red" Ryan – sometimes described as Canada's Jesse James – who had served eleven years of a life sentence and claimed to be a changed man. The institutional injustice in this instance was that the prison had allegedly denied Ryan access to years' worth of letters his wife sent to him. He received the letters only upon his release, by which point his wife had died.

"There will be few to find excuses for a prison system or prison officials capable of evolving and enforcing regulations of such dull and purposeless cruelty," *The Globe*'s editorial said. "So long as there is stupid brutality where there should be justice and humanity, this country's penitentiaries will continue to be crime schools, and not institutions for the reform of criminals."

But the sympathy for Ryan was somewhat misplaced. Less than a year later, he and an accomplice ended up in a shootout in Sarnia, where Ryan killed a policeman before being shot dead.

More recently, *The Globe* again called for reform within the Canadian legal system with a series on solitary confinement led by reporter Patrick White. Among the cases White covered was that of Adam Capay, a twenty-six-year-old from Lac Seul First Nation who spent more than 1,600 days – nearly four-and-a-half years – in solitary confinement after being charged with murder in the stabbing death of Sherman Quisses. A judge later stayed the charge.

"Canadians would like to think that, if a major crime is committed, our justice system can find the accused, detain them in humane conditions, lay the proper charges and carry out a fair trial within a reasonable amount of time," read a January 2019 *Globe* editorial. "Yet in the case of Sherman Quisses and Adam Capay, the system failed on every one of those counts. It failed the accused, it failed the victim and it failed Canadians."

In November of that year, Ottawa announced an end to solitary confinement in Canada – though whether the practice continues to this day under different names is still a matter of fierce debate – a story White and other *Globe* reporters continue to cover.

While *The Globe* can be lauded for taking a stand on the poor treatment of inmates, its crime coverage hasn't always been so high-minded. The lure of the lurid has often run through the paper's pages, from Ryan's killing to the case of Evelyn Dick, who in 1946 became the defendant in one of the most famous murder trials in Canadian history.

Police arrested Dick in Hamilton and charged her with the murder of her estranged husband, whose torso was found by five children on the side of the Niagara Escarpment. Dubbing Dick the "Torso Widow," *The Globe* latched on to the case's many sordid details – which included the discovery of a dead infant in her attic – and ran dozens of stories on the court proceedings, beginning with Dick's trial for the murder of her husband. "The cause of death could not be determined by the postmortem," a reporter wrote, "but it could be presumed that death was caused by injury to the missing head, the pathologist told the court."

In 1946, Dick was convicted and sentenced to death, but her lawyers appealed, and a new jury acquitted her. The following year, she was found guilty of manslaughter in the case of the dead infant and sentenced to life in prison. In 1958, she was paroled and, under a new identity, largely disappeared.

Coverage of the Dick case pales in comparison with perhaps the most notorious Canadian crime story of the past half-century, which began in *The Globe* with a page-one article by Tim Appleby and Donn Downey on February 18, 1993: "Man charged in girls' slayings." For many Canadians, it was the first time they read the name Paul Bernardo.

Bernardo and his estranged wife, Karla Homolka, would eventually be found guilty of some of the most horrific crimes ever detailed in a Canadian courtroom, including the confinement, violent sexual assault and killing of fourteen-year-old Leslie Mahaffy and fifteen-year-old

Kristen French. In the days after Bernardo's arrest, the case was marked by an unpleasant combination of saturated coverage, limited information and publication bans. That secrecy is reflected in myriad *Globe* stories; for example, when police made it clear that there was a second suspect but would give no further details, at least one *Globe* writer assumed the suspect must be a man.

In an effort not to jeopardize Bernardo's looming trial, the Crown issued a strict publication ban on the trial of Homolka, who had taken a plea bargain before a series of gruesome videotapes made clear her level of involvement. But that led to an even greater media circus. In one bizarre incident, hundreds of Canadians drove across the border to get their hands on editions of U.S. newspapers that listed details covered by the ban, while Canadian Customs officials – acting on orders from Ontario's attorney-general – confiscated the papers at the border.

It wasn't until May 18, 1995 – almost two years after Homolka was sentenced to twelve years in prison for manslaughter – that Bernardo's trial formally began. For three months, *The Globe*'s coverage, led by Makin, contained some of the most chilling details ever printed in the paper. Atop one front-page story in June 1995, describing the videotaped assault of one of the victims, editors published a rare cautionary note: "Readers are warned that they may find the following report on evidence presented yesterday at the trial of Paul Bernardo deeply disturbing." It wouldn't be the last time that note would appear.

On September 1, 1995, Bernardo was found guilty and sentenced to life in prison, ending perhaps the most graphic and traumatizing court case in Canadian history.

"Those of us who were together for the entire three months shared the camaraderie of trial veterans, if only because the things we know were often too searing to convey to friends and family," wrote Makin, who estimated there were forty-five or so reporters who covered the entire trial, plus another twenty or thirty who covered it occasionally. "Particularly in the beginning, the mind was unwilling, the tongue unable."

Crime reporting is, by its nature, community reporting. Even the most isolated violence ripples outward in time and place. In this way, nothing exposes a newsroom's wealth or dearth of experience like a crime story.

This became abundantly clear at *The Globe* in June 2006, after one of the biggest anti-terrorism raids in Canadian history. Late on the night of Friday, June 2, heavily armed officers swept up a crew of mostly young men who, it was alleged, had grand and violent plans to do everything from blowing up the CBC's Toronto office to beheading the prime minister. Eventually, the case would come to be known as the "Toronto 18," after the number of suspects. But on that Friday night, it arrived the way almost all crime stories arrive to a newsroom – a terse police statement, a burst of incomplete information.

The following day, news of the arrests made screaming headlines all over the front page of the *Toronto Star*, where reporter Michelle Shephard had been quietly following the lead-up to the arrests. In *The Globe*, it was a minor story on page 2 and didn't even make some editions.

Edward Greenspon, then *The Globe*'s editor-in-chief, summoned staff to an emergency meeting and began issuing directives: go find the ethnic papers in the neighbourhoods where the suspects live; talk to community leaders; find family members; do *something*. For the delicate task of assigning reporters to visit the mosques where many of the suspects were regulars, he looked across the newsroom for any journalists with a Muslim background, a Middle Eastern background, anything that wouldn't cause them to stand out like sore thumbs.

He found two people – Kamal Al-Solaylee, at the time the newspaper's theatre critic, and me, a twenty-five-year-old intern who'd been hired full-time exactly one week earlier.

The Globe found itself with a serious deficit of cultural competence. For several days, in stories about the suspects' first court appearances, *Globe* reporters repeatedly described the wives of the suspects as being dressed in "burqas." They were not; some of them wore niqabs.

In a front-page column about the arrests titled "Ignoring the biggest elephant in the room," Christie Blatchford argued that it was pure self-delusion to say the case had nothing to do with religion, when all the suspects were Muslim. "The accused men are mostly young and mostly bearded in the Taliban fashion," she wrote. "They have first names like Mohamed, middle names like Mohamed and last names like Mohamed."

I remember finding that sentence particularly ironic: my middle name is Mohamed.

In contrast, in February 2010, shortly after serial killer Russell Williams began confessing to multiple murders, sexual assaults and other crimes, *Globe* investigative reporter Greg McArthur learned while interviewing Williams's stepfather that the accused had attended prestigious Upper Canada College. While still on the phone, McArthur passed the detail on to his editor by e-mail. A minute later, the editor responded: "TOUCHDOWN!"

The Globe's editors – white, upper-class Torontonians – couldn't tell the difference between a niqab and a burqa, but UCC alumni were represented in the newsroom in such sufficient numbers that they were able to get Williams's yearbook photos in an instant.

When eight men disappeared from Toronto's Gay Village between 2010 and 2017, Toronto police insisted it wasn't the work of a serial killer – until they arrested Bruce McArthur, who eventually pleaded guilty to eight counts of first-degree murder.

As with Makin's work on the Morin case, the stories written by reporters Justin Ling, Tu Thanh Ha and others on the Village disappearances represented a dogged effort to spell out the truth at a time when policing institutions seemed unwilling to do so. Even as investigators tirelessly pieced together clues and interviewed witnesses, their work took place under the massive, centuries-old shadow of institutional antagonism against Toronto's gay community and within a department whose top brass went to great lengths not to use the phrase "serial killer," despite mounting evidence.

"Sooner or later, Toronto police will have to explain how an alleged serial killer was able to prowl Toronto for years while missing-persons posters spread across the Village," read a *Globe* editorial published after Bruce McArthur's arrest in January 2018, noting that most of the victims were part of one disadvantaged minority or another. "To wonder if those characteristics slowed the police response is inevitable, given the decades of accumulated mistrust between Canadian police departments and marginalized people."

Much of *The Globe*'s best crime coverage shares this same tragic strain of warnings unheeded, of signs missed, care not taken, catastrophe that could have been averted. There is perhaps no more impactful an example of this kind of work than Robyn Doolittle's groundbreaking 2017 series, Unfounded.

Over the course of twenty months, spurred by a victim's story and relying on dozens of interviews and hundreds of access to information requests to police departments across Canada, Doolittle compiled a stunning indictment: every year, potentially thousands of cases of sexual assault are labelled "unfounded" by police, essentially meaning the officers don't believe a crime took place. Cases labelled this way are, in essence, disappeared. Doolittle's reporting revealed that some police departments declare upward of 50 per cent of cases baseless.

"[What] has emerged is a picture of a system that is clearly broken," Doolittle wrote in a piece describing how she uncovered the statistics. "Change isn't going to come about immediately but there are tangible things that can be done to make it better."

As a result of Doolittle's reporting, police around the country initiated a review of more than 37,000 sexual-assault cases. Unfounded won two of the highest distinctions in Canadian reporting, a National Newspaper Award for investigations and the 2017 Michener Award for Public Service Journalism.

Whether covering such stories of systemic failure or cases of individual horror, *Globe* reporters have dedicated years of their lives to the slow collecting and detailing of evidence, the sometimes years-long process of attending daily court hearings – all to get the story right. In the muck of human misery, absent the thick veneer of media relations officers, the professionally vetted press releases and all the tools by which powerful institutions and individuals insulate themselves from honest accounting, crime coverage remains the most unadorned reflection of what journalism actually is – laying bare the character of both a newspaper and the society it covers.

Omar El Akkad is a novelist and former reporter at *The Globe and Mail*.

ABOVE: Sergeant Duncan Rowlands
scans the terrain as fellow soldiers cross
a stream while on patrol in Kandahar
province, Afghanistan, March 18, 2006.
(Louie Palu/*The Globe and Mail*)

Twenty-Five:
A view *on the* world

Since 1956, *The Globe*'s foreign correspondents have covered everything from
wars and famine to business and health
| **Mark MacKinnon**

There they were – and here we are – a gang of scribbling
adventurers, some of us deeply troubled, who believed our
writings could somehow make Canadians care a little more
about what was happening to human beings living far away.
Sometimes we succeeded. A *Globe and Mail* correspondent landed
with Canadian troops in Normandy on June 6, 1944, sending home news
of the D-Day invasion. Two generations later, *Globe* reporting from
Afghanistan shone a light on the complicity of Canadian troops in

prisoner abuse. Dispatches from the 1980s famine in Ethiopia and later from the forefront of the HIV-AIDS crisis helped spur incredible generosity from readers.

Occasionally, the foibles of the journalists sent abroad overwhelmed the rest of their mission. Over the decades, the newspaper's commitment to foreign bureaus rose and fell along with Canada's confidence in itself and with the financial strength of the newspaper.

How *The Globe* covers the world often reflects the ambition, or lack of it, of Canada on the international stage.

Though *The Globe* has delivered news from abroad to its readers for nearly all its 180-year history, the paper only began opening bureaus in the 1950s.

It was a time of international tumult. The Second World War was a decade in the rear-view mirror and the Korean War had ended in a bloody stalemate. A new crisis was emerging centred on the Suez Canal, and Canada, improbably, was the country providing answers, in the form of Lester Pearson's Nobel Peace Prize–winning proposal to create a force of United Nations peacekeepers.

Richard Doyle, then a reporter and later the paper's editor-in-chief, wrote in his memoir *Hurly-Burly* that the 1950s witnessed an "acute consciousness of Canada's rising status as a middle power, with unlimited natural resources, an established manufacturing capacity, and a friendly, even compassionate, interest in world-wide redevelopment."

The first *Globe and Mail* reporter to be permanently based outside Canada had a backstory few of his successors could match. The 1956 announcement of Philip Deane's hiring as the paper's Washington correspondent introduced him as the son of a Greek general who had been born on a troop train "and has more or less been on the move ever since." Deane's real name was Gerassimos Svoronos Gigantes, and later in life he readopted his family name for a career in Greek and then Canadian politics as Philippe Deane Gigantes.

After serving in the British navy during the Second World War, Gigantes's postwar career as a journalist for *The London Observer* landed him in Korea, where he was captured by North Korean troops. "For the next 33 months he suffered the hardships and tortures of a Red prison camp, including a 'death march' and a 17-day ordeal of brainwashing," read the August 9, 1956, announcement "*The Globe and Mail* goes to Washington."

Gigantes's work, and presumably his salary, were shared between *The Globe* and *The Observer*. In his 1976 autobiography, *I Should Have Died*, Gigantes writes that the two newspapers "made a deal" – partly motivated, he suggests, by *The Observer*'s "guilt complex" over his captivity in Korea – that allowed him to serve as the Washington correspondent for them both. It was also *The Observer* that had given him the "Philip Deane" name.

Gigantes was a creature of the *Mad Men* era he lived in – someone who perhaps would have struggled to fit into a more politically correct twenty-first-century newsroom. "What kind of jollies he gets from putting other people down is his secret. He has been known to wear spats on assignment, to strut with a walking stick, and to refuse to sit at press tables," Doyle regaled. Gigantes tired of journalism and set off on a new career in 1961, which would take him from a senior post at the United Nations to the inner circle of King Constantine of Greece to a seat in the Canadian Senate.

Editor-in-chief Oakley Dalgleish's decision to hire an outsider for the new Washington bureau ruffled feathers in the newsroom, but tempers calmed in 1957 when veteran Ottawa columnist George Bain became *The Globe*'s London correspondent.

Of course, Gigantes and Bain weren't the first journalists to report from abroad for *The Globe*. In the paper's earliest days, George Brown received dispatches from a London correspondent. During a nine-month reporting assignment to South Africa at the end of the Boer War, correspondent Frederick Hamilton was "present at every action in which the Canadian infantry has been engaged, and was frequently under fire," *The Globe* claimed in July 1900. Stringer George Ashton sent occasional dispatches from the battlefields of France during the First World War.

The Second World War, meanwhile, transformed sports columnist Ralph Allen into a soldier, after he enlisted in the Royal Canadian Artillery in 1941, and then a "*Globe and Mail* War Correspondent," which was his byline after he was honourably discharged in 1943 so that the twenty-nine-year-old could file reports while embedded with the Canadian Corps.

Allen was one of nine reporters who accompanied Canadian troops as they stormed the beaches of Normandy on D-Day. In a delayed dispatch that was printed in *The Globe* two days after the events, he described the landing as "a short, choppy run to the beaches and we make a wet landing on French soil."

Then came Gigantes and Bain, who were soon joined by others in long-term postings outside Canada's borders. In 1959, *The Globe* would open an office in Beijing (then known in the West as Peking), becoming the first Western newspaper to have a bureau inside Mao Zedong's China.

The Globe finally had a network of correspondents, based abroad and charged with describing the world to Canada.

A long lull followed that flurry of ambitious moves. Not for the last time, both Canada and *The Globe* seemed to pull back from international affairs. The 1960s and seventies were a time of dramatic developments on the home front, from Trudeaumania and the FLQ crisis to the Quebec referendum of 1980 and the repatriation of the Constitution two years later. Coverage of the planet beyond Canada's borders seemed like an accessory.

Interest in the outside world surged again in the late 1980s and early nineties, as Mikhail Gorbachev brought glasnost and perestroika to the Soviet Union, the Berlin Wall started to wobble – along with South Africa's apartheid regime – and even peace in the Middle East seemed within reach.

Flush with advertising revenues, Roy Megarry, *The Globe*'s ambitious new publisher, dispatched Oakland Ross to Mexico City and Michael Valpy to Harare, the latter to cover the unfolding drama in South Africa without paying taxes to the regime there. In 1985, former Washington correspondent Lawrence Martin bashed through the bureaucratic hurdles to open an office in Moscow, the capital of what then–U.S. president Ronald Reagan was calling the "evil empire."

"Roy was an adventurous sort of guy. I made the case to him that 'this is crazy, we're only covering one side of the Cold War,'" Martin recalls. He knew his Soviet government-assigned translator, cook and driver were reporting on his movements, "but it's not as if the KGB were in their glory days with Gorby in power – and I think the staff were picking up on that."

Between 1985 and 1990, shorter-lived bureaus appeared in Tokyo, New York and Los Angeles. And Bryan Johnson, another sports reporter–turned–foreign correspondent, convinced *The Globe* to let him open a temporary bureau in the Philippines, a passion project that saw him produce world-leading coverage of the People Power Revolution that toppled dictator Ferdinand Marcos, as well as groundbreaking reporting about Manila's child-sex trade. *The Globe*'s interest in what was happening in the Philippines dropped off sharply after Johnson quit the paper to open his own go-go bar in Manila's sex district.

In 1991, in the wake of the first Gulf War, Patrick Martin won a years-long battle to convince *The Globe* to open a Middle East bureau, in Jerusalem. John Stackhouse, a future editor-in-chief, created a unique beat that saw him based in New Delhi but focusing on longform reporting on poverty and development around the world. For a few years, *The Globe and Mail* was one of the most important outlets anywhere when it came to covering international news.

"People came to respect at moments like this – and the war in Ukraine is another one – why we have a team on the ground," says Patrick Martin, who served as foreign editor between his two tours of duty in the Middle East. "You build respect over the long haul, not by flying in someone very quickly."

Then came a recession and a new publisher, Roger Parkinson, and editor-in-chief, William Thorsell, who wanted to refocus the paper on its core audience – Bay Street's Report on Business readers and the politicos following every development on Parliament Hill. Foreign news became an expensive luxury, though the paper did regularly send reporters to cover the Balkan wars of the 1990s.

One by one, offices were unceremoniously shuttered, leaving only the original trio of Washington, London and Beijing, plus Moscow.

The trend reversed again after the September 11, 2001, attacks on the United States. Stackhouse, who became foreign editor in the aftermath, believed Canadians would no longer need to be convinced of the importance of events happening a world away. They had tragically seen for themselves why it mattered if a country on the other side of the planet fell into chaos.

Foreign budgets surged with the so-called War on Terror, under a new publisher, Phillip Crawley, a Brit who came to *The Globe* in 1998 from foreign postings of his own, having served as editor of the *South China Morning Post* and managing director of *The New Zealand Herald*. *The Globe* gave full-time coverage to the war in Afghanistan for a decade, with correspondent Graeme Smith living for much of that time in Kandahar, where Canadian troops were based.

Reflecting *The Globe*'s resurgent ambition, Stephanie Nolen, Geoffrey York and I were dispatched to report on the U.S. invasion of Iraq. A Middle East bureau was recreated by Paul Adams (whose wife was posted in Tel Aviv as a Canadian diplomat). Nolen reopened the dormant Africa bureau (based this time in Johannesburg) and delivered world-leading coverage of the HIV-AIDS crisis before moving to New Delhi and then Rio de Janeiro.

It was a thrilling, if dangerous, time to be posted abroad. Smith's office in Kandahar was raided in 2007 by masked gunmen, who beat up the cook and rummaged about before leaving without explanation. Nolen says she found herself "wandering around Mogadishu with my personal militia of fourteen-year-olds with AKs hopped up on qat" while covering Somalia's early 2000s descent into anarchy.

I became perhaps too adept at slipping across international borders, smuggling myself into Taliban Afghanistan (under a pile of carpets) and

Kim Jong-il's North Korea (claiming to be a historian studying the relationship between Moscow and Pyongyang). Years later, I used those skills in reverse to evacuate a source from Russian-occupied Ukraine and – with Smith's help and the support of Crawley and senior management – to bring *The Globe*'s Afghan translators and their families to Canada after the Taliban retook control in 2021.

Even in times of expansion, few women joined the ranks of *The Globe*'s foreign staff. Jennifer Lewington was the first woman posted abroad by *The Globe* when she was sent to Washington in 1984 – something she describes as "a struggle, though other newspapers had sent women abroad years earlier and to genuine battlegrounds" – but only a half dozen other women have followed in her footsteps. It's a problem *Globe* management says can be partly attributed to the fact few women on staff have applied when foreign posts at the paper have come open.

The second woman assigned to a foreign bureau, Latin America correspondent Linda Hossie, found herself caught in the middle of a 1989 gunfight between Salvadoran rebels and U.S. troops and saw a close friend shot and killed in the fray – an experience that friends say troubled her for the rest of her life. When Hossie died in 2020, her *Vancouver Sun* death notice said, "her successes were tempered by the frustrations she and other women encountered trying to make their way in a newsroom that still had many barriers to advancement by women."

Nolen – who now covers global health issues for *The New York Times* – considers it an enormous asset to be a woman working in the field. "I cannot think of a single time when that presented a problem. And I can think of a thousand times that it was enormously useful," she says. "From people not taking me seriously, people not finding me threatening, getting access to 50 per cent of the population in the Muslim world, which my male colleagues generally were not doing. It's just been enormously useful. Why are there not more women in these jobs?"

Even fewer visible minorities have been assigned by *The Globe* to tell Canadians about the changing world around them. At the time of this writing, all six *Globe* correspondents posted outside Canada are white men, albeit led by an all-female team of foreign editor Angela Murphy and her deputy, Belinda Lloyd.

Fixing that problem is complicated by the fact that the paper's international coverage has entered a new era of retrenchment, at least in terms of the number of overseas posts it maintains. The Moscow and Middle East bureaus are both dark. The Africa bureau remains, now staffed by York, making *The Globe* the only Canadian media organization reporting regularly from the continent. But no one followed Nolen into India or Latin America. Instead, *The Globe* increasingly covers overseas news with reporters who live elsewhere and parachute in to cover an event or an issue.

It's a model that's hardly cheaper. *The Globe* spends millions each year maintaining its network of correspondents and paying for them to fly to cover the stories of the day (including myself, based in London but travelling to report on events around the world). It's a system the paper's management sees as more suited to a constantly changing global scene, even as veterans of the craft see a danger in moving away from having correspondents based full-time in the countries they cover.

"If you don't have a commitment to the infrastructure, you're not going to do as good a job covering the trends and events," says Paul Knox, a former *Globe* Latin America correspondent and later foreign editor, who is now a professor emeritus at Toronto Metropolitan University's school of journalism.

Knox defends the need to have Canadians – who understand the audience they're reporting for – tell their country about the world.

"If fewer news outlets are doing their own international reporting on the ground, there's more reproduction of talking points from people who want to influence events – and at a certain point the policymakers are going to be driven by that chatter, rather than the reality of what's actually happening over there," he says.

The Globe is nonetheless bucking the trend by maintaining any reporters abroad. Many rival news organizations have shut down overseas bureaus. CTV announced in 2023 that it was effectively ending its foreign news gathering. For years, none of the *Toronto Star*, Canadian Press or Postmedia organizations have had offices outside North America.

The Globe is the only Canadian media organization with anything like a full-time presence in Ukraine, which Russia invaded in February 2022. The absence of competition and continuing downturns in the fortunes of media companies leave the future of that effort in question even as the war looks set to continue for years.

The October 7, 2023, Hamas attacks on Israel may prove to be a turning point akin to September 11, 2001. Like twenty-two years before, *The Globe* reacted by dispatching a large team of journalists – York, Nathan VanderKlippe, Goran Tomasevic and myself – to cover the eruption of a new war in the Middle East.

Just when it seemed that Canada, and *The Globe*, were on the verge of again turning inward, events half a world away dragged the paper – and its readers – back abroad, to see what happens next.

Mark MacKinnon is a foreign correspondent at *The Globe and Mail*, based in London.

ABOVE: From left, Thomson Corporation chairman Kenneth Thomson, publisher Phillip Crawley and Ivan Fecan, president and CEO, Bell Globemedia, walk through *The Globe and Mail* newsroom on December 2, 2005. (Kevin Van Paassen/*The Globe and Mail*)

Twenty-Six:
Hold *the* front page!

Two great newspaper wars – one involving *The Globe* – helped shaped the landscape of Canadian media | **Roy MacGregor**

An idyllic setting in the eastern Ontario town of Almonte includes a bridge over tumbling falls on the Mississippi River and benches beside the Trans Canada Trail that runs along its banks. One of them is dedicated to Val Sears, who died in Almonte in 2016. The plaque reads "The Most Powerful Words in the English Language . . . 'Let Me Tell You a Story.'"

Val Sears was one of the best storytellers this country has ever known. He was also at the very centre of one of two great newspaper wars that shaped the landscape of Canadian media. *The Globe and Mail* stood on the sidelines of one of those wars but was at the very heart of the other.

The notion of the newspaper war dates from the late nineteenth century, when Joseph Pulitzer, owner of the *New York World*, and William Randolph Hearst, owner of the *New York Journal*, went at it tooth and nail over the Spanish-American War, prohibition and presidential politics.

In the 1950s, Toronto experienced its own great newspaper war, when *The Telegram* and *Daily Star* each sought to triumph over the other. It was a period that Sears, who spent three decades as a writer and editor at the *Star*, captured magnificently in his 1988 book, *Hello Sweetheart . . . Get Me Rewrite: Remembering the Great Newspaper Wars*. Though he had once claimed "the *Telegram* was one paper that came with the garbage already wrapped in it," he later said that was not so. "It wasn't garbage," he wrote. "It was the fragrant leavings of contemporary history. It was the refuse of a battle between the *Star* and the *Tely* that consumed 10 years of our lives, some of our loves, all of our skill. And oh what a lovely war."

The mercurial newspaper baron George McCullagh of *The Globe and Mail* launched the war when he acquired *The Toronto Telegram* in 1946 for the express purpose of taking on "Holy Joe" Atkinson's *Toronto Star*, which conspicuously crusaded for social justice. The two men despised each other.

"The outstanding thing that brought me into this evening-newspaper field was to knock off the *Star*," McCullagh told *Tely* employees the day after he bought the paper. (After Atkinson died in 1948, the *Star* was helmed by president Harry Hindmarsh, whom McCullagh also despised, and then publisher Beland Honderich, whom Sears called "a tough, unforgiving man.")

McCullagh, who fought mental illness his whole adult life, was found dead in a pond near his home in 1952, having most likely died by suicide. His role as publisher of *The Telegram* was filled by a young John Bassett from the *Sherbrooke Record*, a newspaperman Sears described as "a big, powerful, wide-striding, high-rolling man, with piercing blue eyes that could make nuns and virgins wistful."

Globe and Mail city editor Doug MacFarlane became *The Telegram*'s editor, "inspiring in reporters an equal mixture of fear and worship," recalled Sears. MacFarlane's counterpart at the *Star* was soft-spoken Borden Spears, who would later tell a biographer, "I knew at the time what we were doing wasn't respectable. But it was so much goddam fun."

During this period, the fight escalated between the *Star* (circulation approximately 400,000) and the *Tely* (approximately 200,000). *The Telegram* mastered the art of the sensationalist headline: "Radioactive human roams Toronto streets"; "Boyd, killer pals on loose – police 'shoot on sight.'" It created entertainment pages and an "action line" column to advocate for readers who had run-ins with businesses. The *Star* expanded its classified ads to great success. The *Tely* pushed to get the first woman to the North Pole.

The two papers were profoundly different from *The Globe and Mail*, which stayed largely above the fray, focusing on expanding its business and national coverage. "Unlike writers on the other papers," wrote Michael Enright in *Canadian Newspapers: The Inside Story*, "*Globe* reporters shunned the personal approach to stories. A cardinal sin was the use of the personal pronoun in a story. The *Star* and the *Tely* thrived on the first person, I-was-there approach, thinking it brought the reader closer to the writer and the newspaper."

The *Star* and *Tely* fought over coverage of the notorious Boyd Gang's string of bank robberies and prison escapes. When seventeen-year-old Marion McDowell went missing from Lovers' Lane, the *Tely* brought over "Fabian of the Yard." With a young Sears assigned to accompany him, Robert Fabian, who had once headed up Scotland Yard's murder squad, drifted about the city and its bars, finding nothing.

The best tale of the wars concerned a young swimmer named Marilyn Bell, who was the most famous Canadian of her time. Only sixteen years old, she was determined to swim across Lake Ontario, a distance of fifty-two kilometres. As a 1954 promotion, the Canadian National

Exhibition had decided to sponsor English Channel swimmer Florence Chadwick in a solo crossing, but Bell wanted to race Chadwick.

They set out on September 8. At midnight, Bell passed Chadwick, who by dawn was vomiting and had to be pulled from the water.

Bell was instantly the biggest story in the country – and the *Star* had it, having signed a contract for exclusive access that included a *Star* reporter in the boat accompanying her. Bassett had turned down a chance to sponsor her for $5,000 and was now deeply regretting it. The swim was a sensation. About 150,000 people had gathered at Sunnyside Beach to await her arrival.

MacFarlane came up with a plan to dress reporter Dorothy Howarth as a nurse and have her sneak into an ambulance to interview the swimmer. The *Star* thwarted the scheme, whisking Bell off to a suite in the Royal York Hotel.

No matter. The *Tely* decided to tell her story anyway. Howarth wrote the account as though she were Bell herself. The front-page piece appeared over Bell's faked signature: "Marilyn's story – I felt I was swimming forever."

It was compelling stuff: ". . . the eels kept coming around me," Howarth (as Bell) wrote. "I could feel them. One of them fastened on my leg. I could feel its sucking mouth. It slowed me a little and finally I kicked it off . . ."

Years later, Bell would tell MacFarlane that "I liked my story better in the *Tely* than my story in the *Star*."

But the *Star*'s emphasis on growing revenue through classified ads proved more successful than the *Tely*'s attention-grabbing headlines. In 1971, Bassett folded the paper. In perhaps the greatest of all Canadian newspaper wars, the *Star* was the clear winner.

The Globe and Mail could not remain aloof during a later great Canadian newspaper war, because it was the target.

By the late 1990s, rising media mogul Conrad Black's Hollinger Inc. had taken over both the Southam chain, which included many of the major dailies across the country, and the *Sun* tabloids. Unable to purchase *The Globe and Mail* from the Thomson family, Black determined that his company would create its own national newspaper that would both compete with *The Globe* and dominate the national-news dialogue.

The idea was to build a general daily called the *National Post* around the existing *Financial Post*, which Black also owned. The *Post* would offer a conservative alternative to *The Globe*, which Black and others perceived to be too aligned with the liberal establishment. It would push to unite the right – at that point fractured between the old Progressive Conservative Party and the Reform movement that had risen in the West – and it would be distributed across the country through the facilities of the various Hollinger dailies.

Though Black considered it a favourable time for such an undertaking, others had misgivings. As former *Globe and Mail* editor-in-chief John Stackhouse wrote in his 2015 book, *Mass Disruption: Thirty Years on the Front Lines of a Media Revolution*, newspaper advertising peaked in the United States in 1999 at US$65.8-billion annually. Fifteen years later, that number had plunged by more than half, as emerging internet giants such as Google and Facebook captured the market.

Undeterred, Black acquired a brilliant young Canadian magazine editor, Ken Whyte, who set about assembling an all-star cast of writers and columnists, cherry-picking freely from the best of the regional papers. He hired Toronto's Christie Blatchford as the paper's general columnist, Edmonton's Cam Cole as its sports columnist and dozens of others, myself included, to cover everything from Parliament Hill to personal grooming.

It was a grand time to be a Canadian journalist. Those who initially balked at accepting Whyte's invitation were offered tens of thousands of dollars in raises as well as a leased car to change sides.

Whyte brought in a brash and nervy young Brit, Martin Newland, from Black's *The Daily Telegraph* to be his managing editor. Another recruit from the *Telegraph*, David Walmsley, would become *The Globe*'s editor-in-chief fifteen years later.

The first edition of the *National Post* appeared on October 27, 1998. The paper looked slick and smart. Alberta premier Ralph Klein pushed to "unite the right" in the lead news item. The paper was well designed and immensely readable.

A newspaper war was on.

The *Post* was bright and sharp and sexy. "Like Coke versus Pepsi, or McDonald's versus Burger King, the *Post* frequently drew *The Globe* into its wake, at least for a time," Stackhouse wrote. "Where Christie Blatchford went, [*The Globe*'s] Jan Wong might follow. The *Post* hired Rebecca Eckler to be its flirtatious female columnist. *The Globe* countered with Leah McLaren."

Cost was not a factor in the early years at the *Post*. Most staff travelled business class. Black and his wife, columnist Barbara Amiel, celebrated the paper's first anniversary with a huge gala held at the Royal Ontario Museum. They told staff that they could have an extra week off in summer to do anything they wished, so long as they wrote about it. (I took my son Gordon on a fly-fishing adventure.) When the Concorde took its final flight in 2003, the *Post* sent Blatchford to London to buy a multi-thousand-dollar ticket and write about the experience.

"It was really no-expense-spared from the beginning," said Michael Cooke, an experienced editor Black brought in from the *Vancouver Province* to work on the early prototypes.

The *Post* was unabashedly pro-America and was so anti-Liberal that Prime Minister Jean Chrétien's wife, Aline, banned it from 24 Sussex Drive. *Ottawa Citizen* reporter Chris Cobb documented those early years in *Ego and Ink: The Inside Story of Canada's National Newspaper War*, published in 2004. The new paper, Black told Cobb, "gelignited the fetid little media log-rolling and back-scratching society in Toronto." Once readers looked up "gelignite," they agreed that the *Post* had "exploded," not just in Toronto but across the country.

The *Post* had its detractors. Ottawa-based satirical magazine *Frank* called it the "Daily Tubby," a shot at Black's girth. *Toronto Star* executive editor James Travers described the content of the new paper as "tits and analysis." But it worked, at least for a while. As Cobb wrote, "the *National Post* knocked the 154-year-old *Globe and Mail* off kilter with staggering speed and apparent ease."

Cobb wrote that in the *Post*'s "hottest year," 2000, the new paper generated $130-million in revenue, compared with *The Globe*'s $250-million. However, the *Post* was spending so much money and giving away so many free copies that $190-million went out the door, an ominous sign.

Fighting back, *The Globe*'s owners had brought in Phillip Crawley as publisher. A Newcastle native who had worked everywhere from Fleet Street to New Zealand, Crawley was tough, creative and fearless. On the eve of the *Post*'s launch, Stackhouse later wrote, "Crawley held his first town hall with *Globe* staff, explaining the newspaper's finances and market position and warning that any breaches of confidence would be met with the offending party swinging from the rafters."

Crawley also believed that *The Globe* had grown stodgy and stuck in its ways, a self-inflicted victim of largely unchallenged success. He hired Richard Addis, a Fleet Street editor who was, as Stackhouse put it, "unapologetic about his ignorance of Canada," as editor-in-chief. (At one point, Addis asked senior editor Edward Greenspon, "Who is Wayne Gretzky, and why would we put him on the front page?")

The paper brought in colour in a break with its bland black-and-white tradition. Crawley brought back a proper sports section, something that had withered on the vine since the glory days of Scott Young and Dick Beddoes. Addis had the paper redesigned by London's David Hillman, who had a soaring reputation following his overhaul of *The Guardian*.

In the late summer of 2001, CanWest, owned by the Asper family of Winnipeg, took full ownership of the *National Post* and the rest of Black's Canadian dailies. Mere weeks later, on September 17, more than 130 staffers were laid off. The paper shut down its sports and lifestyles departments, leaving only columnists to give a sense of coverage.

Morale plummeted. The layoffs, a week after the terrorist strikes of September 11, were a body blow. Reaction to the changes from advertisers was so negative that the Aspers soon reinstated dropped departments such as sports and arts and lifestyle. Nonetheless, many of the paper's most prominent journalists began to leave, some of them moving to *The Globe*, myself included. By spring 2003, the *Post* was on its way to a $23-million loss. Circulation had fallen from a high of 327,108 to 243,000. Deliveries to much of Atlantic Canada were suspended. Whyte was told he was being "transitioned" out.

In 2010, Postmedia, a newly formed group headed by *National Post* CEO Paul Godfrey, assumed ownership of the *Post* and the other Asper papers, two-thirds of the sale paid for by a New Jersey hedge fund. With the *Post* reeling, *The Globe* began to rise perceptively above the fray. Addis was replaced by Greenspon, who recruited several new columnists. The paper modernized its presses, though its more lasting innovation was to transition to a revenue model based largely on digital subscriptions.

By the middle of the last decade, the *Post-Globe* newspaper war was essentially over. It had been fun for those reporters involved, though things never got as wild as the *Star-Tely* battle of the 1950s. For the owners at Postmedia, as losses mounted, it was no fun at all.

"The biggest factor in the decline of the newspaper industry in the last twenty-five years, not only in Canada, has been ownership instability," Crawley said in the spring of 2023. "Businesses that were once in good hands, like the Southam and Sifton families, were replaced by owners who lost the plot and destroyed value for readers and shareholders alike. *The Globe and Mail* remained successful because the Thomson family stuck to its principles."

Chris Cobb, looking back in 2023, finds it "a sad irony that the introduction of a new daily newspaper in 1998 caused a domino effect that has contributed to the death and decimation of so many others – and with it, an uncertain future for the role of all levels of professional journalism across this wealthy G7 democracy.

"Unintended consequences. Every war has them."

Roy MacGregor is an author and former columnist and feature writer at *The Globe and Mail*.

ABOVE: David Walsh, president of
Bre-X, in his Calgary office,
February 23, 1996. (Mike Ridewood/
The Globe and Mail)

Twenty-Seven:
Flagrant fraud, cautionary tales

The Globe continues to have an important role in exposing corporate malfeasance | **Rita Trichur**

I t was surely one of the clumsiest attempts ever to rewrite history. In 1996, Calgary-based Bre-X Minerals Ltd. spent months assuring investors it owned most of Busang, a mammoth gold deposit in Indonesia. But the following February, CEO David Walsh flipped the script. "Some have mistakenly thought that we somehow owned 90 per cent of this property," Walsh said at the time. "This was never the practical reality, nor was it ever a basis for the valuation of Bre-X stock."

Hogwash. Bre-X's previous assertions that it owned 90 per cent of the bonanza were exactly what juiced its stock. And when *The Globe and*

Mail reported five months earlier that Bre-X had lost its grip on Busang, Walsh repeatedly denied the story, doubling down on his majority-stake narrative. It wasn't until the Indonesian government forced Bre-X into a development deal that left the miner with a 45-per-cent stake that Walsh contradicted himself. But ownership issues were just the tip of Bre-X's $6-billion fraud.

Business journalism is often derided as boring – or worse, sycophantic. But an independent financial press is fundamental to the efficient functioning of free markets. Reporters are an important check on corporations, analysts and regulators by ensuring a free flow of information that enables ordinary people to make informed investing decisions.

The role of the press in exposing corporate malfeasance is particularly vital in Canada, where constitutional divisions of power have prevented the creation of an effective national securities regulator. And in a time when many workers must manage their own retirement investments, we need more than ever a functioning press able to identify and call out Ponzi schemes, deceptive practices and other forms of corporate fraud.

After all, the next time the press alerts investors to financial wrongdoing, one of those investors could be you.

In retrospect, it seems unfathomable that a rinky-dink miner run by a ragtag cast of characters fooled so many people into believing it had the world's biggest gold find.

Walsh and his wife, Jeannette, created Bre-X in 1988, and by the following year it was trading as a penny stock on the Alberta Stock Exchange. But it wasn't until 1993 that a chain-smoking Canadian geologist named John Felderhof helped the company acquire its first stake in Busang and recruited Michael de Guzman, a Filipino geologist, to join his crew.

Bre-X initially told investors that Busang could contain one million ounces of gold. But over the years that estimate ballooned to a whopping two hundred million ounces. In 1996, the company's stock migrated to the Toronto Stock Exchange's flagship 300 index of leading companies.

And when the company announced there was too much gold to mine on its own, Barrick Gold and Placer Dome were among those who competed fiercely to become its partner.

"It got adulation from Bay Street and, above all, from Wall Street – virtually without exception," recounts Douglas Goold, a former *Globe* journalist who co-authored the book *The Bre-X Fraud* with colleague Andrew Willis.

Retail investors, too, became seduced by gold fever. In St. Paul, Alberta, a town about two hundred kilometres northeast of Edmonton with a population of 5,200 at the time, an estimated one in fifty residents owned shares of Bre-X. "I've got the contract to build a 20-storey building for everyone to jump off of when Bre-X crashes," Jack Kindermann, a local electrical contractor, quipped to a *Globe* reporter in March 1996.

In fact, people everywhere were hanging on every twist and turn of the Bre-X story. "I was stopped in the street all the time and asked, 'What do you think is going to happen?'" Goold says.

The Globe's scoops – which included revelations that Bre-X no longer had a valid exploration permit or clear title to Busang – helped the public separate fact from corporate fiction. But not everyone appreciated the newspaper's unflinching coverage. "Your paper is anti-Bre-X," Felderhof told Goold in an interview in Jakarta on February 28, 1997.

Less than two weeks later, the Bre-X fraud began to unravel with shocking speed. U.S.-based Freeport-McMoRan Inc., which conducted its own sampling, couldn't square its findings with Bre-X's results. It called on de Guzman, who was in Toronto, to return to Busang to provide answers.

While travelling to the site on March 19 of that year, de Guzman fell out of a helicopter. His badly decomposed body was found four days later, and conspiracy theories began to swirl online suggesting the forty-one-year-old geologist had faked his own death because he knew the jig was up. It would later be revealed that de Guzman was running from the truth in his personal life, too, after secretly marrying four wives. His health was also deteriorating because of malaria, typhus and hepatitis B.

On March 26, Bre-X finally conceded that its gold estimates may have been overstated, tanking its shares. But rather than scrutinizing the company's increasingly unsustainable claims, the Ontario Securities Commission's acting chairman, Jack Geller, rushed to Bre-X's defence, lashing out at the media for creating a "feeding frenzy" that also hurt the TSE. He specifically criticized *The Globe* and the *Financial Post*, accusing them of engaging in an "orgy of speculation, printing, and even encouraging, the wildest surmises so as to keep the story on the front burner."

"I think the biggest challenge with Bre-X was the sort of home-team challenge," says Paul Waldie, who was one of the reporters covering the story. "Any time you wrote something negative about Bre-X at the peak of its market cap, you were sort of dissing Canada somehow."

On May 4, an independent audit by Strathcona Mineral Services Ltd. determined that Bre-X's samples were subject to widespread tampering. A separate report would later name de Guzman and four other Filipino workers as the culprits who salted the samples with grains of gold. "The fraud itself was so primitive," explains Willis. "They were grinding apart wedding rings and using that to salt the samples early on. Then they were buying river gold and throwing it in the bags."

Two days later, a *Globe* editorial called for the creation of a national securities commission, arguing that junior companies like Bre-X needed proper vetting before being included on benchmark stock indexes: "The first and last line of defence for investors is information. The more investors have, and the quicker they have it, the better off they will be."

Provincial governments, jealously guarding their jurisdictional turf, refused to cede that authority to Ottawa, though regulators did change some rules for junior miners.

Bre-X succeeded in bilking investors around the world with its bogus claims of bullion in Busang. It also earned Canada infamy as the Wild West of investments regulation.

The Bre-X affair was by no means the first time that a flagrant fraud caught securities regulators and the TSE flat-footed. Back in 1964, there

was an embarrassing scandal involving Windfall Oils and Mines –
another junior company turned stock-market darling.

Windfall exaggerated claims about mineral finds, including copper,
in Northern Ontario and then rode a wave of market speculation. Its
shares soared from 56 cents to $5.60 on the TSE, then cratered after the
company came clean.

In that sense, Bre-X was simply a new spin on an old-fashioned mining fraud. But because Bay Street's minders rejected other proposed
reforms to tighten oversight, another scandal soon erupted on their
watch. YBM Magnex International Inc. – an industrial magnet maker that
once had a stock market capitalization of nearly $1-billion – collapsed
in the spring of 1998 after revelations the company had links to Russian
organized crime.

YBM started out as a Channel Islands company with alleged ties to
Sergei Mikhailov, a suspected Russian crime godfather. After a complex
series of mergers and combinations, the company emerged on the Alberta
Stock Exchange in 1995 as YBM Magnex International Inc., migrating
to the TSE the following year. Former Ontario premier David Peterson
joined YBM's board, which bolstered the company's credibility and helped
fuel a cultish following among institutional investors and analysts.

But it all came to an end on May 13, 1998, when the FBI raided YBM's
Pennsylvania head office after the company's auditors raised concerns
about alleged criminal activities, forcing the OSC to issue a cease-trade
order.

That same month, *Globe* journalists Karen Howlett and Waldie, after
digging deep into YBM's past, linked the company to another Russian
mob boss, Semion Mogilevich, who owned almost one-third of its
shares, along with five of his associates. What's more, British police had
been investigating Mogilevich's alleged mob activities since at least
1994, and securities regulators in Alberta were aware of that probe. "It
spoke to how naive Canadian capital markets were at that time," Waldie
says. "Americans were all over it, the British were all over it and the
Canadians did nothing."

In December 1998, *The Globe* reported details about YBM's money-laundering operation, and in February 1999, the paper published another bombshell: the OSC and TSE received damning information about YBM from the RCMP more than a year before the FBI raid. On April 18, 1997 – the very day that YBM was added to the TSE 300 index – the Mounties warned regulators that YBM's financial statements appeared to be bogus. YBM's stock continued to trade even as the OSC received reams of corroborating information, including from a company whistle-blower.

The OSC sat on that intelligence and kept investors in the dark for thirteen months while squabbling with the TSE about who should lead the investigation. What's worse, regulators also gave their blessing for YBM to raise $100-million from investors. "It was a real black eye for our securities regulators," Howlett says. "They actually had information handed to them on a platter."

The YBM case – which should have been a watershed moment for securities-law enforcement – ended with five of the company's eight former directors getting a slap on the wrist. Peterson was among those who escaped sanction.

Today, most corporate fraud remains undetected because of relatively low levels of enforcement in Canada, says Alexander Dyck, a professor of finance at the University of Toronto's Rotman School of Management. "A national securities regulator would help," he says. The financial press plays a critical role in uncovering corporate fraud, he adds, noting that the reflex of CEOs, directors and even some external auditors is to keep misrepresentations under wraps.

Poonam Puri, research chair in corporate governance at York University, agrees that "an independent financial press is of utmost importance" in holding corporate Canada to account. Governments and regulators have multiple obligations. Retail investors have little time to scrutinize potential investments. "Business reporters fill this gap," she says. "They combine the expertise, capacity and reputational heft needed to get to the bottom of scandals."

———

Technological innovations are shaking up the investment industry. Online platforms enable retail investors to bypass go-betweens like investment advisers and brokers, while digital technologies have given rise to new asset classes, including cryptocurrencies. But securities regulators are still struggling to catch fraudsters who hide in plain sight, as illustrated by the collapse of QuadrigaCX – formerly Canada's largest cryptocurrency exchange.

Launched in 2013 by Gerald Cotten and Michael Patryn, the Vancouver-based exchange billed itself as an easy-to-use platform for people to buy bitcoin and other high-flying crypto assets. Quadriga attracted customers from Canada and abroad, some turning over their life savings. In 2018, Cotten boasted to *The Globe* that Quadriga had 350,000 users. Who knows if he was telling the truth?

The Globe and other media, however, had already started reporting on signs of trouble. Clients faced lengthy delays in retrieving their money, which the exchange initially played down. By October of that year, *Globe* capital markets reporter Alexandra Posadzki had the backstory: the Canadian Imperial Bank of Commerce had frozen several accounts belonging to Quadriga's payment processor, Costodian Inc., sequestering $28-million because it was unclear who owned the money.

After reporting this revelation, Posadzki became the target of a SIM-swap scam; criminals hijacked her cellphone number to access her online accounts. "People assumed maybe I had crypto as well," she says. "But I did not have any crypto, and they didn't get anything."

Undeterred, she, Joe Castaldo and other reporters stayed on the story as Quadriga's financial crisis spiralled. After bitcoin's price crashed that November, there was a full-blown run on the exchange. Then in December, Cotten died suddenly at age thirty from complications of Crohn's disease while on his honeymoon in India. By February 5, 2019, Quadriga was no more.

In the end, more than 76,000 former clients received only a pittance of what they were owed. The OSC later determined that Cotten operated Quadriga like a Ponzi scheme, plundering client accounts to fund his posh lifestyle and fraudulent trading that resulted in steep losses.

This time, the osc didn't chastise the press for exposing a homegrown fraud. *Globe* journalists broke scoop after scoop about this made-in-Canada scam, including the fact that Patryn was a convicted criminal formerly known as Omar Dhanani, who had served eighteen months in a U.S. prison for his role in an online identity-theft ring, and that Cotten had flogged get-rich-quick schemes since he was a fifteen-year-old high school student in Belleville, Ontario. "It was such a wild story because the characters were kind of larger than life," says Posadzki, who was one of three *Globe* reporters featured in a Netflix documentary about Quadriga.

As with Bre-X's de Guzman, there's been no shortage of online conspiracy theories suggesting that Cotten faked his own death. *The Globe* sent then–Asia correspondent Nathan VanderKlippe to India to piece together Cotten's final hours. He gleaned exclusive details from the doctor who treated Cotten and the police officer who ruled out foul play.

Bre-X, ybm Magnex and Quadriga are cautionary tales about the dangers of undetected corporate frauds. *The Globe* has covered many more over the years, including Livent, Nortel, Sino-Forest and others. The common theme in all these scandals is that people lose their money, but no one goes to jail or is otherwise seriously punished for deceiving the investing public.

Although *The Globe*'s journalism has spurred regulatory changes over the years, Canada still doesn't have a national securities regulator, which impedes enforcement. And whistle-blowers have insufficient incentives to report corporate malfeasance. Meanwhile, Canadian companies seek growth in overseas markets and the internet is blurring international borders – trends that demand better oversight and risk management.

Against that backdrop, a retirement-savings crisis looms. As workplace pensions become less generous, ordinary people are shouldering more responsibility to manage their money, including through investments. Retail investors in the digital age may have a wealth of information at their fingertips, but that hasn't made them less susceptible to scams.

Accountability journalism is needed like never before, even as the ranks of business reporters are shrinking across the country. "I worry very much about the deteriorating economics of the business press," Dyck says. "Our capital markets are better because you exist."

Rita Trichur is a columnist for Report on Business.

ABOVE: Flooded farms along the
Trans-Canada Highway near Abbotsford,
British Columbia, November 22, 2021.
(Darryl Dyck/The Canadian Press)

Twenty-Eight:
Shades *of* green

The Globe has often, if not always, been a fierce advocate for environmental solutions proposed by our best scientific minds | **Gary Mason**

When record-breaking rains fell on British Columbia in November 2021, Wayne and Rhonda MacDonald braced for the worst. It had been that kind of year.

Four months earlier, the couple watched anxiously as a massive wildfire approach their Bar-FX cattle ranch in the Nicola Valley, in the province's southern Interior. This was after another earlier blaze levelled the town of Lytton, British Columbia, on June 29, a day after the small community saw the temperature soar to a Canadian record 49.6 C. The BC Coroners Service later said that 619 people in the province died from the extreme heat that lasted from June 25 to July 1, the deadliest weather event in Canadian history.

The MacDonalds lost thirty-two animals and 70 per cent of their rangeland in the fire that raged through the Nicola Valley, but they managed to save their home. Others weren't so lucky. Wildfires throughout B.C. that month forced thousands to flee their properties and placed tens of thousands more on evacuation alert, ultimately destroying nearly nine thousand square kilometres of forest – about one-and-a-half times the size of Prince Edward Island.

Then the rains came. On November 13, an elongated strand of moisture-laden air – known as an atmospheric river – unleashed its cargo on the province. More rain fell over three days than normally falls in the entire month of November, destroying highways and bridges and cutting off vital supply links to the rest of the country. The damage totalled in the many billions of dollars.

In the valley, the Nicola River spilled its banks, swallowing two hectares of the MacDonalds' property, including a calving barn. The flood destroyed their irrigation system. The fire-scarred landscape couldn't contain the moisture, repelling much of it down mountainsides to create even greater devastation. A half-dozen neighbouring homes were washed away.

"We were so afraid of the fire," Rhonda MacDonald told *The Globe* in the aftermath. "But it was the flood that ended up taking us out."

If the country needed an illustration of what the future might look like as the planet continues to warm, it was on full display in B.C. that year. "Extreme heat, fire, drought, record rain, floods: It feels biblical. And it is all interconnected and made worse by climate heating," *The Globe*'s editorial board wrote on November 18, 2021. "Canada is heating twice as fast as the global average . . . the No. 1 thing to do is to reduce greenhouse gas emissions as quickly and as soon as possible."

Throughout its history, *The Globe* has chronicled the many environmental threats facing Canada. Beyond reporting on these events, the paper has often, if not always, been a fierce advocate for changes proposed by our best scientific minds, as the country and the world confronted everything from the use of insecticide DDT to acid rain and the growing hole in our ozone layer.

But *The Globe*'s position on some matters, especially climate change, would anger parts of the country, particularly Alberta, where governments accused the paper of being out of touch with the province's economic realities even while global fossil fuel production put the planet in an increasingly precarious position.

Others would point to the contradiction of warning about global warming on one page, while endorsing the latest proposed oil or gas pipeline on the other. The paper has often struggled to balance local interests and global concerns.

In the 1880s and nineties, *The Globe*'s environmental coverage largely concentrated on the proper management of the country's forests. The mentality of the time was to "clear them as speedily as possible," said a story on May 31, 1875, titled "The destruction of forests." But the story offered hope for a day "when their preservation and renewal will have to be as much a matter of public policy as of private advantage."

In the first half of the twentieth century, environmental coverage focused on the protection of habitat. "The United States and Britain both teach a lesson that may be studied with advantage by those who would open the way to timber and game pillage and expose our Northern heritage to needless fire hazards," said a 1933 editorial. Bison, whooping cranes and other species – even the iconic beaver – were all at risk.

The publication in 1962 of *Silent Spring*, a book by U.S. biologist and ecologist Rachel Carson, helped launch the modern environmental movement, with its warning of the deadly effects of the pesticide DDT. Carson's findings alarmed *The Globe*, which warned in a July 1962 editorial that insecticides "dangerously disturb the balance of nature and may release upon humanity more harmful forces than the pests they destroy."

In the 1970s, *The Globe*'s first environmental beat reporter, Peter Whelan, covered topics such as high mercury levels in Ontario lakes that contaminated fish stocks. Then came Victor Malarek, who warned in a July 1979 story that "as many as 50,000 Canadian lakes may be seriously endangered over the next two decades because of acid rain."

In many respects, the debate that enveloped acid rain was a harbinger of things to come with climate change. The federal government warned that industries needed to clean up their act or Ottawa would step in with punitive action.

Many corporations blamed pollution wafting up from the U.S. for the problem, but science didn't bear out that claim. "A report from the Great Lakes Advisory Board has estimated sulphur dioxide is responsible for $1.7-billion in health costs and $2-billion in architectural damage annually in the United States," a *Globe* editorial said in October 1979.

Eventually, industries on both sides of the border began drastically reducing toxic emissions, even as Canada and the U.S. established an air-quality agreement in 1991 to address transboundary pollution.

Along with acid rain, a growing hole in the Earth's ozone layer alarmed environmentalists and government officials. Scientists determined that hydrochlorofluorocarbons (HCFCS) – gases used in refrigeration, air conditioning and aerosol products – were damaging the Earth's stratospheric ozone layer, vital for protecting humans from potentially deadly ultraviolet solar radiation.

Then–prime minister Brian Mulroney helped spearhead what became known as the Montreal Protocol, signed in September 1987. As of this writing, nearly two hundred countries have ratified the accord, which phased out several gases that were depleting the ozone layer.

"We like to think that this moves us down the road to the day when industry and the environment will not be locked in combat, each blindly defending or promoting a set of interests," a *Globe* editorial said of the accord. The ozone layer continues to gradually heal and recover.

In the 1990s, the eyes of the environmental world focused on a pristine swath of old-growth forests on the west side of Vancouver Island known as Clayoquot Sound. The B.C. NDP government of Mike Harcourt announced a plan to allow commercial logging in almost half of the area and limit logging in another 18 per cent of the territory. The decision touched off the War in the Woods, one of the largest environmental protests in the country's history, culminating in the arrests of 856 people in the summer of 1993.

In a July 1993 editorial, *The Globe* acknowledged the balancing act the B.C. government faced between allowing commercial logging to take place and protecting virgin forests. However, the government "leaned too far toward placating an already existing local industry and not enough toward protection of an ecologically valuable resource." That said, the paper had little appetite for histrionic protests, stating in a July 1995 editorial that demonstrators needed to stop equating logging "with the rape of the environment and recognize it for what it is: a sensible, sustainable way of taking wood from the woods."

A compromise in 1996 saw the area in which logging could occur drastically reduced. In 2000, UNESCO designated the entire sound a Biosphere Reserve.

The protests at Clayoquot typified the growing phenomenon of aggressive environmental activism. Young Canadians in particular considered themselves guardians of the Earth, giving rise to numerous environmental organizations, particularly in B.C. The most famous was Greenpeace, which had its beginnings in Vancouver in 1971.

In one of its earliest expeditions, a boat crew headed for the Aleutian island of Amchitka in Alaska, seeking to disrupt U.S. plans to detonate five megatons of nuclear explosives below the Pacific Ocean. In a September 1971 editorial, *The Globe* called the protest "a useful gesture by a courageous group even merely as a means of drawing world attention to the Amchitka experiment."

The paper was also on Greenpeace's side when one of its vessels was rammed by the French navy in 1971 during an excursion to protest nuclear testing at the Mururoa atoll in French Polynesia. "We don't usually have much sympathy for Greenpeace, whose grandstanding tactics usually induce companies and governments to do the wrong thing (curtail the Atlantic seal hunt; scrap, not sink, a North Sea oil platform). But in this case, the cause is good and the tactics, so far, acceptable."

In the following decades, *The Globe* would often support Greenpeace's position on various environmental issues, while opposing its tactics.

The organization held a particularly profound meaning for *Globe* reporter Justine Hunter, whose father, Bob, co-founded the organization. In a poignant piece published in 2015, she talked about finally finding peace with the distant relationship she had with her father, who was so often away on one long adventure after another, leaving her missing him.

Ten years after Bob Hunter's death from cancer, Justine brought his ashes to Hanson Island, one of the gateways to the Great Bear Rainforest and a place that held a special meaning for him.

"I took a handful of ashes and swung my open hand over the waters of Blackfish Sound, and let go."

On August 3, 1970, *The Globe* published its first story chronicling the concerns of scientists about the warming effect of pollutants on the stratosphere. At the time, the paper was skeptical. "The effect of increasing quantities of carbon dioxide in the atmosphere (believed to raise temperatures by the 'greenhouse effect') has resulted in little climate change this century," the story concluded.

But as the decade unfolded, the tenor of those stories changed, warning with increasing alarm of the potential catastrophic impact of climate change. By the 1980s, scientists began removing all doubt about what lay ahead if action wasn't taken to curb greenhouse gas emissions.

Michael Keating remembers his first major story on climate change, published on October 22, 1983, under the headline "Greenhouse effect: what happens in Canada?" It ran on the front page.

"Experts predict parts of Canada will be flooded, others turned into dustbowls and balmy temperatures could moderate the bitter winters," he wrote. "Prince Edward Island will likely be cut in half by the rising Atlantic Ocean, but the Northwest Passage could open to summer shipping. There will be less water in the Great Lakes and droughts in the prairies."

"What I find impressive is how well they were able to predict changes back then," Keating says now. "It shows the science was already well established but had escaped public attention."

Between the formation in 1988 of the United Nations' Intergovernmental Panel on Climate Change and the start of 2023, *The Globe* editorial board wrote nearly four hundred pieces that mentioned climate change. Many called for domestic and global action on the issue.

But provincial governments that depended on revenue from the fossil fuel industry, such as Alberta, resisted aggressive action to cut emissions. There were some in the country who believed governments were creating a panic where one did not need to exist.

And as a business newspaper, *The Globe* often sided with industry over the contentious issue of pipelines. Over the years, the paper backed the building of plenty of them. In a September 2011 editorial, the paper threw its support behind the Keystone XL pipeline expansion, which would have carried Albertan oil to points south. The paper said that pipeline opponents, including then–U.S. president Barack Obama, seemed intent on "blocking something that will create a continuing and jointly shared economic benefit." An August 2013 editorial called the proposed Energy East pipeline "a laudable initiative, one that the Quebec government should see fit to back." A December 2013 editorial said "concern about climate change should not be a reason to oppose" the proposed Northern Gateway pipeline. Oil, the paper said, "is going to move, one way or the other," and the degree of risk of an oil spill should determine whether a pipeline was approved. All three pipelines were cancelled or not approved.

No one stirred more ire over *The Globe*'s coverage of environmental issues than star columnist Margaret Wente.

A noted contrarian, Wente wrote about Danish statistician Bjorn Lomborg, who questioned the "doomsayers" who maintained the planet was heading for oblivion because of global warming. In another piece, she wrote that serious scientists "have given up trying to explain why the entire edifice of global warming was an intellectual house of cards."

She had letter writers and bloggers up in arms.

In an interview, Wente stands by her columns. "Climate change and global warming account for more cultism and groupthink than any other issue of our time," she says. "Don't get me wrong. Global warming is certainly for real . . . but the hysterical doom-mongering and predictions of apocalyptic collapse are not science-based."

Some environmentalists were dismayed with *The Globe* for not taking a tougher stand on global warming. "On climate change, I would suggest that *The Globe* has . . . erred on the side of politics and short-term economic agendas over the science and urgency," says Tzeporah Berman, co-founder of Stand.earth and one of the world's leading climate activists.

The climate-related calamities that hit B.C. in 2021 gave the country a look at what the future might hold if the planet continues to warm at current rates. The MacDonalds of the Bar-FX ranch in the Nicola Valley emerged from the year alive but faced difficult questions about a way forward. Did they even want to stay where they lived?

Others faced the same dilemma, as they struggled to come to terms with surroundings that were now completely different.

"I saw in people, especially older folks, a kind of mournful disorientation with the world around them," recalls *Globe* reporter Nancy Macdonald, who covered all three 2021 climate-related disasters in B.C. "I later learned there is a term for this – 'solastalgia' – which was coined by Australian philosopher Glenn Albrecht. It is a form of homesickness one gets when one is still home, but the environment has been altered and feels unfamiliar."

We may all feel solastalgic in the years ahead, as climate change renders our world more unrecognizable by the day.

Gary Mason is a national affairs columnist at *The Globe and Mail*, based in Vancouver.

TOP: Demonstrators on Parliament Hill protest the War Measures Act, October 18, 1970. (Peter Bregg/The Canadian Press)

BOTTOM: Police remove blockading protesters opposed to vaccine mandates at the Ambassador Bridge in Windsor, Ontario, February 12, 2022. (Barbara Davidson/*The Globe and Mail*)

Twenty-Nine:
The subject *who* is truly loyal . . .

The story of Junius at *The Globe*
| Tony Keller

"T he subject who is truly loyal to the Chief Magistrate will neither advise nor submit to arbitrary measures – Junius."

Those words first appeared on the front page of the first edition of *The Globe*, on March 5, 1844, and they've been in the paper ever since, now on the editorial page. Junius is, and always has been, the notional author of the newspaper's unsigned editorials.

George Brown chose those words, and that author, because they spoke to his beliefs about the dividing line between legitimate government and illegitimate rule. The original Junius was an eighteenth-century British Whig who wrote under a pseudonym to avoid winding up in court, or jail, for his broadsides against the British government of the day and what he saw as its abuse of power against the rights of Parliament and the people. In Canada, where the burning issue of 1844 was whether the country would get responsible government – government accountable to Parliament – Junius's dictum must have struck Brown as particularly apt.

The governor-general of the Province of Canada at the time, Sir Charles Metcalfe, was attempting to govern without the support of the majority in the colony's legislature. For Brown, it meant that the Crown's representative in Canada was claiming powers that the Crown in Britain had long ago surrendered to Parliament. However, Upper Canada's Tories were supportive of the governor, and he of them. They accused opponents of being radicals and revolutionaries, disloyal to Canada and Britain.

Brown would become famous for his editorials (many, in fact, penned by his younger brother, Gordon), which bulldozed opponents with a torrent of logic, facts and, often, mockery. But before he published his first *Globe* editorial, he came up with an editorial motto whose meaning readers would have grasped instantly, at least in 1844.

Brown used the original Junius's words to say that if anyone was loyal, it was Junius of *The Globe* – and if anyone was disloyal, it was the governor and the Tories. Ruling without the support of the representatives of the people was unconstitutional in Britain, so how could it be desirable in British North America? The subject who was truly loyal would not consent to arbitrary government, nor would he advise the Crown to govern arbitrarily. Yet arbitrary government is what the governor and the Tories were advising and practising. In such circumstances, what was true loyalty? Opposition.

"Let me exhort and conjure you," the original Junius had warned readers in 1772, "never to suffer an invasion of your political constitution, however minute the instance may appear, to pass by, without a determined, persevering resistance." He said the best protection against such invasions was a free press – "the palladium of all the civil, political and religious rights." That made newspapering, and editorial writing, not just a business for Brown but a high calling.

In the years before Confederation, Junius became Upper Canada's leading voice for free trade with the United States (but firmly against talk of annexation); British-style parliamentary government (but not American-style Jacksonian democracy, with its elected upper house and elected judges); separation of church and state (opposed by Anglicans and Catholics); representation by population (opposed by Quebec, which feared the growing English-speaking majority); and joining the Atlantic provinces, British Columbia and the vast territories of the Hudson's Bay Company to Canada (ditto).

Junius had big dreams, but Canada's two decades before Confederation were marked by political paralysis because of seemingly irreconcilable "racial" differences between French and English. Some said separation was the answer; Junius called that "the advice of the coward." Separation would landlock Ontario and "place our foreign commerce at the mercy of Brother Jonathan" – an earlier personification for Uncle Sam – "and Jean Baptiste." And a divided Canada, lacking "the strength to command respect," risked being swallowed by the U.S.

"To be a great state, we must continue our alliance with Lower Canada," insisted Junius. But how? The answer Junius came to embrace was federalism. Federalism made Confederation possible.

On July 1, 1867, Junius celebrated the new Dominion of Canada. The editorial was the only thing on the front page, and its nine columns of dense type consumed page 2 and turned to page 3. In nine thousand words, written by Brown himself, Junius laid out Canada's possibilities – which, in a particularly Canadian move, he saw in America's reflection.

The Dominion Day editorial offered a compendium of comparisons between the infant America of 1776 and a nascent Canada in 1867. The United States had gone from fragile experiment to continent-spanning colossus – could not Canada do the same? Canada already had "a population greater than that with which the United States began their career ninety years ago," and like the U.S. could one day extend all the way to the Pacific. Junius saw a future of "teeming millions who in ages to come will people the Dominion of Canada from ocean to ocean."

In the run-up to Confederation, Junius and Brown alienated French Canadians and Catholics with strident calls for secular schools and rep-by-pop, yet they also learned to compromise, even on big issues, in pursuit of the larger goal of a greater country. And for the next century and a half, keeping that country whole, by balancing competing desires across the sectional divide, remained top of mind for Junius. Sometimes Junius found the balance. Sometimes not.

On the North-West Rebellion of 1885, Junius was sympathetic to the plight of the Métis, arguing that the Conservative government of Sir John A. Macdonald had ignored their legitimate claims, year after year, leaving them no choice but to take up arms.

With Louis Riel on trial, the headline on a July 27, 1885, editorial was "One criminal tried by a greater." On October 7: "Blame the real criminal." And on October 24, after Riel was sentenced to hang, Junius wrote: "The responsibility for the rebellion, and for all the bloodshed in the North-West, rests upon SIR JOHN MACDONALD." Junius called the PM "the first criminal in this case" and "the greatest criminal, because his cold-blooded criminality was the cause of all the crimes of all these unfortunate Metis."

Attacking Macdonald and the Conservatives was par for the course for *The Globe* of that era, for it was not just a liberal paper but a Liberal paper. Nevertheless, these were remarkably strong words, and many readers would not have appreciated them. Junius took a position in line with that of most French Canadians – who were outraged by the treatment of the mostly francophone and Catholic Métis – but against majority opinion in mostly Protestant English Canada, particularly in deeply Orange Toronto.

Junius wasn't always so solicitous of the francophone minority. When Ontario brought in Regulation 17, forcing French speakers to go to school mostly in English, Junius was supportive. In an editorial on February 26, 1916, Junius said that *Le Devoir* founder Henri Bourassa, by demanding "the principle of equality of rights for both races all over the land," was trying to create "a racial cleavage." Junius argued that forcing French children into English classrooms was for their own good.

"Quebec is likely to be bilingual for all time but Ontario is firmly resolved to maintain English as the official language."

By the early 1960s, Junius worried that "Canada must surely be the first nation in history that courted elimination because its citizens could not work up the interest to keep it alive." Junius wondered if Canadians might be "perfectly willing to submerge their Canadianhood in the great nation to the south, and add a few more stars to Old Glory in place of the Canadian flag they never got around to creating."

But as for that new flag, Junius was opposed. He called Prime Minister Lester Pearson's push to replace the Red Ensign "a silly issue" that risked igniting conflict. When the conflict caught fire, Junius was not surprised: the prime minister had "chosen to press the divisive issue of a national flag at a time when emotions are already deeply stirred by the question of national unity – or rather, by the lack of unity."

Through the winter and spring of 1964, Junius urged Pearson to drop the flag business. Then as the debate reached a peak, Junius reversed position. Recognizing the danger of an unbridgeable gap being opened between French and English, Junius asked the opposition Conservatives, and no doubt many *Globe* readers, to make a gesture of reconciliation, and back a new flag. Why? Because "they must concede that they have no real alternative to a flag designed around the maple leaf. French-speaking Canada can no more be persuaded to accept a flag in which the Union Jack is the dominant symbol than English-speaking Canada could be persuaded to acknowledge a flag in which the fleur-de-lis was pre-eminent . . . if we have to choose a flag at this time – and the Government is forcing the choice – we must look for a symbol that is offensive to none and acceptable to all."

Junius also weighed in as Canada fought two era-defining federal elections on free trade with the United States, in 1911 and 1988. In both, Junius backed free trade as economically beneficial. In both, the opposition attacked free trade as an assault on Canada's essence.

In 1911, the Conservatives argued that the soul of Canada – which for many Canadians of that era meant Britishness and the imperial connection – would be undone by free trade. Rudyard Kipling, in a letter published in *The Montreal Star*, argued that "it is her own soul that Canada risks." Junius disagreed, but Junius's side lost.

Three-quarters of a century later, Britishness was no longer part of the catechism of sacred Canadianess, but the claim that the nation's immortal soul was in peril was still central to the anti-free-trade campaign, now led by the Liberals. Four days before the vote, on November 17, 1988, Junius wrote:

> We had thought, perhaps naively, that the debate would turn on economic matters – benefits and losses under free trade (for of course there will be some of both), the quality of future jobs, the consequences for different regions and the like. Instead, Canadians listening to the debate have been told that their medicare system will be destroyed . . . Frightened old people have been told their pensions are at risk . . . Radioactive waste will be dumped in Saskatchewan, and on and on.
>
> All these things are possible in an imperfect world, of course – so are floods, killer bees and the heartbreak of psoriasis – but none will be caused by the free-trade agreement. John Turner, Ed Broadbent, hysterical editorialists and the plaster saints of our cultural world have a lot to answer for here.

But the plaster saints did not carry the day. Junius celebrated and highlighted what would not change: "The Conservative victory does not, however, transform Canada into a Thatcherite or Reaganite society. Canada has its own dynamics which put a premium on consensus, a feeling of community and concern for those in need. These values are deeply rooted and entirely consistent with a vigorous market economy."

For more than sixteen years, I was Junius, or a Junius, as an editorial writer from 1991 to 1999 and the editorials editor – *Junius inter pares?* – from 2013 to 2022. Writing an editorial – they run about seven hundred words these days – is as much about what you say as what you leave out. The latter is the hardest part. In this essay, I have of necessity left out much.

I don't want to go without mentioning Junius's most famous turn of phrase – that the state has "no right or duty to creep into the bedrooms of the nation" – which Pierre Trudeau lifted, edited and improved to: "There's no place for the state in the bedrooms of the nation." Or how Junius backed conscription in both world wars, which was in line with military necessity and the wishes of most voters in English Canada but put near-fatal strains on national unity. Or how a sincere liberalism had Junius favouring alcohol prohibition in the early twentieth century but backing marijuana legalization in the twenty-first century.

And then there's the fact that early Junius, though a moderate in most things, was a radical who brooked no compromises when it came to slavery. In 1849, he urged Canadians to welcome freedom seekers from the U.S. because, though Canada was poor, "we are possessed of a jewel more valuable than all the riches in the world, and that we present to many a poor and wearied fellow man – the jewel of *freedom*. These treasures we can give without limit."

Reading through 180 years of editorials, I've been struck by how often history repeats and rhymes, and how events separated by generations often trod well-worn paths that, for Junius, raised recurring concerns.

Consider the invocation of the War Measures Act in 1970 and the use of the Emergencies Act in 2022. I was in Junius's chair for the latter, and when I went back and read *The Globe*'s editorials from the fall of 1970, I discovered that an earlier Junius had wrestled with the same questions, gone through a similar thought process and reached similar conclusions.

After FLQ terrorists kidnapped James Cross in 1970 Junius urged the Pierre Trudeau government to safeguard public figures and public order. The FLQ had been carrying out terror bombings for years, and documents had earlier been discovered showing plans for a kidnapping campaign. Why had Ottawa not acted sooner, and why was it not moving more forcefully to uphold the law?

Junius took a similar position in 2022 with regard to blockades at the borders: of course they were illegal, and government and police had to put an end to them. "Protest is a legal right," said the headline of the

February 4 editorial, "but a blockade isn't a legal protest." Junius has often been that Canadian paradox, the law-and-order liberal.

But when Ottawa in 1970 went from inaction to the most drastic action – invoking the War Measures Act – Junius had reservations. "Only if we can believe that the Government has evidence that the FLQ is strong enough and sufficiently armed to escalate the violence that it has spawned for seven years now," wrote Junius on October 17, the day after invocation, "only if we can believe that it is virulent enough to infect other areas of society, only then can the Government's assumption of incredible powers be tolerated." Junius extended the government some initial benefit of the doubt, but day by day raised the degree of doubt.

In 2022, Junius similarly questioned whether the government was overreacting and abusing the law. "The Parliament Hill park-in has been a long, loud, illegal imposition on Ottawa residents," said the editorial of February 16. "But a bunch of parked vehicles and drivers in hot tubs is not exactly an existential threat to the country."

Two days later, Junius asked, "If COVID-19 didn't clear the bar for the Emergencies Act, does this?" After three days more, pointing to the dubious suspension of habeas corpus in 1970, Junius described the freezing of bank accounts in 2022 as "a suspension of financial habeas corpus. Is that constitutional? Is it something Canadians want?"

The words on the masthead, already old when George Brown borrowed them, are still fresh.

Tony Keller is a columnist for Report on Business.

ABOVE: Publisher George McCullagh
and his wife christen the *Globe and
Mail*'s new airplane, known as "The
Flying Newsroom," June 10, 1937.
(John H. Boyd/*The Globe and Mail*)

Thirty:
The unlikely country

Canada is as impossible to describe as it is to cover. *The Globe* keeps trying.

| Ian Brown

Which is the greater miracle: that *The Globe and Mail* has lasted 180 years as Canada's self-styled national newspaper, or that a country as unlikely as this (vast and varied and frozen and underpopulated) ever came to be, never mind survived? Both prospects were long bets. But this we can say: one wouldn't have existed without the other, not in the form they take today. Canada has always been as improbable as the challenge of covering it.

The parallels between the two endeavours are almost spooky. As has been made sparklingly clear in this series of essays, George Brown, the founder of *The Globe*, was an impatient, stubborn, bull-headed thrasher whose ambitions for his four-page, 1844 weekly paralleled – or were at least congenitally intermixed with – his hopes for the nascent country he had emigrated to from class-locked Scotland.

Brown's bombastic editorship of *The Globe* was described by a contemporary as a "long reign of literary terror." (It wasn't the last one either.) But he had a vision. He instinctively understood that a new, bursting, eager-to-expand town – one that had been controlled for too long by a small and wealthy establishment known as the Family Compact – was fertile ground for a fresh and rambunctious newspaper. *The New York Times* had a similar mission, but Brown's *Globe* – started at a cost of £250 then, or about $68,000 in 2023 dollars – predated the *Times* by seven years. Brown was always ahead of the mainstream.

Toronto in 1844 was still a hick town, with a tenth of the population of New York. Water was still sold door to door. Gaslight was only just being installed, and electric power was unknown (though *The Globe*'s editorials would later be instrumental in the creation of Ontario Hydro). Railways were little more than a promise: goods and people got around by stagecoach – that is, if there was a plank road for the stagecoach to follow, a luxury that in 1844 still didn't extend to nearby Hamilton. "Local" was the only purview to be had.

Toronto was all future, a newly incorporated city of under twenty thousand souls. In the ensuing four decades, that number quadrupled. *The Globe*'s circulation jumped quickly, from an initial run of three hundred for its first weekly edition to 2,300 within three months. By the time *The Globe* went daily in 1853, with a circulation of six thousand, it was the largest local newspaper in British North America.

How did that happen? As John Ibbitson makes very clear in his essay about the paper's founder, Brown – as was the practice in journalism at the time – had zero compunction about using *The Globe* to further his Reform (now Liberal) Party campaigns against his archenemy, Sir John A. Macdonald, the leader of the Conservative Party. *The Globe and Mail* styles itself today as the daily read of ambitious professionals and high-end executives, the paper of the establishment. But at the outset, it was the rag of the upstarts, the runty but ardent organ of Brown's English-speaking, pro-British, righteously Presbyterian ilk. Its strong views appealed to the yearning middle classes, stoking their resentments and justifying their acquisitiveness.

Brown hitched his newspaper to two novel developments in the Province of Canada. The first was new technology. Brown was Canada's earliest early adopter. Within three years of *The Globe*'s founding, Brown was publishing telegraph news from as far away as Buffalo, in upstate New York. The telegraph shifted public consciousness then the way the internet has challenged the mainstream media today: it made the world at once bigger and smaller and more reactive. This was especially true in wildly underpopulated Canada, where annexation by the Americans was still widely feared and occasionally threatened (as was the case during their Civil War). Connected to the larger world via telegraph, *The Globe* would warn us if the Yankees were coming.

The other mainstay of Brown's *Globe* was his non-stop campaign for a larger and more diversified (that is, less centralized and less protectionist, more business-friendly) Canada. Like most ideologues and idealists, Brown was a born malcontent. No solution was ever quite good enough. But he was also a product of the Scottish Enlightenment (the same movement that gave us the *Encyclopedia Britannica* and Edmund Burke) and therefore convinced of the rightness of human reason. *The Globe* didn't start calling itself Canada's national newspaper until 1909, but in Brown's large dome of a head, it was the country's rational newspaper from day zot. When Brown wasn't going after Macdonald's cronies for malfeasance (see Doug Saunders's recap of the Pacific Scandal), he was rounding up all the reasons rational men ought to want a bigger and more sprawling Canada, as Tony Keller notes in his deft history of Junius, the notional author of *The Globe*'s unsigned editorials. A divided Canada risked being swallowed up, piece by piece, by the United States.

To that end, by 1859, Brown was lobbying hard in *The Globe* for a united federal Canada that (eventually) encompassed the Maritimes, the North-West and Rupert's Land (what is now Manitoba, Saskatchewan and Alberta and beyond), part of which territory Brown helped wrest from the hands of the Hudson's Bay Company by 1870. Brown may have been a Father of Confederation, but he was also its obstetrician, and *The Globe* was the forceps he used to yank the newborn country into being.

Whereupon, in an early example of what public intellectual Noam Chomsky later dubbed "manufacturing consent," *The Globe* immediately declared Confederation a complete success. "The unanimity and cordiality with which all sections of the people of Canada accept the new Constitution, give the happiest omen of its successful operation," *The Globe* declared on our very first Dominion Day, July 1, 1867. The paper went on to proclaim "the inauguration of *a new nationality* [my italics] to which we committed the interests of Christianity and civilization in a territory larger than that of the ancient Roman Empire."

Which was disgracefully presumptuous (what about the new country's Indigenous forefathers?) and largely untrue. As Alexander Willis notes in *History of the Book in Canada*, there were 380 "newspapers" in British North America in 1865, each one espousing the point of view of a different regional, political, religious or cultural interest group. The Conservatives had their megaphones, as did the Liberals, as did the French-Canadian Liberals (the anti-clerical Rouges), the French-Canadian Conservatives (George-Étienne Cartier's Bleus) and many others. This "second legislature," as the cacophony it created was called, was still arguing violently about the pros and cons of Confederation when Confederation happened. Meanwhile, in the Maritimes, both Nova Scotia and New Brunswick instantly regretted their decision to leave the bosom of Britain and join Canada. Haligonians marked the nation's first Dominion Day by burning their premier, Sir Charles Tupper, the Father of Confederation who persuaded them to join the party, in effigy, alongside a live rat. The country was a nation in name alone. In a lot of ways, it still is.

Having used his newspaper to birth the improbable Frankenstein called Canada, Brown and *The Globe* set about trying to describe the monster.

Never mind covering it thoroughly, or fairly, or justly, or consistently: the essays of Jana G. Pruden and Ann Hui and Gary Mason and Marsha Lederman and Dakshana Bascaramurty and Rachel Giese and Willow Fiddler all offer plenty of evidence of the contradictory, biased, racist, sexist, ignorant and even excellent reporting and opinionating *The Globe and Mail* has committed over its lifespan. Brown was an abolitionist, ardently anti-slavery, and a keen defender of prison reform. But his newspaper was still capable of comparing the arrival of thousands of Irish Catholic famine refugees in Toronto to the descent of the locusts on Egypt. Six years later, the newspaper was writing in support of them: they were, after all, potential readers and potential Liberal voters. Brown's beloved daughters (he married late, in his forties) were two of the first women to graduate from the University of Toronto, but *The Globe* was always a hesitant fan of feminism, even balking at the use of Ms. roughly a century and a half later, as Elizabeth Renzetti notes in her essay on the rise of the women's movement. The real news isn't that *The Globe* covered all these subjects well and poorly, fairly and otherwise. The surprise is that *The Globe* attempted to cover the whole country at all.

Geography alone made it impossible. George McCullagh, who merged *The Globe* with *The Mail and Empire* and became the first publisher of *The Globe and Mail* in 1936, flew copies of the paper to Vancouver by plane every day to justify the claim that *The Globe* was a national newspaper. But we know from Temur Durrani's essay, which tracks *The Globe*'s embrace of technology, that it wasn't until the introduction of satellites into the production process in 1980 – a move that "confirms the destiny of *The Globe*," publisher Roy Megarry brashly declared at the time – that the newspaper could claim with any honesty to be a national publication. (The satellite instantly increased the paper's circulation by forty thousand readers.) And even then, with a page a minute being transmitted to printing plants across the country, delivering those printed papers through Canadian weather was a gargantuan challenge, and still is.

Fog and snow and floods shut down B.C.'s Coquihalla Highway at least half a dozen times a year, preventing the six-hour daily run of 1,200 newspapers – at the time of writing – from Delta, British Columbia, to Vernon and stops along the way. The driver, who makes the return trip six days a week, goes through a truck a year delivering *The Globe*: he has smashed into mountains and moose and more. *The Globe* has long flown copies of the newspaper to Iqaluit and Yellowknife, which only underlines the economic absurdity of publishing a national newspaper.

And then there was the impossible task of reporting on a country as large and diverse as Canada.

That reporting was bound to be criticized, even as *The Globe* became more profitable in the early decades of the twentieth century and could finally afford to be more politically independent. The pallid history of the opening of *The Globe*'s domestic bureaus, staffed by its own reporters, is a case in point. It was 1954 before *The Globe* established its first out-of-province bureau, in Quebec City. (It was the first newspaper outside Quebec to do so.) It was 1956 before the paper opened its first foreign bureau in Washington, D.C. As Nathan VanderKlippe explains in his essay, *The Globe* was the first Western newspaper to open a bureau in Beijing in 1959; was that so much more important (or profitable) than opening a Vancouver bureau, which happened only later that year? Halifax, Edmonton, Calgary and Winnipeg had to wait until 1970, 1979, 1980 and 1981, respectively. That's how young, how unexamined, how uninvestigated, how untold this country still is, from a national news perspective.

How could it be otherwise? Consider the challenge of covering the North, which Patrick White outlines in his essay about Northern Canada and its presence in our national consciousness. A subcontinent that hadn't changed much in ten thousand years is suddenly, because of climate change and southern capitalists, changing so fast that even its residents don't fully grasp the consequences. "You're literally dealing with a culture here that's evolving so quickly that it's happening before your eyes," a mining executive on Baffin Island told a *Globe* reporter a decade ago. On weekends, his crew of newly trained Inuit equipment operators took classes in how to work an ATM and how to make a budget to help them manage the $75,000 salaries they were suddenly receiving. There are now twenty-five communities in Nunavut, none of which are as yet connected by roads of any kind.

In 2012, *Globe* photographer Peter Power and I traversed the Arctic from Iqaluit to Inuvik, stopping along the way to write about the region. This is what a national newspaper is supposed to do, after all: cover the land. It took us six weeks. Our flights alone cost $100,000. Despite such hindrances, a succession of *Globe* writers has brought stories of the North to the consciousness of southerners. Our reports read like dispatches not just from the pioneer days but from a previously undiscovered (and sometimes not particularly admirable) stage of human evolution: the year the federal government allowed Inuit to buy liquor (1959), the year federal ballot boxes arrived up north (1962), the stretch during which Ottawa assigned the Inuit identification numbers (which they wore around their necks, on leather thongs, now collector's items) so Canada could claim geographic sovereignty over the North by dint of the fact that it was "populated."

The Inuit were strangers to us, and we were strangers to them, albeit often friendly. George Qulaut, one of the founding fathers of Nunavut, told *The Globe* that he remembered his father approaching him, in all seriousness, and asking, "George, what is this place, Canada, that I keep hearing about? What is a Canadian?" That was in 1971, for God's sake, well within living memory. These days, the federal government's subsidy of Nunavut amounts to $57,273 per resident. Is that a tenable situation? It had better be, because the "inhabited" Canadian North is the only entity that lies between us and the northern marauding of Russia and China.

One reason this country's stories still feel only partly told, despite the repeated efforts of the national newspaper, is because the stories are too complicated, too evolving, to be told in any simple, fixed way. As Konrad Yakabuski makes clear in his crisp but comprehensive overview of Canada's two solitudes, the separation of English and French cultures was built into Canadian life from its outset. The separateness never goes away, entirely, which is perplexing, but it always abates and then resurges, which is just as perplexing. Is the rise and fall of interest in separatism as much a function of simple demographics, of the average age of the population, as it is of any deeper cultural dissatisfaction?

In 1850, Brown's *Globe* was omnidirectionally hostile to Quebec's early political domination of the Province of Canada. But by 1863, Ontarians outnumbered Quebeckers, and a subtler and more experienced Brown, with Confederation in his sights, had become more understanding of francophone Canada's existential nervousness. That anxiety has been ponging back and forth from side to side, like a germ that will not die, ever since. The Constitution Act recognized the use of both languages in Parliament back in 1867, but the Official Languages Act wasn't passed until 1969, by which time there were seven million francophones in Quebec.

There are now 150,000 Manitobans who can claim French heritage, fifty thousand of whom list French as their first language – but for sixty years Manitoba schools were officially English-only, a crisis of political paranoia Evan Annett outlines in his essay on the Manitoba Schools Question. In 1992, after a decade of constitutional wrangling and only months before the (ultimately unsuccessful) Charlottetown Accord, Don Getty, the unilingual premier of Alberta, declared his government's intention to abandon official bilingualism. Alberta's Conservatives soon faced a much wider challenge to their narrow definition of who is and isn't an Albertan: the most frequently spoken language after English in Calgary today is either Tagalog or Punjabi. That further complicates the always jittery (and some would say unanswerable) question of provincial and national self-definition, of who we are as a place, if we are ever just any one thing at all. The more narrowly you define a nation, the more arguments you will have as to whom it belongs.

The West, as Kelly Cryderman astutely observes in her contribution to the collection, has in fact become Canada's third solitude, the breeding ground of its own populist and separatist alienation, some of which manifested in the now-infamous 2022 national park-in of Ottawa, aka the truckers' convoy. Maybe that alienation was inevitable:

the 4.5 million square kilometres that became the west and northwest of Canada were jammed on in a panic to serve the interests of central Canada by creating space between the westward-expanding Americans and the money-grasping, London-based Hudson's Bay Company, which did not want to let go of its territory.

Is it any surprise that central Canada – and even "the Toronto *Globe and Mail*," as westerners sometimes call it – has on occasion (but certainly not always) treated the West as an economic colony? And has done so in spite of the region's distinct farming and ranching and resource-based economy, that in turn has produced its own proud political traditions, such as socialized medicine. Old mistrusts die hard. Alas, the standoff is infinitely more complicated today, because it isn't just Bay Street that wants to control Alberta's oil patch. It's the entire planet, suffering as it is from human-caused, fossil-fuel-induced climate change.

Whether it takes the form of a website or a podcast or a physical object printed on a byproduct of harvested trees, a daily newspaper today performs the same function it always has: it is a compressor of time and space that curates an illusion of order out of the chaos of random happenstance.

In that way it is not unlike a national identity, another equally artificial organizing principle. Benedict Anderson, the late, undersung Anglo-Irish political scientist and author of *Imagined Communities: Reflections on the Origin and Spread of Nationalism*, thought the two were related. He likened the reading of a daily newspaper to a "mass ceremony" whose purpose was to consecrate and make real the abstract entity we know as a nation. (One current fear is that if you demolish the ceremony – as online technology has undermined the newspaper business – you weaken the cord of connection.) Anderson's point was that every nation is an artificial creation, imagined into being by almost hilariously selective details of geography, history, religion, ethnicity, civic-mindedness, military might and financial convenience. We hope the arrangement of values is just and convince ourselves it will last, but in a young, (relatively) underpopulated country as wide and tall as Canada, the past is still too geographically scattered and recent to have the heft of solid tradition. Hence the steady bickering and nattering existential doubts that characterize our politics and so much of *The Globe*'s reporting over a mere 180 years. Everyone wants to own this place, and only the callow and the careless think they actually can or do.

Which is the weird and somehow reassuring thing: the unlikelihood of Canada turns out to be its most distinguishing feature, so far. All the reasons Canada ought not to exist, chronicled by *The Globe* over the decades – its physical immensity and tiny population, the dissimilarity of its regions, its tense and complicated mix of ethnicities and languages, its penchant for apology and compromise, its bland civic idealism and watery political system, its often feckless and dependent economy, the lies and contradictions of its touted but also real inclusivity, to say nothing of the precariousness of living on top of the unhinged but thrilling, hyper-argumentative but bracingly confident, gun-toting but world-defending meth lab of capitalism known as the United States of America – are the same reasons Canada survives.

Brown described Confederation as a coming together of dissimilar regions under the unifying authority of a brand-new federal government. But as one of his successors, former *Globe* editor William Thorsell, once pointed out, Confederation was actually an agreement of mutual separation. The French and the English, the East and the West, the Liberals and the Conservatives, didn't triumph over one another or even resolve their differences. They simply agreed to co-exist by ignoring one another, by – to put it a slightly more flattering way – giving each other enough space to co-exist. They decided to honour not their sameness but their tolerance for difference, which was their most impressive sameness.

That may be justification enough to proceed with the wobbly but continuing Canadian project. It's the identity of no identity, the definition of a place that is wary, for very practical reasons, of definitions. *The Globe and Mail* has now spent 180 years trying to discover and describe the details of that undefinability, and the job still isn't finished, because the country keeps warping and moving and growing and changing. That's actually the good news.

Ian Brown is a feature writer at *The Globe and Mail*.

Bibliography

Abella, Irving, and Harold Troper. *None is Too Many: Canada and the Jews of Europe, 1933-1948*. Toronto: University of Toronto Press, Scholarly Publishing Division, 2017.

Anderson, Benedict. *Imagined Communities: Reflections on the Origin and Spread of Nationalism*. London: Verso, 1991.

Bassnett, Sarah, and Sarah Parsons. *Photography in Canada, 1839-1989: An Illustrated History*. Toronto: Art Canada Institute, 2023.

Blatchford, Christie. *Spectator Sports*. Toronto: Totem Books, 1987.

Bobier, Richard. "Africville: The Test of Urban Renewal in Halifax, Nova Scotia." *Past Imperfect* 4 (February, 1995). https://doi.org/10.21971/P75K5M.

Bourrie, Mark. *Big Men Fear Me*. Windsor: Biblioasis, 2022.

Braz, Albert. "United in Oppression: Religious Strife and Group Identity in the Cavan Blazers." *Literature and Theology* 16, no. 2 (June 1, 2002): 160–71. https://doi.org/10.1093/litthe/16.2.160.

Careless, J. M. S. *Brown of the Globe*. Toronto: Macmillan of Canada, 1959.

Careless, J. M. S. *Careless at Work: Selected Canadian Historical Studies*. Toronto: Dundurn Press, 1996.

Carson, Rachel Louise. *Silent Spring*. London: Hamish Hamilton, 1962.

Chambers, Stephanie, Jane Farrow, and Maureen FitzGerald, eds. *Any Other Way: How Toronto Got Queer*. Toronto: Coach House Books, 2017.

Clippingdale, Richard, and Joe Clark. *The Power of the Pen: The Politics, Nationalism, and Influence of Sir John Willison*. Toronto: Dundurn Press, 2012.

Cobb, Chris. *Ego and Ink: The Inside Story of Canada's National Newspaper War*. Toronto: McClelland & Stewart, 2004.

Coleman, Jim. *Long Ride on a Hobby-horse: Memoirs of a Sporting Life*. Toronto: Key Porter Books, 1990.

Dickson, Paul Douglas. *A Thoroughly Canadian General: A Biography of General H.D.G. Crerar*. Toronto: University of Toronto Press, 2007.

Downie, Jill. *A Passionate Pen: The Life and Times of Faith Fenton*. Toronto: HarperCollins, 1998.

Doyle, Richard J. *Hurly-Burly: A Time at the Globe*. Toronto: Macmillan of Canada, 1990.

Enright, Michael. "A Writer's Newspaper." Essay. In *Canadian Newspapers: The Inside Story*, 99–110. Edmonton: Hurtig Press, 1980.

Freeman, Barbara M. *Kit's Kingdom: The Journalism of Kathleen Blake Coleman*. Montréal: McGill-Queen's University Press, 1989.

Friesen, Gerald. *River Road: Essays on Manitoba and Prairie History*. Winnipeg: University of Manitoba Press, 1996.

Gerson, Carole. *Canadian Women in Print, 1750-1918*. Waterloo: Wilfrid Laurier University Press, 2011.

Gibbons, Kenneth M., and Donald C. Rowat. *Political Corruption in Canada: Cases, Causes and Cures*. Toronto: McClelland & Stewart, in association with the Institute of Canadian Studies, Carleton University, 1976.

Gigantes, Philip Deane. *I Should Have Died*. New York: Atheneum, 1976.

Goold, Douglas, and Andrew Willis. *The Bre-X Fraud*. Toronto: McClelland & Stewart, 1997.

Hayes, David. *Power and Influence: The Globe and Mail and the News Revolution*. Toronto: Key Porter Books, 1992.

Hodgetts, John E., and Eugene Forsey. *The Sound of One Voice: Eugene Forsey and His Letters to the Press*. Toronto: University of Toronto Press, 2000.

Humphries, Mark Osborne. *The Last Plague: Spanish Influenza and the Politics of Public Health in Canada*. Toronto: University of Toronto Press, 2013.

Jacobs, Jane. *The Death and Life of Great American Cities*. New York: Random House, 1961.

Kapica, Jack. *Shocked and Appalled: A Century of Letters to the Globe and Mail*. Toronto: Lester & Orpen Dennys, 1985.

Knowles, Valerie. *Strangers at Our Gates: Canadian Immigration and Immigration Policy, 1540-2015*. Toronto: Dundurn Press, 2016.

Levine, Allan. *Toronto: Biography of a City*. Toronto: Douglas & McIntyre, 2022.

Malarek, Victor. *Haven's Gate: Canada's Immigration Fiasco*. Toronto: Macmillan of Canada, 1987.

Sakamoto, Mark. *Forgiveness: A Gift from My Grandparents*. Toronto: HarperCollins, 2018.

Saunders, Doug. *Maximum Canada: Why 35 Million Canadians Are Not Enough*. Toronto: Alfred A. Knopf Canada, 2017.

Sears, Val. *Hello Sweetheart...Get Me Rewrite: Remembering the Great Newspaper Wars*. Toronto: Key Porter Books, 1988.

Stackhouse, John. *Mass Disruption: Thirty Years on the Front Lines of a Media Revolution*. Toronto: Random House Canada, 2015.

Thorsell, William. *Crest to Crest: Riding the Boomer Wave*. William Thorsell, 2022.

Willis, Alexander J. "Shifting Boundaries: Newspapers and the Confederation Debate." Essay. In Vol. 2 of *History of the Book in Canada: 1840-1918*, 306-309. Toronto: University of Toronto Press, 2004.

Willison, John. *Reminiscences, Political and Personal*. Toronto: McClelland & Stewart, 1919.

Willison, John. *Sir Wilfrid Laurier and the Liberal Party: A Political History*. Toronto: G.M. Morang, 1903.

Index

Library and Archives Canada Cataloguing in Publication

Title: A nation's paper : the Globe and Mail in the life of Canada / edited by John Ibbitson.
Other titles: Globe and mail in the life of Canada
Names: Ibbitson, John, editor.
Identifiers: Canadiana (print) 20240304691 | Canadiana (ebook) 2024030473X | ISBN 9780771006289 (hardcover) | ISBN 9780771006296 (EPUB)
Subjects: LCSH: Canada—History—Press coverage. | LCSH: Globe and mail—History. | LCSH: Canadian newspapers—History. | LCGFT: Essays.
Classification: LCC FC165 .N38 2024 | DDC 971—dc23

Jacket and book design by Kate Sinclair
Jacket art: (newsprint) RapidEye / Getty Images;
(paper coil) MirageC / Getty Images

Typeset in FreightText Pro by Sean Tai
Printed in Canada

Published by Signal,
an imprint of McClelland & Stewart,
a division of Penguin Random House Canada Limited,
a Penguin Random House Company
www.penguinrandomhouse.ca

1 2 3 4 5   28 27 26 25 24

Penguin
Random House
Canada